MW01592900

Social Injustice

What Evangelicals Need to Know About the World

Editors
Michael T. Cooper
William J. Moulder

Foreword
Ronald P. Hesselgrave

i

Social Injustice: What Evangelicals Need to Know About the World

William J. Moulder and Michael T. Cooper

Social Injustice: What Evangelicals Need to Know About the World

Copyright © 2011 William J. Moulder and Michael T. Cooper

Published by the Timothy Center Press
The publisher of the Timothy Center for Sustainable Transformation
736 N. Western Ave
Lake Forest, Illinois 60045
USA

www.thetimothycenter.org

All rights reserved. No part of this book may be reproduced in any form – mechanical, electronic retrieval system, photocopy, etc. – without permission in writing from the publisher, except in the case of brief quotations embodied in books, critical articles, or reviews. Permission to reproduce the book or its contents can be secured by contacting the publisher.

This book is published in an electronic format and is licensed for your personal reading only. It may not be re-sold, given away to other people or posted in any electronic format on the Internet. If you have received a copy of this book without purchasing, please consider a donation to the Timothy Center. Thank you for respecting the hard work of these authors and thank you for choosing Timothy Center Press books.

Electronic edition 2011

ISBN: 978-1-4524-1633-5

Paperback edition 2011

ISBN: 978-0-578-09049-8

[sacredtribes] The electronic version is published in partnership with Sacred Tribes Press, the academic publisher for the Western Institute for Intercultural Studies, 358 South 700 East, Suite B356, Salt Lake City, UT, 84102, USA. Visit the website at www.sacredtribespress.com.

Table of Contents

About the Contributors

SARAH BUSHMAN is graduate of Trinity International University where she earned a Master of Arts in Cultural Engagement with an emphasis in Social Entrepreneurship. While at Trinity, Sarah focused her passion and studies on development in Haiti. After an April 2010 visit to Haiti, she realized the need for creation care practices and sustainable social entrepreneurial ventures. As a result, she developed a business plan for a recycling initiative in Haiti to provide for Haitians and the environment and is currently working to implement the business.

MICHAEL T. COOPER is associate professor of Religion and Contemporary Culture and program director of the Master of Arts in Cultural Engagement at Trinity Graduate School in Deerfield, Illinois. He earned his BED from Texas A&M University, his MA from Columbia Biblical Seminary and School of Mission, and his PhD from Trinity Evangelical Divinity School. He has contributed numerous articles and chapters dealing with Christian engagement of Western society. He is the author of *Contemporary Druidry: A Historical and Ethnographic Study* (Sacred Tribes Press 2010) and editor of *Perspectives on Post-Christendom Spiritualities: Reflections on Western Spiritualities and New Religious Movements* (Morling Press 2010) and *The Peaceable Christian: Five Evangelicals Reflect on Peace* (The Timothy Center Press 2011). He is founder of the Timothy Center for Sustainable Transformation and a research fellow of the Western Institute for Intercultural Studies as well as an academic advisor for the Lausanne Committee's Issue Group addressing new spiritualities in a postmodern world.

PAIGE COMSTOCK CUNNINGHAM is Executive Director of The Center for Bioethics & Human Dignity. She is also a Fellow at the Institute for Biotechnology and the Human Future and a Trustee of Taylor University. Cunningham is Adjunct Professor of Law and Bioethics at Trinity Graduate School. She was an adjunct instructor at Wheaton College for eight years. She graduated from Taylor University (*summa cum laude*), and earned her J.D. from Northwestern University Law School, and an M.A. in Bioethics from Trinity International University. Cunningham lectures and has published numerous articles, editorials and book chapters in the areas of law, bioethics and public policy, and has testified before congressional committees at the state and national level, and has appeared frequently on radio and television.

STEPHEN PAUL KENNEDY received his Ph.D. in Social Ethics from the University of Southern California. He was a Congressional Fellow in the United States Senate in 1986 and for the next three years was a speechwriter in the U.S. Department of Health and Human Services. He has taught at Georgetown University, Concordia University (Irvine), Fuller Theological Seminary, Trinity Graduate School and Trinity Law School. He is currently adjunct faculty at Biola and Trinity Law School and a leading evangelical expert on international human rights and serves on the board of the Timothy Center for Sustainable Transformation.

RAJKUMAR BOAZ JOHNSON was raised in one of the slums of New Delhi, among the poorest of poor – among kids who were sold into slavery. He was trained in a radical Hindu grammar and high school. While in high school, he read the works of a Hindu Brahmin convert to Jesus, Pandita Ramabai. She had rescued hundreds of young girls from sexual slavery. He also met Bhai Bhakt Singh, an extremist Sikh whose life was radically changed by Yesu Masih (Jesus Christ). Thereafter, he was given a copy of the Gospel of John. The picture of the life and death of Yesu Masih completely captured his mind. No Hindu god or guru showed such pure and selfless love. This was a life changing encounter for him. Jesus, it became clear to him was the only answer to poverty and slavery in India, and the complexity of issues facing the world. He alone could bring about comprehensive and radical change.

YELENA LOPUGA as a first generation immigrant from Ukraine, has firsthand experience in the transformative power of education. She holds a Bachelors of Arts in Christian Ministry from California Christian College and a Masters in Communication and Culture from Trinity Graduate School in Deerfield, Illinois. As a human rights advocate, she hopes to use her knowledge to further just treatment of the poor and disadvantaged.

TERESSA MAHL is a graduate of Trinity International University where she pursued a degree in masters degree in Communication and Culture. She received her undergraduate degree in Organizational Communications from Cedarville University, and currently works at TIU in the Office of Alumni & Community Relations as the Coordinator for Communications and Events. Teressa lives with her husband Aaron in Deerfield, Illinois.

WILLIAM J. MOULDER is professor of biblical studies at Trinity International University's Trinity College. Dr. Moulder received the Bachelor of Arts in biblical education at Columbia Bible College, the Master of Divinity at Trinity Evangelical Divinity School, and the Doctor of Philosophy in New Testament languages and literature from St. Andrews University in Scotland. His areas of expertise include Bible interpretation, biblical research, and Greek. He is an occasional member of the Chicago Society for Biblical Research and Institute for Biblical Research. Dr. Moulder has a variety of teaching experiences over the last twenty-five years which include: Moffatt College of Bible, Kenya; Union Biblical Seminary, India; North Park Seminary, Chicago; Trinity Torch Graduate School of Theology, Seoul; and Trinity Evangelical Divinity School. In addition, Dr. Moulder has written many articles regarding the Old Testament and the New Testament.

ALEX SHAVER originally from Wellington, Ohio, holds a Bachelor of Arts in Student Ministry from Geneva College in Beaver Falls, PA and a Master of Arts in Communication and Culture from Trinity Graduate School in Deerfield, Illinois. He currently serves as an Resident Director at Grove City College in Grove City, Pennsylvania.

MICHAEL J. SLEASMAN is the managing director and research scholar for The Center for Bioethics & Human Dignity and an affiliate professor in the Graduate School at Trinity International University. He regularly teaches courses at the graduate and undergraduate levels in philosophy, theology, and ethics. His particular specialization is the intersection of technology and culture. He is co-editor with Kevin Vanhoozer and Charles Anderson of *Everyday Theology: How to Read Cultural Texts and Interpret Trends*. Dr. Sleasman serves on the Board of Reference for the Christian Institute on Disability for Joni & Friends, International. He has been interviewed on a range of bioethical issues by media sources in print and on the radio, and has delivered workshops and lectures for a variety of audiences.

JAMES J. STAMOOLIS is a consultant to educational and missionary organizations. A convert from Greek Orthodoxy to evangelical Protestanism, he was a missionary in South Africa, a Theological Secretary for the International Fellowship of Evangelical Students, Graduate Dean of Wheaton College, Senior Vice President and Dean of the College at Trinity International University and CEO of a mission. He has been adjunct faculty at Wheaton College, Northern Baptist Theological Seminary, Trinity International University and Columbia International University. Author of *Eastern Orthodox Mission Theology Today* (Orbis), Gen. ed. of *Three Views on Eastern Orthodoxy and Evangelicalism* (Zondervan) and numerous journal and encyclopedia articles.

Foreword

WHEN I WAS A FIRST-YEAR seminary student I personally wrestled with the view that the institution of slavery was the means God used to bring the gospel and Christian civilization to the heathen in Africa. Slavery in the South was, according to this argument, a good thing for the enslaved. Similar arguments have been made to justify the unjust treatment of the American Indians and the wedding of missionary activity to colonialism. At the time I was exposed to this position, Timothy Smith was visiting professor at the seminary I attended. I remember having a conversion with him, during which I asked him what he thought about the subject. He was aghast that Christians could seek to justify slavery from a biblical and theological standpoint. It was from this dialogue with him that I learned of his seminal and ground-breaking book, *Revivalism and Social Reform: American Protestantism on the Eve of the Civil War* which clearly showed that evangelical revivalists in mid-19th century played a key role in the movement to abolish slavery and other forms of social injustice.

Still today, there is confusion within the institutional church about the relationship between the gospel and a concern for justice. Religious conservatives emphasize our responsibility for evangelism but often neglect issues of social injustice, while theological liberals champion causes of justice and human rights but ignore the earthly and eternal consequences of sin for people without a personal Savior. Twenty years ago the noted evangelical theologian Carl Henry stated:

> If the church preaches only divine forgiveness and does not affirm justice, she implies that God treats immorality and sin lightly. If the church proclaims only justice, we shall all die in unforgiven sin without the Spirit's empowerment for righteousness. We should be equally troubled that we lag in championing justice and in fulfilling our evangelistic mandate. We should realize that the Great Commission is dwarfed and even maligned if one implies that God is blindly tolerant of social and structural evil, that he forgives sinners independently of a concern for justice. . . The local church should identify the most grievous injustices—local, regional, and national—and strive to rectify them, in concert with all who seek to right the wrong. (Interview with Carl F. H. Henry, "A Summons to Justice," Christianity Today, 1992)

Today, perhaps as never before, we live in world characterized by oppression, war, terrorism, growing poverty and unrestrained greed. The gap between the world's rich and the poor is ever increasing. Human trafficking—encompassing sexual exploitation, debt bondage and forced labor—has become the modern day form of slavery. These are issues that the Church ignores at its own peril.

William Moulder and Michael Cooper have done us a great service in compiling these essays on justice from an evangelical perspective. The first three essays in this timely and important book lay out the biblical, theological and historical foundations of justice. The next seven essays address the practical application of biblical principles of justice to a wide range of issues in the global context: (1) human trafficking in India; (2) bioethics and exploitation in the global medical enterprise; (3) education and freedom in Ethiopia; (4) the care of Haitian orphans: (5) literacy in Afghanistan; (6) food production and our relationship to the land as a gift from God; and (7) membership rights. The theme running through all of these essays is perhaps best summed up in these words by Boaz Johnson: "It is the encounter with the text of the Bible, and the God of the Bible, and the Messiah of the Bible that gives true freedom from systemic injustice and slavery" (p. 89). *but what does "freedom" look like?*

The ten essays in this book force us to re-examine from a biblical standpoint what it means to love mercy and act justly (Micah 6:8) in response to the needs of the poor and oppressed of the world. Again, I will attempt to illustrate this with a personal anecdote. When I was a student at Trinity College in Deerfield, IL in the late 1960s, I would go with a friend to witness to homeless people living in the flop houses along Madison Street in Chicago. This was an experience that left an indelible impression on me. When I became professor of sociology at Trinity I made it a point to take students on tours of the inner city, which included walks down the same street where I had witnessed to the homeless years before. By then the flop houses were gone, but the homeless were still there. In recent years, Madison Street has undergone a transformation. The homeless and various ministries and shelters that served them have been pushed out to make way for gentrification, or the movement of wealthier people into the community. Upscale condos and apartment buildings and large single-family homes with well-manicured lawns line newly paved streets. But over the years since my days as a college student, the problem of homelessness in Chicago has increased, not decreased. More homeless live on the streets and back-alleys of our major cities now than ever before. This is a reminder that issues like poverty and homelessness are complex and multifaceted. The desperately poor need more than a well-intentioned pat on the back and cheery "God loves you;" or a few coins in a Styrofoam cup; or a box of food from a food pantry. There must be a total restructuring of the Church and rethinking of what it means to do ministry in a broken world. This book points us in the right direction.

Ronald P. Hesselgrave, Ph.D
Educational Resources Coordinator
Evangelical Free Church of America TouchGlobal

← "ACT JUSTLY"

Chapter One

Evangelicals and Social Justice: Setting the Global Context

Michael T. Cooper

CHRISTMAS 2009 FOUND the Coopers in Nicaragua. We spent the holiday with family enjoying the warmth of the Central American sun, zip-lining through the rain forest canopy, and sailing on the Pacific Ocean. Nicaragua is a beautiful country with lush countryside filled with sugarcane and spectacular volcanoes that are still active. It was certainly a pleasurable change from the freezing temperatures we were accustomed to in Chicago. One evening as we were settling down I asked our three kids about their experience. They were indeed enjoying the time with their cousins, but they also noticed the disparity between how we were living compared to the Nicaraguans. Up to this point in their young lives and in spite of travelling through much of the United States and Europe, they had never experienced what poverty looked liked. We did live in one of the poorest countries of Europe for ten years, but the two oldest were one and two when we returned to the States and hardly have a memory of it.

Of course the kids know about poverty. We have been involved with providing bed nets to families in sub-Sahara Africa in a fight against malaria. Our daughter, who was 12 at the time, raised money as a class project to provide two families with bed nets. Our youngest son (9 at the time) wrote a school essay about how he would use a million dollars to provide bed nets to families. It impressed his teacher so much that she had to tell us and other teachers. Apparently it is not every day that a fourth grader would use his money for the poor. It was our oldest son (almost 13 now), as we were sitting on the bed that evening, who shared that the people were really poor. Many of the houses had dirt floors and corrugated tin roofs. Children ran around without shoes and younger ones without clothes. Poverty became something real to them on that trip. They saw what it looked like and they knew it was not fair.

Over the course of the past several decades evangelicals have wrestled with their role in efforts to address global issues of injustice. Historically speaking, early Christianity was on the side of social good. There is clear indication that

1

Christians cared for the diseased and hungered as much as the enslaved and oppressed. Such care was an impetus to the early church's growth.[1] The situation changed, however, after the institutionalization of the church at the time of Emperor Constantine.[2] Saint Jerome, writing in the fifth century, iterates the sentiment of the church's shift to power, "Parchments are dyed purple, gold is melted into lettering, manuscripts are dressed up in jewels, while Christ lies at the door naked and dying" (*Ep.* 22, 32). Despite its new authority, much can be said for the development of hospitals, orphanages and poor-house by the hands of European Christians as evidence for the continued care for the marginalized. Indeed, Christianity has a long and distinguished history of such care.

For decades non-governmental organizations like the Red Cross and Red Crescent, among many others, have provided a means by which people could engage in voluntary and financial participation in current issues affecting people either locally, nationally or globally. In the last century, governments have united to help resolve such global issues. Among the noteworthy participants, the United Nations is instrumental in leading the way toward identifying and addressing social concerns. For example, in September 2000 world leaders gathered to set goals to reduce extreme poverty. These goals now referred to as the Millennium Development Goals (MDG) are utilized by many NGOs, both Christian and other, for their development programs.

This chapter is going to raise awareness about what evangelicals need to know is happening in the world today. I originally prepared this chapter as part of a missions conference sermon at Johnston Evangelical Free Church in Iowa in February 2010. It was later refined and used as a lecture for a symposium at Trinity International University in April 2010. I have used portions of it in graduate courses on cultural engagement. Everywhere that I have been able to talk about the global context of social justice issues and how evangelicals can be involved I have met with a similar response: I didn't know that was going on. This chapter, in fact the entire book, looks at the world and the numerous issues that confront us. I have become convinced that if evangelicals only knew the dire conditions of billions of people that we would rise up and respond out of compassion for those who were created in God's image.

Becoming Conversant with Social Justice

In the 21st century, the church is confronted with the reality of injustice as never before. In a global community were information is readily available, we are increasingly aware of the plight of people in places that were once simply loca-

2

tions on a map. Recent tragedies like the devastating earthquake in Port-au-Prince, Haiti or the oil slick crisis caused by the destruction of a $700 million oil platform in the Gulf of Mexico have brought the plight of the suffering into our living rooms and onto our computers. As I write this paragraph, I am sitting in a parking lot of a school in Grayslake, Illinois where I could get access to news around the world in an instant. In fact, earlier this morning I received a telephone message from a student working in the second largest urban slum in Africa updating me on her progress in Kibera near Nairobi, Kenya. We live in a different time and there is little excuse for us lacking awareness about what is going on in the world.

Social justice is not an avant-garde term awaiting the arrival of another neologism to replace it. The great 20th century evangelical theologian Carl F.H. Henry wrote in 1964, "In an hour of widespread revolution, when political forces are reshaping the larger frontiers of modern life, the Church's concern with the problem of social justice is especially imperative."[3] Nevertheless, the term certainly conjures up old debates about the social gospel. While the evangelical movement successfully turned the tide away from the social gospel in the late 19th and early 20th centuries, it came, at times, at the expense of care for the very people that might be called "neighbor" as it focused on a rather Gnostic-like worldview emphasizing the primacy of the spiritual with the uneasy consequence being the physical well-being of people.

The issue of evangelical social involvement has been an uncomfortable one since such involvement has often been associated with the social gospel. The social gospel, at its core, is a gospel that focuses on the betterment of society as prerequisite to, or even in place of, soul salvation. In the early 20th century its focus was on social movements and causes which emphasized improving human conditions as has been practiced in liberal Protestant and Catholic churches. However, the social gospel cannot be limited to simply liberal social concern. The conservative counterpart of contemporary fundamentalism and some segments of evangelicalism are often as guilty of practicing a social gospel as they place an emphasis on social change through political involvement that legislates morality (i.e. capital punishment, school prayer, abortion, etc.). Such involvement has the hope that people will be born again. *Does it? or is it simply stating what is right or wrong?*

Still, the question of Christian involvement remains. On the one hand, some argue that Christians should be involved in extending help in the name of Christ as he himself model and taught (Matt 25:31-46). On the other hand, some say that any help should focus on Christian brothers as seems apparent from the Apostle John's first epistle (1 John 3:17). At the same time, the argument is put forward that social justice is a part of the gospel itself and should be sought wherever the gospel is proclaimed (Luke 4:16-22). Still others posit that social justice should be a result of Christian behavior after the gospel proclamation. However it is understood, it certainly encompasses what Robert Coleman iterated years ago, "Persons with a Gospel priority cannot be indifferent to the cry for justice across the world, and many, by virtue of their calling, will take leading roles in shaping public policy."[4]

While many are talking about social justice, few have offered a definition so let me attempt at least a working one. Social justice is the application of the gospel in both word and deed (Matt 25-28). This dual proclamation of God's kingdom combines the message of the gospel with the power of the gospel for the physical, social, emotional and spiritual well-being of people (Luke 4:16-19) created in the image of God (Gen 1:26; James 3:9). Social justice recognizes the sociality of people in their relationship with God and others.[5] Because of God's love for humankind, the Christian is commanded to work together with God (2 Cor 6:1) to reconcile those relationships in respect to Christ's ministry of reconciliation (2 Cor 5:18-19). The biblical mandate compels the Christian to act with care for the widowed, orphaned and enslaved (1 Tim 5:3; 6:1-2; James 1:27), to give to the poor (Acts 11:29-30; 24:17) and to remember the imprisoned and mistreated (Heb 13:3). In other words, social justice is the comprehensive call of the gospel to live and work as Christ in the world. A critical aspect to evangelical involvement in social justice is awareness of not only what it is but what the injustices are.

Current State of the Globe[6]

Having been asked about the greatest challenges facing the world, former president Jimmy Carter indicated in his Nobel lecture after being awarded the Peace Prize in 2002, "I decided that the most serious and universal problem [in the world] is the growing chasm between the richest and poorest people on earth."[7] There are approximately 6.8 billion people in the world today.[8] Nearly a quarter (1.4 billion) of the world's population lives on less than $1.25 per day.[9] The United Nations estimates that the number of those living in extreme poverty will decrease to 920 million by 2015. However, the situation does not seem to be moving toward improvement with a global economy still feeling the pangs of recession.[10] The problem is acutely felt in parts of the world where Islam, Hinduism and Buddhism are dominant. The countries of these regions are experiencing the fastest population growth and constitute eighty percent of the world's impoverished.

Poverty is one of the leading factors to numerous social issues. For example, one third of the child mortality of 8.8 million in 2008 was caused by under-nutrition. In fact, in 2008, an estimated 1.1 billion people were undernourished. Poverty places people in extreme circumstances and contributes to the increasing numbers of individuals caught in unfair labor practices. An estimated 12 to 27 million people are enslaved in conditions where they are unable to acquire free-dom due to constraints placed on them by employers.[11] Such slave conditions occur primarily with women and children and many are often used in the sex in-dustry. Some 900,000 people are trafficked annually as slaves, 50,000 of those come through the United States and 18,000 end up being enslaved in the United States. In one instance, according to UN International Labour Organization (ILO), in 2005 approximately 9.49 million people were used in forced labor in the Asia-Pacific region. UNICEF estimates that 2,000 Haitian children are trafficked to the Dominican Republic. Human trafficking is the third most profitable illegal mo-neymaker in the global economy.[12] There are currently more people enslaved in the world than there were taken from Africa during the trans-Atlantic slave trade in the 16th-19th century.

While the countries of the developed world have taken notice and provided monetary relief to improve social situations, they have often done so blindly. Africa has benefited from foreign aid and has emerged in pop culture as a pre-ferred cause for individuals and corporations alike. Sub-Saharan African nations are at the heart of the MDG discussion being the home of 50 percent of the world's poorest people.[13] Aid relief in Africa has provided some relief; however, 70 percent of African governments are dependent on foreign aid. The US sends $40 billion in aid to Africa while only $17 billion is directed to investment. This has created a climate of self-perpetuating bureaucracies and disincentives for de-velopment. The result is devastating. Sixty years ago about 10 percent of the continent lived on a dollar a day and today over 70 percent live on a dollar a day.[14] Many African nations that have been on the receiving end of about $1 tril-lion over the past half-century are as poor or poorer than they were 40 years ago.[15]

Poverty is exacerbated by the number of refugees who cannot or do not work. Today there are an estimated 15.2 million refugees and 27.1 million inter-nally displaced people. Lack of educational opportunities perpetuates poverty as well. In 2008, 69 million children did not have or were denied access to educa-tion. Nearly half of out-of-school children have never had any education. Over half of them are girls. This lack of educational opportunities forces families into situation where children are exploited for forced labor, both physical and sexual.

Disease is also a contributor to poverty. When people are ill they are unable to work. Many illnesses today are easily preventable. Clean water would help in many situations where diseases run rampant. Reality is, however, that 13 percent of the world's population relies on unimproved water sources for drinking, cooking and bathing. In 2008, an estimated 2.6 billion people lacked access to improved sanitation and open defecation is practiced by 1.1 billion people.

In a world were nearly one million people die each year from this preventable disease, simple insecticide treated bed nets have proven to be an effective means for the control of malaria in sub-Sahara Africa. Still, approximately 243 million people are infected annually.[16] Sadly, every 30 seconds a child dies from this preventable infection. HIV/AIDS continues to be a burden. While there are cultural peculiarities tied to this disease, two-thirds of the victims live in sub-Sahara Africa. Fifteen million children world-wide lost a parent to AIDS in 2007. Over 47 million children in Sub-Sahara Africa have lost one or both parents to the disease. Just in 2008, 17.5 million children lost a parent to AIDS.

In such conditions of poverty peace and stability are threatened. Muhammad Yunus, the Bangladeshi micro-lender, stated in his 2006 Nobel Peace Prize address,

> Peace is threatened by an unjust economic, social and political order, absence of democracy, environmental degradation and absence of human rights. Poverty is the absence of all human rights. The frustration, hostility and anger generated by abject poverty cannot sustain peace in any society. For building stable peace we must find ways to provide opportunities for people to live decent lives.[17]

With increased awareness of these issues and others such as organ trafficking, conflict minerals, and child soldiering religious organizations are playing critical roles in helping confront social concerns. Religious groups such as International Justice Mission, World Vision and Food for the Hungry give an explicitly evangelical voice to social justice. Other groups such as Interfaith Youth Core, Malaria No More, both founded by Muslims as inter-religious organizations, are also actively working to confront issues that are important for the global community.

Christianity and Social Concern

There are certainly practical Christian application and command to engage social issues. Such application and command will have to include an evaluation of the way in which we utilize our financial resources. It is estimated that the sum of all the salaries of Christians in the United States amounts to four trillion dollars.[18] One can figure that if Christians were simply to tithe a tenth of their income they alone could address some of the extreme issues of the world. However, the reality is that Christians give less than three percent to the church.

Thirty-nine percent of the US adult population attend one of an estimated 340,000 congregations once a week or more (87.75 million people).[19] Assuming that half of the total adult population who attend church once a week or more is the number of Christian households (43.875 million) then if every household tithed there would be in excess of $200 billion in revenue. Instead, Christians only give about $66 billion to the church. Five billion dollars goes to foreign missionary work while the rest stays in the United States.[20]

To figure it differently, 26 percent of the US adult population identifies as evangelical. That translates to 58.5 million people.[21] If we were to take the median income of lower-to-upper middle class evangelicals we would have 31 million making between $30,000-99,999 per year. If only those evangelicals were to tithe there would be approximately $202 billion in revenue.[22] Through financial donations, evangelicals could be a powerful force for alleviating much of the world's poverty altogether. Instead, in 2009 evangelicals spent an estimated $158 billion on entertainment, $127 billion on clothing and accessories and $53 billion on pets, toys, hobbies and playground equipment.[23]

Evangelicals alone could alleviate extreme poverty, provide clean water and nutrition for the world if they were simply to tithe. Richard Stearns, president of World Vision, U.S.A., has observed,

> If every American churchgoer tithed, we could literally change the world. In fact … $65 billion…could eliminate the most extreme poverty on the planet for more than a billion people. Universal primary education for children would cost just $6 billion; the cost to bring clean water to most of the world's poor, an estimated $9 billion; and basic health and nutrition for everyone in the world, $13 billion.[24]

When figured in this manner there would be $109 billion of the tithe left over to cover the $5 billion for missions and $61 billion for ministries in the United

States. However, it often seems like Christians in the USA fit with what St. Jerome observed in the Roman Empire. A contemporary paraphrase might be expressed in this manner: "Our clothes are made by slaves, our jewelry is mined by children, and our church buildings are draining our resources, while Christ lies in the slums naked and dying."

The point here is not to place guilt on the American Christians' financial management, although a dose of guilt would not necessarily be bad. In spite of the fact that the American church is the richest church in the history of Christianity, simply giving money is not enough. We need to be involved both personally and financially. The Apostle John tells us as much, "But if anyone has the world's goods and sees his brother in need, yet closes his heart against him, how does God's love abide in him. Little children, let us not love in word or talk but in deed and in truth" (1 John 3:17-18).

Christian Engagement in Social Justice

Christianity has a long and distinguished history engaging social justice. Tertullian, writing around 200 AD, described the activities of the church in *Apology*. After defending the manner in which Christians worship he noted, "It is our care of the helpless, our practice of loving kindness that brands us in the eyes of many of our opponents. 'Only look,' they say, 'look how they love one another'" (*Apology* 39). The pre-Constantinian growth of Christianity is well documented in the writings of the early church. As Rodney Stark has argued, that growth was largely due to the Christian concern for the other.[25] This certainly seems intuitive.

From Constantine to the Reformation, Christians continued to express concern for others. While at times it was manifested in social control, there was a benevolent aspect as well. Although not an exclusively Christian nor Western idea as examples are found across the globe, the bishops gathered at the first ecumenical council in 325 at Nicaea and ordered hospitals to be constructed in every city.[26] The council was equally concerned for the care of the poor who at times were being exploited by the wealthy.[27] Care was a hallmark of the early church. Indeed, Craig Carter profoundly wrote, "Somebody else can run the government, fight the wars, and struggle for power, money, and fame. Christians have better things to do. We need to imitate our Lord and strive to live lives of forgiveness, reconciliation, and service to the poor. We need to live together in community and put the needs of each other ahead of our own selfish desires."

Such care has marked evangelicals as well. While often under resourced, evangelicals have historically engaged in issues of social justice. What might perhaps be a watershed of evangelical expression of social concern took place in Lausanne, Switzerland in 1974. Convened at the call of Billy Graham, more than 2,000 Christian leaders from around the globe gathered to discuss the continuing mission of world evangelization. The Lausanne Covenant resulted and expressed a consensus of evangelical conviction to proclaim the gospel world-wide. While many significant statements exemplify the covenant, there was recognition that gospel proclamation cannot be devoid of Christian social responsibility. The covenant states,

> We affirm that God is both the Creator and the Judge of all people. We therefore should share his concern for justice and reconciliation through-out human society and for the liberation of men and women from every kind of oppression. Because men and women are made in the image of God, every person, regardless of race, religion, colour, culture, class, sex or age, has an intrinsic dignity because of which he or she should be res-pected and served, not exploited. Here too we express penitence both for our neglect and for having sometimes regarded evangelism and social concern as mutually exclusive. Although reconciliation with other people is not reconciliation with God, nor is social action evangelism, nor is po-litical liberation salvation, nevertheless we affirm that evangelism and socio-political involvement are both part of our Christian duty. For both are necessary expressions of our doctrines of God and man, our love for our neighbour and our obedience to Jesus Christ. The message of salva-tion implies also a message of judgment upon every form of alienation, oppression and discrimination, and we should not be afraid to denounce evil and injustice wherever they exist. When people receive Christ they are born again into his kingdom and must seek not only to exhibit but al-so to spread its righteousness in the midst of an unrighteous world. The salvation we claim should be transforming us in the totality of our per-sonal and social responsibilities. Faith without works is dead.[28]

A Rationale for Christian Engagement in Social Justice

The Lausanne statement on Christian social responsibility provides a founda-tion upon which to build a rationale for engaging in social justice. Such a rationale focuses on a biblical understanding of God and humanity. Christians hold a high view of humanity as created in the image of God. No matter their re-ligious or socio-economic situation, people matter to God and should matter to Christians as well. When the Apostle Paul engaged philosophers in Athens (Acts 17:16-34) we learned that people were spiritual in nature and should be respected

(v. 22). In addition, Paul's speech at the Areopagus illustrated his perspective that people are created by God and are his offspring (vv. 26, 29). The very notion that we are offspring demands that we believe we bear some resemblance to the creator. God has determined the boundaries of people groups and permitted cultures to emerge while remaining near to them (vv. 25, 27). This conviction of God's care for people led Paul to proclaim the need to come to Christ.

Christians also believe that God is concerned with issues of social justice. It grieves the heart of God that people live in the impoverished situations when resources are available to help. Christians also believe that the proclamation of the gospel comes in both word and deed. The two cannot be separated (Matt 25-28). Christians must always keep in mind that behind the social issues are people who need Christ. So while we might work to eradicate poverty, lasting change will not occur until we engage people. Such people have both material and spiritual needs. Henry observed,

> A distinctive feature of New Testament ethics is its call to every believer to serve God and neighbor. Within family and community redeemed man stands in social relationship to both divine and human society. This dual relationship motivates his social responsibilities and by it he is linked to the whole enterprise of civilization.[29]

To engage in these areas requires thoughtful identification of issues of both local and global concern. As such, the Christian must be aware of one's society as well as the issues shaping the sundry cultures in society. An awareness of such issues comes by deliberate observation of and dialogue with these cultures. In addition, awareness comes by the study of the development of the issues and the worldviews of the people. Identifying cultural aspects of issues will always have in mind that behind them is an individual who has the need for Christ.

Because Christians are concerned for the spiritual dimension of the person, engaging social issues must be from a distinctly Christian perspective. Believing that God is omnipresent and omniscient as well as the plenipotentiary continued work of the Holy Spirit, the social issues in the world are not unknown to him. In fact, God continues to be at work in societies across the globe. It is the responsibility of the Christian to identify where God is at work and participate in what he is doing with concerted efforts to proclaim Christ's redeeming work in culture. Thus, it is necessary to have a solid theological foundation in order to address the world's social problems.

Conclusion

I have had opportunity over the past two years to visit some of the poorest places in the Western Hemisphere. As mentioned, in December 2009 I was in Nicaragua, the second poorest country in this hemisphere with a *per captia* GDP of just over $1,000, where I heard of child trafficking in both labor and sex. In March 2010 I was on the Pine Ridge Indian Reservation, which has the lowest life expectancy in the Western Hemisphere (between 47-56 years old) with very little industry.[30] Early in April 2010 and then again in October I was in Haiti, the poorest country in this hemisphere with a *per capita* GDP of less than $800, 90 percent unemployment and a life expectancy of 60 years old; where people continue to suffer from the devastating effect of the earthquake and extreme poverty. All three areas had one question in common: Where is the hope? Many in the world today have the same question.

It has been a long personal journey to arrive at social justice and probably not the typical manner by which one becomes involved in such issues. Over the course of the past several years I have been conducting research on a new religious movement known as contemporary Druidry.[31] Along the way I have gathered numerous interviews with Druids as well as others in an attempt to understand why people practice the religions they do. One interesting fact that emerged from the research was the number of people who were once Christian. When I first began this research I was quite surprised that many who left Christianity did so due to the impression that Christians were not acting like Christians. After eight years of such research and countless conversations I am no longer surprised, but have come to expect it. In fact, not only has my research found this to be true, the research of others has as well. This impression might be summed up by a comment that a Lakota recently made to me, "There is no honor in being a Christian." A now famous Haitian prayer, thanks to Pat Robertson erroneous reference to Satan, communicated a similar notion back in 1791,

> The god who created the sun which gives us light, who rouses the waves and rules the storm, though hidden in the clouds, he watches us. He sees all that the white man does. The god of the white man inspires him with the crime, but our god calls upon us to do good works. Our god who is good to us orders us to revenge our wrongs. He will direct our arms and aid us. Throw away the symbol of the god of the whites who has so often caused us to weep, and listen to the voice of liberty, which speaks in the hearts of us all.[32]

11

Of all religions of the world Christianity offers hope, but unfortunately the way that Christians have acted has inspired hopelessness. The true hope that Christianity offers is not only a future hope, it is a present hope. I believe that if the church is aware of the needs around the world she will rise to the call to bring the gospel in both word and deed. That is what this book is about. I hope you will be inspired to consider your part.

---

[1] Rodney Stark, *The Rise of Christianity: How the Obscure, Marginal Jesus Movement Became the Dominant Religious Force in the Western World in a Few Centuries* (San Francisco: Harper Collins, 1996), 73-94.

[2] Michael T. Cooper, "From Christendom to Post-Christendom: The Continuing Evolution of the Western Religious Landscape and the Emergence of New Religious Identities," in *Perspectives on Post-Christendom Spiritualities: Evangelical Reflections on New Spiritualities*, ed. Michael T. Cooper (Sydney: Morling, 2010), 1-18.

[3] Carl F.H. Henry, *Aspects of Christian Social Ethics* (Grand Rapids: Eerdmans, 1964), 21. See also Richard J. Mouw, "Carl Henry was Right," *Christianity Today* (January 2010): Internet resource available from http://www.christianitytoday.com/ct/2010/january/25.30.htm. Mouw, president of Fuller Theological Seminary, stated, "Christianity Today's first editor grasped what I as a young theologian failed to understand about church involvement in social justice."

[4] Robert E. Coleman, *The Master's Plan of Discipleship* (Old Tappen, N.J.: Fleming H. Revell, 1987), 96.

[5] Stephen P. Kennedy, "From Secular Rights to Sacred Rights," in *Perspectives on Post-Christendom Spiritualities: Reflections on New Religious Movements and Western Spiritualities*, eds. Michael T. Cooper (Sydney: Morling Press, 2010).

[6] The data for this section is extracted from the Millennium Development Goals Report 2009 (http://www.un.org/millenniumgoals/pdf/MDG_Report_2009_ENG.pdf) and 2010 (http://www.un.org/millenniumgoals/pdf/MDG%20Report%202010%20En%20r15%20-low%20res%2020100615%20-.pdf).

[7] Jimmy Carter, "Nobel Lecture," Oslo, Norway 10 December 2002. Internet resource available from http://nobelprize.org/nobel_prizes/peace /laureates /2002/carter-lecture.html.

[8] To put this number in perspective, it would take someone 215 years of non-stop counting to arrive at 6.8 billion.

---

[9]An increase from 1.37 billion in 2006, but a decrease from 1.5 billion in 2009.

[10]Despite global economic growth in the early part of this decade and the concomitant increase in employment, the unemployment rate began to climb in 2008. From a low of less than 2 percent in 2007, unemployment spiked in 2009 to 6.6 percent. While the global economy is recovering, unemployment is expected to be at 6.5 percent in 2010.

[11]See for example Kevin Bales, *Disposable People: New Slavery in the Global Economy* (Berkeley: University of California Press, 2004), 8-9.

[12]See U.S. Department of State, *Trafficking in Persons Report* (Washington, D.C.: U.S. Department of State 2004).

[13]Dambisa Moyo, *Dead Aid: Why Aid Is Not Working and How There Is a Better Way for Africa* (New York: Farrar, Straus and Giroux, 2009), 5.

[14]Mindy Belz and Alisa Harris, "Minding Africa's Business," *World*, (10 October 2009):34-40.

[15]Moyo, *Dead Aid*, 5-35.

[16]This represents a decline from 330 in 2007.

[17]Muhammad Yunus, *Creating a World Without Poverty: Social Business and the Future of Capitalism* (New York: Public Affairs, 2007), 238-239.

[18]There are ca. 138.1 million employed people in the United States. Seventy-six percent of the US population identifies as Christian leaving nearly 105 million employed people who identify themselves as Christian. The median weekly wage in 2009 was $739. When worked out, Christians earn approximately 4.018 trillion dollars a year. Data from, Steven F. Hipple, "The Labor Market in 2009: Recession Drags On," U.S. Labor Market, 2009 Internet resource available from http://www.bls.gov/opub/mlr/2010/03/art1full.pdf. Accessed 22 April 2010.

[19]The average household income in 2007 was $50,233.

[20]See A. Scott Moreau, "Putting the Survey in Perspective," Linda J. Weber and Dotsey Welliver, eds., *Mission Handbook 2007-2009* (Wheaton: Evangelism and Missions Information Services, 2007), 12-13.

[21] Their incomes are broken down as such: 19.89 million make less than 30,000 per year; 14.04 million make between 30-49,999 per year; 10.53 million make between 50-74,999 per year; 6.435 million make between 75-99,999 per year; 7.605 million make more than 100,000 per year.

[22]This number excludes the 19.89 million evangelicals who make less than 30K/year and the 7.605 million who make more than 100K/year.

[23]Data from the US Bureau of Labor Statistics. Available from http://www.bls.gov/cex/2009/Standard/cucomp.pdf

[24]Ibid., 218.

[25]Stark, *The Rise of Christianity*.

[26]Canon LXX.

[27]See for example Canons XIV, LXXV

[28]The covenant cites the following passages: Acts 17:26,31; Gen. 18:25; Isa. 1:17; Psa. 45:7; Gen. 1:26,27; Jas. 3:9; Lev. 19:18; Luke 6:27,35; Jas. 2:14-26; Joh. 3:3,5; Matt. 5:20; 6:33; II Cor. 3:18; Jas. 2:20.

[29]Henry, *Aspects of Christian Social Ethics*, 31.

[30]Evelyn Nieves, "On Pine Ridge, a String of Broken Promises," *Washington Post* (October 21, 2004). Internet resource available from http://www.washingtonpost.com/ac2/wp-dyn/A49822-2004Oct20?language=printer

[31]Michael T. Cooper, *Contemporary Druidry: A Historical and Ethnographic Study* (Salt Lake City: Sacred Tribes Press, 2010).

[32]Markel Thylefors, "'Our Governemnt is in Bwa Kayimon:' A Vodou Ceremony in 1791 and its Conteporary Significance," *Stockholm Review of Latin American Studies*, 4 (2009): 78.

Chapter Two

Toward a Theology of Social Justice

William J. Moulder

IT MIGHT SEEM SUPERFLUOUS to write about the responsibilities of believers to act justly and for justice since such requirements are writ large in both old and new covenants. But the frequency with which the Hebrew prophets and the Christian apostles confronted their faith communities with their failures to keep the covenant obligations and challenged them to act as God has instructed them suggests that the need to speak of the requirements of justice and mercy is perennial. Indeed, the history of the Christian church is also punctuated by the voices of reformers and prophets calling God's people back to righteous and just living. It will be worthwhile therefore to review what the old covenant and later the new covenant required of God's people and what the theological foundations of these requirements were. It may be good also to ask what some contemporary applications of these requirements might be and to ponder how the Spirit of God continually renews and energizes the church for its worship, witness, and work in the world. I suggest that acting right(eous)ly and justly is the responsible and faithful response to God's acting right(eous)ly and justly and to his intimate love under both old and new covenants. It may be good to begin with some definitions.

Definitions for Understanding Justice

The Hebrew word for "peace" is well known—*shalom*. TDNT defines it thusly, "At root it means 'well-bearing,' with a strong emphasis on the material side.[There are a] great number of passages in which shalom denotes relationship rather than a state."[1] Similarly, *NIDOTTE* definition includes, "The nom. Shalom is also used to express the social or communal relations between friends, parties, and nations . . . representing ...a friendly alliance."[2] The NT word for peace is *eirene*, meaning "a state of rest," has taken on the content of the Hebrew shalom since *eirene* in the LXX translated almost all of the OT passages where shalom occurs.[3] In sum, peace connotes wholeness in relationships--to God, to people, to the environment.

Peace is more than the absence of war; it cannot be reduced to the maintenance of a balance of power between opposing forces nor does it arise out of despotic dominion, but it is appropriately called the "effect of righteousness" (Isaiah 32:17). It is the fruit of that right ordering of things with which the divine founder has invested human society and which must be actualized by humans thirsting after an ever more perfect reign of justice. Peace cannot be obtained on earth unless human welfare is safeguarded and people freely and trustingly share with one another the riches of their mind and their talents. A firm determination to respect the dignity of others and other peoples along with the deliberate practice of love are absolutely necessary for the achievement of peace. Accordingly, peace is also the fruit of love, for love goes beyond what justice can ensure.

Therefore, all Christians are earnestly to speak the truth in love (cf. Ephesians 4:15) and join with all who love peace in pleading for peace and trying to bring it about. In the same spirit we cannot but express our admiration for all who forgo the use of violence to vindicate their rights and resort to those other means of defense which are available to weaker parties, provided it can be done without harm to the rights and duties of others and of the community.

Insofar as all are sinners, the threat of war hangs over them and will so continue until the coming of Christ; but insofar as they can vanquish sin by coming together in charity, violence itself will be vanquished and they will make these words come true: "They shall beat their swords into plowshares, and their spears into pruning hooks; nation shall not lift up sword against nation, neither shall they learn war any more" (Isaiah 2:4)[4]

Soong-Chan Rah, cites Walter Brueggemann's distinction between "*shalom* of the haves and of the have-nots.*" He commented, "A theology of blessing [celebration] for the well off 'haves' is very different from the theology of salvation [suffering] for the precarious 'have-nots.'" Rah insists that, just as "a proper kingdom theology demands the intersection between the now and the not yet—a proper shalom theology dictates that there is an intersection between suffering and salvation."[5]

The words "just(ice)" and "right(eousness)" essentially mean conformity to a standard; in OT this standard is the law of God which is fundamentally an expression of God's essential nature. To be just or righteous [Heb. *zedek*] therefore means to observe the law of God conscientiously. Those who are just/righteous therefore reflect the character of God who gave the law. "Be holy as I am holy" (Lev. 19:2b) expresses this idea in its simplest form. Inasmuch as God cares for the poor, the orphan, the widow, and the stranger, the law of God requires this

16

same care for the most vulnerable (Dt. 10:17-21).[6] *NIDNTT* states, "Righteousness in the OT is not a matter of actions conforming to a given set of absolute legal standards, but of behavior which is in keeping with the two-way relationship between God and man. Thus the righteousness of God appears in his God-like dealings with his people, i.e. in redemption and salvation (Isa. 45:21; 51:5f.; 56:1; 62:1)."[7] Consequently Israel is to imitate God's righteous behavior: ". . . Yahweh's righteousness implies the same kind of right conduct . . . in Israel; the justice appropriate to Israel on her side is determined by her position as the covenant people. . . ."[8]

Especially significant is the use of the Greek word *dikaios* in the LXX where the word is used of God himself. "The fact that in Hellenistic Judaism, too, God can be called *dikaios*, the One who is infallibly consistent in the normative self-determination of His own nature, and who maintains unswerving faithfulness in the fulfillment of His promises and covenant agreements, prepares the ground for the crucial religious importance of the term in the NT."[9] Not surprisingly the Messiah is also called *dikaios*. "The Messiah is called righteous because His whole nature and action are in conformity with the norm of the divine will."[10]

The rabbinical interpretation of Hab. 2:4 is significant. Righteousness is "a comprehensive fulfillment of the commandments in meritorious faithfulness."[11] But it should also be noted that in the LXX the *relational* aspect of righteousness is especially important: "A man is righteous when he meets certain claims which another has on him in virtue of relationship. Even the righteousness of God is primarily His covenantal rule in fellowship with His people."[12] God's righteousness in relationship is particularly linked with the idea of "help" or "salvation," God's intervention for the oppressed.[13] In this respect righteousness is closely to "stedfast-love", "mercy" [Heb. *Hesed*, Gk. *Eleos*] which the LXX sometimes uses to translated *zekek*. "It thus signifies the commitment to an act of loving service which arises within a social relationship (tribe, friendship or covenant)."[14] This thought is expressed in Mt. 6:33: "Seek first the kingdom of God and its righteousness." This statement "refers to that which brings the disciple into harmony with the will of God. . . . Righteousness is here closely linked with God and His kingdom . . . ."[15]

"Compassion" is inseparably related to "justice:" *"Compassion is the interiorisation of justice.* Compassion is the motivating force that drives us on to do justice spontaneously, willingly and perseveringly. It is the compassion of Jesus who began his ministry with the mission of bringing good news to the poor, liberty to captives, recovery of sight to the blind and release to prisoners (Luke 4:18)"[16] In Psalm 83:10 ("Righteousness and peace have kissed") the personifica-

17

tion of these two values vividly underscores their intimate relationship: there can be no real justice without peace and no real peace without justice![17]

Hebrew Covenantal Obligations and Their Theological Foundation

In the Torah (Law, Pentateuch)

In Ex. 20:2 the Ten Commandments are rooted in God's character: "I am the LORD your God, who brought you out of the land of Egypt, out of the house of slavery" (cf. Deut. 5:6). The action of God toward Israel . . . precedes the commandments and is the justification for them."[18] The same foundation is given in Deut 5:9-10 You shall not bow down to them or worship them; for I the LORD your God am a jealous God, punishing children for the iniquity of parents, to the third and fourth generation of those who reject me, [10] but showing steadfast love to the thousandth generation of those who love me and keep my commandments (Ex 20:5-6) Likewise in Dt. 10:17-21 God's fairness and compassion for the most vulnerable (orphans, widows, and strangers) is the basis for justice that should characterizes God's people:

> [17]For the LORD your God is God of gods and Lord of lords, the great God, mighty and awesome, who is not partial and takes no bribe, [18] who executes justice for the orphan and the widow, and who loves the strangers, providing them food and clothing. [19] You shall also love the stranger, for you were strangers in the land of Egypt. [20] You shall fear the LORD your God; him alone you shall worship; to him you shall hold fast, and by his name you shall swear. [21] He is your praise; he is your God, who has done for you these great and awesome things that your own eyes have seen.

In Num 35:34 God says of the land that it is "the land in which I also dwell," God's presence in the land requiring justice be done there. "Dwelling in the land as [God] does, Israel partakes of God's righteousness (Ps.24[23]:5) and such righteousness may actually be referred to in spatial terms (Pss. 89[88]:16; 69[68]:28)."[19] What might be the implications of this for land use and possession? What might be the contemporary application to Israeli-Palestinian conflicts? Leviticus 19:2b states, "I am holy" and "I am the Lord" (vv.3, 4, 10, 12, 14, 16, 18, 25, 30, 31, 32, 34, 37) provides the divine sanction for the various laws, including especially love for neighbor (v. 18) and even love for the alien as for oneself (v.34)!

In the Prophets

D. Hill commented, "The prophetic teaching [is] essentially a recalling of Israel to the covenant and to the standards and way of life which should characterise national and individual existence within the covenant."[20] For example, in Amos 8 the promised land becomes another Egypt--place of slavery!--(v.8) through the greedy exploitation of the poor (vv. 5-6). Micah 6:6-8 reads:

> With what shall I come before the LORD, and bow myself before God on high? Shall I come before him with burnt offerings, with calves a year old? Will the LORD be pleased with thousands of rams, with ten thousands of rivers of oil? Shall I give my firstborn for my transgression, the fruit of my body for the sin of my soul? He has told you, O mortal, what is good; and what does the LORD require of you but to do justice, and to love kindness, and to walk humbly with your God?

Here the prophet clearly states that doing justice is a ***primary*** element in Hebrew religion. Isaiah agrees [note the italicized portions]: 1:15ff.

> When you stretch out your hands, I will hide my eyes from you; even though you make many prayers, I will not listen; your hands are full of blood. [16] Wash yourselves; make yourselves clean; remove the evil of your doings from before my eyes; cease to do evil, [17] *learn to do good; seek justice, rescue the oppressed, defend the orphan, plead for the widow.* [18] Come now, let us argue it out, says the LORD: though your sins are like scarlet, they shall be like snow; though they are red like crimson, they shall become like wool. [19] If you are willing and obedient, you shall eat the good of the land; [20] but if you refuse and rebel, you shall be devoured by the sword; for the mouth of the LORD has spoken. [21] How the faithful city has become a whore! *She that was full of justice, righteousness lodged in her-- but now murderers!* [22] Your silver has become dross, your wine is mixed with water. [23] Your princes are rebels and companions of thieves. Everyone loves a bribe and runs after gifts. *They do not defend the orphan, and the widow's cause does not come before them.*
>
> [24] Therefore says the Sovereign, the LORD of hosts, the Mighty One of Israel: Ah, I will pour out my wrath on my enemies, and avenge myself on my foes! [25] I will turn my hand against you; I will smelt away your dross as with lye and remove all your alloy. [26] And I will restore your judges as at the first, and your counselors as at the beginning. Afterward *you shall be called the city of righteousness,* the faithful city. [27] Zion shall be redeemed *by justice, and those in her who repent, by righteousness.*

In the Writings

The righteous life that pleases God is describes by Job in his attempts to understand the meaning of his unmerited suffering:

> [11] When the ear heard, it commended me, and when the eye saw, it approved; [12] because I delivered the poor who cried, and the orphan who had no helper. [13] The blessing of the wretched came upon me, and I caused the widow's heart to sing for joy. [14] I put on righteousness, and it clothed me; my justice was like a robe and a turban. [15] I was eyes to the blind, and feet to the lame. [16] I was a father to the needy, and I championed the cause of the stranger. [17] I broke the fangs of the unrighteous, and made them drop their prey from their teeth; (Job 29:11-16)

> [16] "If I have withheld anything that the poor desired, or have caused the eyes of the widow to fail, [17] or have eaten my morsel alone, and the orphan has not eaten from it-- [18] for from my youth I reared the orphan like a father, and from my mother's womb I guided the widow-- [19] if I have seen anyone perish for lack of clothing, or a poor person without covering, [20] whose loins have not blessed me, and who was not warmed with the fleece of my sheep; [21] if I have raised my hand against the orphan, because I saw I had supporters at the gate; [22] then let my shoulder blade fall from my shoulder, and let my arm be broken from its socket. [23] For I was in terror of calamity from God, and I could not have faced his majesty. [24] "If I have made gold my trust, or called fine gold my confidence; [25] if I have rejoiced because my wealth was great, or because my hand had gotten much; [26] if I have looked at the sun when it shone, or the moon moving in splendor, [27] and my heart has been secretly enticed, and my mouth has kissed my hand; [28] this also would be an iniquity to be punished by the judges, for I should have been false to God above. (Job 31:16-28)

Psalm 49 speaks of the folly of trusting in riches:

> [5]Why should I fear in times of trouble, when the iniquity of my persecutors surrounds me, [6] *those who trust in their wealth and boast of the abundance of their riches?* [7] Truly, no ransom avails for one's life, there is no price one can give to God for it. [8] For the ransom of life is costly, and can never suffice [9] that one should live on forever and never see the grave. . . . [16] Do not be afraid when some become rich, when the wealth of their houses increases. [17] *For when they die they will carry nothing away; their wealth will not go down after them.* [18] Though in their lifetime they count themselves happy-- for you are praised when you do well for yourself-- [19] they will go to the company of their ancestors, who will never again see the light. [20] Mortals cannot abide in their pomp; they are like the animals that perish.

20

Anderson commented, "God cannot be bought off, and no wealth, however great, can alter the purposes of God." (A.A.Anderson, *Psalms, NCB*,376)

Recognizing how important it is for the leaders of God's people to practice justice, several psalms pray for Israel's king. **Psalm 72** is one example (cf. Prov. 29:14).

> [1]Give the king your justice, O God, and your righteousness to a king's son. [2]May he judge your people with righteousness, and your poor with justice. [3]May the mountains yield prosperity for the people, and the hills, in righteousness. [4]May he defend the cause of the poor of the people, give deliverance to the needy, and crush the oppressor. . . . [7]In his days may righteousness flourish and peace abound, until the moon is no more.
>
> [12]For he delivers the needy when they call, the poor and those who have no helper.
>
> [14]From oppression and violence he redeems their life; and precious is their blood in his sight.

Likewise in **Psalm 113** God is praised for his care for the poor and the needy:

> [1] Praise the LORD! Praise, O servants of the LORD; praise the name of the LORD. [2] Blessed be the name of the LORD from this time on and forevermore. [3] From the rising of the sun to its setting the name of the LORD is to be praised. [4] The LORD is high above all nations, and his glory above the heavens. [5] Who is like the LORD our God, who is seated on high, [6] who looks far down on the heavens and the earth? [7] He raises the poor from the dust, and lifts the needy from the ash heap, [8] to make them sit with princes, with the princes of his people. [9] He gives the barren woman a home, making her the joyous mother of children. Praise the LORD!

The biblical standard for political leaders—righteousness/justice and care for the poor--is reflected in these words of Shakepeare's King Lear when he finds himself homeless:

> Poor naked wretches, wheresoe'er you are,
> That bide the pelting of this pitiless storm,
> How shall your houseless heads and unfed sides,
> Your looped and windowed raggedness, defend you
> From seasons such as these? O, I have ta'en
> Too little care of this! Take physic, pomp;
> Expose thyself to feel what wretches feel,

That thou mayst shake the superflux to them,
And show the heavens more just." *King Lear*, III, iv, 28-36

In Psalm 82 *God speaks and confronts those who practice injustice:* verses 1-4 God has taken his place in the divine council; in the midst of the gods he holds judgment:

> [2] "How long will you judge unjustly and show partiality to the wicked? Selah [3] Give justice to the weak and the orphan; maintain the right of the lowly and the destitute. [4] Rescue the weak and the needy; deliver them from the hand of the wicked."

Dahood comments, "The psalmist had been under the impression that the pagan deities were of some importance, but now realizes that they are nothing, because they are quite incapable of defending the poor and rescuing the downtrodden."[21]

Psalm 104 speaks of *God's generous provision of food* for people and animals alike.

> [14] You cause the grass to grow for the cattle, and plants for people to use, to bring forth food from the earth, [15] and wine to gladden the human heart, oil to make the face shine, and bread to strengthen the human heart. [16] The trees of the LORD are watered abundantly, the cedars of Lebanon that he planted. [17] In them the birds build their nests; the stork has its home in the fir trees. [18] The high mountains are for the wild goats; the rocks are a refuge for the coneys. [19] You have made the moon to mark the seasons; the sun knows its time for setting. [20] You make darkness, and it is night, when all the animals of the forest come creeping out. [21] The young lions roar for their prey, seeking their food from God. [22] When the sun rises, they withdraw and lie down in their dens. [23] People go out to their work and to their labor until the evening. [24] O LORD, how manifold are your works! In wisdom you have made them all; the earth is full of your creatures. [25] Yonder is the sea, great and wide, creeping things innumerable are there, living things both small and great. [26] There go the ships, and Leviathan that you formed to sport in it. [27] *These all look to you to give them their food in due season;* [28] when you give to them, they gather it up; when you open your hand, they are filled with good things. [29] When you hide your face, they are dismayed; when you take away their breath, they die and return to their dust. [30] When you send forth your spirit, they are created; and you renew the face of the ground.

This point is made also in Psalm 145:[15] The eyes of all look to you, and *you give them their food in due season.* [16] You open your hand, satisfying the desire of every living thing. [17] *The LORD is just in all his ways, and kind in all his doings.*

Similar statements are found in the Proverbs. For instance, "The good leave an inheritance to their children's children, but the sinner's wealth is laid up for the righteous. [23] The field of the poor may yield much food, but it is swept away through injustice" (Prov 13:22-23).

Prov. 14:20-21 speaks of and challenges the perennial tendency of humans to value people accounding to their wealth: "The poor are disliked even by their neighbors [cf. 19:7], but the rich have many friends. [21] Those who despise their neighbors are sinners, but happy are those who are kind to the poor.

Prov. 29 speaks of both people and ruler as righteous when they regard the poor:

> [7] The *righteous know the rights of the poor*; the wicked have no such understanding.

> [13] The poor and the oppressor have this in common: the LORD gives light to the eyes of both. [14] *If a king judges the poor with equity, his throne will be established forever.*

One of the most important statements made in the writings shows the strong connection between a person's treatment of the poor and their attitude toward God: "*Those who mock the poor insult their Maker*; those who are glad at calamity will not go unpunished" (Prov. 17:5).

New Covenant Obligations and Their Theological Foundation

In the Gospels

Jesus called disciples to follow him and become like him. The word "disciple" means "someone who learns." This meaning is clear in Mt.11:28-:28, "Come to me, all you that are weary and are carrying heavy burdens, and I will give you rest. [29] Take my yoke upon you, and learn from me; for I am gentle and humble in heart, and you will find rest for your souls. [30] For my yoke is easy, and my burden is light."

Davies sees in this passage that Jesus is the equivalent to Torah in Judaism: "The Sages learned Torah, the disciples learn Jesus", including all that Jesus had said and done (11:2, 19-20).[22] He added, "In this passage, Jesus reveals that he is the revealer. That is, he reveals that, as the meek and humble Son of the Father, he fulfills the calling of Israel, embodying in his own person Torah and Wisdom and thus making known the perfect will of God."[23] It is the person of Jesus also

23

which provides the motivation to follow him as a disciple. As N.T. Wright says, "The longer you look at Jesus, the more you will want to serve him in his world."[24]

The disciples, those who are taught and who learn, are commissioned to teach others what Jesus had taught them (Mt. 28:19-20). In John the Baptist's question and Jesus' reply (Mt 11:2-11) it is clear that caring for those most in need were Jesus' major priority.

In Lk. 4:16-21, Jesus' first recorded sermon, giving in the synagogue in Capernaum, he read the servant song of Isa 61:1f., which describes the messianic figure of the Servant of the Lord, one who cares for the vulnerable, Jesus said that this scripture was being fulfilled in his ministry.

> [16] When he came to Nazareth, where he had been brought up, he went to the synagogue on the sabbath day, as was his custom. He stood up to read, [17] and the scroll of the prophet Isaiah was given to him. He unrolled the scroll and found the place where it was written: [18] "The Spirit of the Lord is upon me, because he has anointed me to bring good news to the poor. He has sent me to proclaim release to the captives and recovery of sight to the blind, to let the oppressed go free, [19] to proclaim the year of the Lord's favor." [20] And he rolled up the scroll, gave it back to the attendant, and sat down. The eyes of all in the synagogue were fixed on him. [21] Then he began to say to them, "Today this scripture has been fulfilled in your hearing."

Isaiah 42 includes similar statements about the messiah.

> [1]Here is my servant, whom I uphold, my chosen, in whom my soul delights; I have put my spirit upon him; he will bring forth justice to the nations. [2] He will not cry or lift up his voice, or make it heard in the street; [3] a bruised reed he will not break, and a dimly burning wick he will not quench; he will faithfully bring forth justice. [4] He will not grow faint or be crushed until he has established justice in the earth; and the coastlands wait for his teaching. [5] Thus says God, the LORD, who created the heavens and stretched them out, who spread out the earth and what comes from it, who gives breath to the people upon it and spirit to those who walk in it: [6]I am the LORD, I have called you in righteousness, I have taken you by the hand and kept you; I have given you as a covenant to the people, a light to the nations.

Both in his teaching and his manner of life Jesus taught what it means to be his disciple and consequently what it means to live a life of justice/righteousness and peace. This means more than simply following the letter of the law. "Woe to you, scribes and Pharisees, hypocrites! For you tithe mint, dill, and cummin, and have neglected the weightier matters of the law: justice and mercy and faith" (Mt 23:23). It is these you ought to have practiced without neglecting the others. As Davies notes tithing is not invalidated by "weightier" matters of the law but rather subordinated to them: it is the misplaced priorities of the Pharisees Jesus criticizes, not Jewish tradition itself.[25]

Jesus continues:

> [24]You blind guides! You strain out a gnat but swallow a camel! [25] "Woe to you, scribes and Pharisees, hypocrites! For you clean the outside of the cup and of the plate, but inside they are full of greed and self-indulgence. [26] You blind Pharisee! First clean the inside of the cup, so that the outside also may become clean. [27] "Woe to you, scribes and Pharisees, hypocrites! For you are like whitewashed tombs, which on the outside look beautiful, but inside they are full of the bones of the dead and of all kinds of filth. [28] So you also on the outside look righteous to others, but inside you are full of hypocrisy and lawlessness." (Mt 23:24-28)

Davies puts it eloquently: "The scribes and Pharisees play on the sea shore of religion while the great ocean of fundamental truth lies all undiscovered before them."[26] Jesus' call to love others included even enemies (Mt. 5:43-8; but Torah also called for love of aliens, Lev. 19:33-34). Because this exhortation is both the climactic and the most difficult command,[27] it leads to the call to "be perfect as your Father in heaven is perfect" (5:48)!

In the parable of the vineyard (Mt. 20:1-16) what the landowner considered "right/just" turns out to be what is "generous"; this means giving people what they *need*, not what they can earn. This "righteousness/justice" of the God's kingdom is what believers are to seek *first*, Mt. 6:33. Because the instruction in Mt.5-7 is hard teaching, Jesus reminds his disciples that they have a Father in heaven who gives good gifts to his children (6:25-34; 7:7-11).[28]

And seeking first the Kingdom of God means understanding the nature of the King and his kind of rule/reign—a reign of justice (as described by Mary in her Magnificat, Lk. 1:47-55). It also means being agents of this kingdom and of its coming.

Jesus words to the "rich young ruler" in Mt. 19:21, "Sell what you have and give it to the poor and you will have treasure in heaven" suggest an antipathy between earthy wealth and heavenly wealth—one cannot have both! Similarly in Mt. 5:19,

> Do not store up for yourselves treasures on earth, where moth and rust consume and where thieves break in and steal; [20] but store up for your-

selves treasures in heaven, where neither moth nor rust consumes and where thieves do not break in and steal. [21] For where your treasure is, there your heart will be also.

How does one "store up treasure in heaven"? The explanation is found in the broader context of Mt. 5-7: the Father rewards those described in the Beatitudes (5:3-12), those who practice their piety in secret (6:1), give alms, pray, and fast in secret (6:4, 6, 18) and love their neighbors as themselves (7:12). (Davies, I, 632)

Maura Eichner's poem brings this down to earth.

Continually think of those
who were truly great
who in their lives fought
for life, who wore
at their hearts, the fire's
center. Feel the meanings
the words hide. Make routine
a stimulus. Remember
it can cease. Forge
hosannahs from doubt.
Hammer on doors with the heart.
All occasions invite God's
mercies and all times
are his season.[29]

With regard to money Jesus puts the matter bluntly in Lk. 16: 13 No slave can serve two masters; for a slave will either hate the one and love the other, or be devoted to the one and despise the other. You cannot serve God and wealth." Fitzmyer comments: "The saying puts the attitude toward money very radically: God or mammon! Which is going to govern one's life? For no one can serve both of them! If one allows oneself to get involved in the servile pursuit of wealth and reduces oneself to a slave of it, then one cannot really serve God. Mammon thus becomes the god that one serves. So the saying puts the question to the Christian reader: Which do you want to serve?"[30]

Then significantly we learn in v. 14 that "The Pharisees, who were lovers of money, heard all this, and they ridiculed him." This comes after the parable of the unjust steward, the point of which is that "the children of the kingdom" should be wise in the use of material resources to achieve heavenly ends. In the parable of the rich man and poor Lazarus, the sin of rich man is not that he made Lazarus poor. Rather, being aware of Lazarus' need and having abundant means of helping, the rich man neglected him. (Lk. 16:19-31) Fitzmyer noted T.W.Manson's

(*Sayings*, 301) felicitious description of this section of Luke as "the Gospel of the Outcast", asking of the disciples of Jesus their "generous and gracious help for all the victims of poverty, sickness, and any other ill."[31] Manson and others see Luke making "a deliberate attempt to show God's concern for those human beings whom people tend to despise or condemn."[32] This emphasis in Luke is developed in Cassidy, *Jesus, Politics, and Society*, who notes Jesus' particular concern for the outsider and despised: women, children, gentiles, and the poor.

The often quoted statement "the poor you have always" is sometimes take as a resolution to the status quo and that relieving poverty should not be a priority. But this clearly not what Jesus intended as is made apparent in Mark's account: For you always have the poor with you, and you can show kindness to them whenever you wish; but you will not always have me. (Mk. 14:7) "He was not diminishing the importance of relieving the suffering of the poor. In Deuteronomy 15:11, to which Jesus may have been alluding, the observation that 'there will never cease to be some in need on the earth' is tied to the command to 'open your hand to the poor.' The issue is not a forced choice between worship and ministry; there is a time for each, and the poor will always be better served by the spontaneous generosity of the unnamed woman than the calculating plans of those who were critical of the beautiful thing she did for Jesus." (Culpepper, *Mark*, 486).

In the parable of the sheep and the goats in Mt. 25:31-46 Jesus gives the criteria for the last judgment: feeding the hungry, clothing the naked, taking in the homeless, and visiting prisoners. Ron Sider's *Rich Christians in an Age of Hunger*, outlines the modern application of this concern for the poor and the hungry. As Kenneth Leech says, "The gospel demand is a practical demand. It is useless to worship the God who is present everywhere, and ignore his presence somewhere. To fail to recognize Christ in the hungry and thirsty, in the stranger and the naked, in the sick and the prisoner, is to deny the incarnation."[33]

John emphasizes this point very clearly in chapter 13: Jesus, "having loved his own, loves them to the end/to the utmost", demonstrates his love in humble service by washing their feet (before giving his life on the cross); then he calls his disciples to do the same. "Jesus' love for his own was capable of any act of service or suffering. . . . [and] Jesus loved his own up to the last moment of his life."[34] The healings and other miracles of compassion are in John's Gospel seen as *signs* that Jesus is the Son of God (John 20:30-31; 21:25)

Being Jesus' disciple means remaining intimately related to Jesus, keeping his commandments, bearing the fruit of good works, and remaining in Jesus' love and loving others. As a result the Father is glorified (John 15:1-17): v. 8 My Father is glorified by this, that you bear much fruit and become my disciples.v.9 As the Father has loved me, so I have loved you; abide in my love.

In Acts and the Epistles

Peter describes the life of Jesus as one of caring for the needy, evidence that Jesus is the Messiah. "You that are Israelites, listen to what I have to say: Jesus of Nazareth, a man attested to you by God with deeds of power, wonders, and signs that God did through him among you, as you yourselves know" (Acts 2:22).

He says the same thing to the first gentile convert, Cornelius:

> You know the message he sent to the people of Israel, preaching peace by Jesus Christ-- he is Lord of all. [37] That message spread throughout Judea, beginning in Galilee after the baptism that John announced: [38] how God anointed Jesus of Nazareth with the Holy Spirit and with power; how he went about doing good and healing all who were oppressed by the devil, for God was with him. [38] how God anointed Jesus of Nazareth with the Holy Spirit and with power; how he went about doing good and healing all who were oppressed by the devil, for God was with him. (Acts 10:36)

The early church is described in Acts as giving, sharing community and one in which healing made for powerful witness (Acts 2:43-47). The Greek verbs in 2:45 are in the imperfect tense: "Luke is describing a state which persisted for some time."[35] Elsewhere in Acts, the charitable and miraculous works of the apostles and the church had a powerful effect on those who witnessed the believers' life together and their emulation of Jesus' compassion and service (Acts 3:9-10; 4:13-14; 4:32-37; 5:12-16). Barnabas sold his property and gave the proceeds to the church, unlike Ananias and Sappira who only pretended to do so (Acts 4:34-5:11).

The practical applications of Paul's great exposition of "justification by faith" in Romans are spelled out in a series of brief exhortations characteristic of the early apostolic correspondence. These applications give particular attention to those in need, as in Rom. 12:13, 20-21: "Contribute to the needs of the saints; extend hospitality to strangers."

> [14] Bless those who persecute you; bless and do not curse them. [15] Rejoice with those who rejoice, weep with those who weep. [16] Live in harmony with one another; do not be haughty, but associate with the lowly; do not claim to be wiser than you are. [17] Do not repay anyone evil for evil, but take thought for what is noble in the sight of all. [18] If it is possible, so far as it depends on you, live peaceably with all. [19] Beloved, never avenge yourselves, but leave room for the wrath of God; for it is written, "Ven-

geance is mine, I will repay, says the Lord." [20] No, "if your enemies are hungry, feed them; if they are thirsty, give them something to drink; for by doing this you will heap burning coals on their heads." [21] Do not be overcome by evil, but overcome evil with good."

Similar practical expression of faith is given at the end of Hebrews: 13:1 Let mutual love continue. Heb 13:2 show hospitality; remember those in prison, Heb 13:3 keep yourselves free from the love of money, Heb. 13:5; 13:16 Do not neglect to do good and to share what you have, for such sacrifices are pleasing to God. "Brotherly love" (v.1), which was understood necessarily to involve the sharing of possessions,[36] is to be extended to strangers as well (hospitality, v. 2) and prisoners. "Hebrews opposes "being content with what you have" to greed. . . . Such contentment is the prerequisite for the ability to share one's possessions . . . [13:16]" (p. 343). This contentment comes from placing one's trust in God, not in possessions.

My brothers and sisters, do you with your acts of favoritism really believe in our glorious Lord Jesus Christ? [2] For if a person with gold rings and in fine clothes comes into your assembly, and if a poor person in dirty clothes also comes in, [3] and if you take notice of the one wearing the fine clothes and say, "Have a seat here, please," while to the one who is poor you say, "Stand there," or, "Sit at my feet," [4] have you not made distinctions among yourselves, and become judges with evil thoughts? [5] Listen, my beloved brothers and sisters. Has not God chosen the poor in the world to be rich in faith and to be heirs of the kingdom that he has promised to those who love him? [6] But you have dishonored the poor. Is it not the rich who oppress you? Is it not they who drag you into court? [7] Is it not they who blaspheme the excellent name that was invoked over you? [8] You do well if you really fulfill the royal law according to the scripture, "You shall love your neighbor as yourself." [9] But if you show partiality, you commit sin and are convicted by the law as transgressors. [10] For whoever keeps the whole law but fails in one point has become accountable for all of it. [11] For the one who said, "You shall not commit adultery," also said, "You shall not murder." Now if you do not commit adultery but if you murder, you have become a transgressor of the law. [12] So speak and so act as those who are to be judged by the law of liberty. [13] For judgment will be without mercy to anyone who has shown no mercy; *mercy triumphs over judgment.* [14] What good is it, my brothers and sisters, if you say you have faith but do not have works? Can faith save you? [15] If a brother or sister is naked and lacks daily food, [16] and one of you says to them, "Go in peace; keep warm and eat your fill," and *yet you do not supply their bodily needs, what is the good of that?* [17] (James 2:1-17)

So faith by itself, if it has no works, is dead. James is describing the pious response of one who prays for the needy to be provided for but offers the hungry nothing but a prayer! The verb translated "eat your fill" is used of fattening cattle (meaning well fed): James is giving a caricature[37] of the one who prays but does not act!

Genuine love, God's love, is necessarily expressed in deeds done to help those in need: "How does God's love abide in anyone who has the world's goods and sees a brother or sister in need and yet refuses help?" (I Jn. 3:17). The word translated "sees" appears only here in the Johannine epistles. "It implies a prolonged look at a needy brother, rather than a casual glance. . . . The subject . . . has ample time to take in the plight of the other person; and this means he has less justification than ever for turning away.[38] As Schnackenburg says, "The author puts all his emphasis on the *deed* of love" [italics added].[39] The phrase "love of God" could mean love for God, God's love for us, or love like God's love. Smalley says, "the context demands . . . that we should understand we should the primary meaning as 'a love like God's.'"[40] Putting James and 1 John together, it appears that caring for those in need is a *sine qua non* of both *faith* and *love*!

As we learn in 2 Pet 3:13, righteousness will characterize the world to come: "But, in accordance with his promise, we wait for new heavens and a new earth, where righteousness is at home." This is what we pray for when we say the Lord's prayer: "Your kingdom come. Your will be done, on earth as it is in heaven." (Mt. 6:10).

In Revelation may be found one of the strongest indictments of the wicked world which God judges in his wrath. Included in the list of items of trade in an economically wealthy but spiritual impoverished "Babylon" is the statement "and human souls" (Rev. 18:13)! That humans can be bought and sold as merchandise is stated in a sort of matter-of-fact manner intended to shock the reader of Revelation. That the world today traffics in humans in the sex trade and other forms of modern human slavery challenges the followers of Jesus to act to oppose this great evil.

The crass materialism described here is also relevant to our modern situation, particularly in the affluent West. G.E. Ladd said of this text, "The language used implies an attitude of arrogance on the part of Babylon's merchants. Her sin did not consist always in the fact of her wealth, but in the overwhelming pride and self-exaltation induced by her wealth. . . . Her sin was not alone in wanton luxury, but a crass materialism which led her to exalt herself over God and persecute the people of God."[41] One wonders whether the lack of persecution of Christians in

developed nations is due to the fact that those who profess to follow Jesus are not sufficiently different from in non-believers in their attitudes toward wealth and their materialistic lifestyle. Were Christians to be radically counter-cultural in devoting themselves to simple living, thereby threatening the consumer economy in which they live, might persecution indeed be the result?

Foundational for a lifestyle of doing justice is the character of God. This point is reiterated many times in Holy Scripture. "Be holy as I am holy" (Lev. 19). "Be perfect as your Father in heaven is perfect" (Mt. 5:48) "Be imitators of God, as beloved children and live in love as Christ loved us and gave himself up for us, a fragrant offering and sacrifice to God" (Eph. 5:1-2). Above all it is in the person, work, and words of Jesus the Christ that the character of God is most clearly seen and the ultimate model of the kind of life that most pleases God. Disciples of Jesus therefore reflect the character and believer of their Lord: "You call me Teacher and Lord-- and you are right, for that is what I am. So if I, your Lord and Teacher, have washed your feet, you also ought to wash one another's feet. For I have set you an example, that you also should do as I have done to you" (Jn. 13:13-15).

Gerard Manley Hopkins expresses this idea clearly:

> AS kingfishers catch fire, dragonflies dráw fláme;
> As tumbled over rim in roundy wells
> Stones ring; like each tucked string tells, each hung bell's
> Bow swung finds tongue to fling out broad its name;
> Each mortal thing does one thing and the same: *5*
> Deals out that being indoors each one dwells;
> Selves—goes itself; *myself* it speaks and spells,
> Crying *Whát I do is me: for that I came.*
> Í say móre: the just man justices;
> Kéeps gráce: thát keeps all his goings graces;   *10*
> Acts in God's eye what in God's eye he is—
> Chríst—for Christ plays in ten thousand places,
> Lovely in limbs, and lovely in eyes not his
> To the Father through the features of men's faces.

Conclusion

In conclusion, *caring for the poor is not an option for the Christian, it is an OBLIGATION!* It is a matter of obedience to the obligations under both old and new covenants. It is a matter of following Jesus, obeying Jesus, being like Jesus. It is the criterion of the Last Judgment, proof of being truly one of Jesus' disciples (Mt. 25). It is a matter of being like God who cares for the poor, a matter of loving others as God has loved humans, and a matter of seeking first the Kingdom of God.

There are some concrete steps to take in response to these reminders of the Christian's responsibility under God.

1. A first step is to recognize and acknowledge the believer's obligation. This is not, of course, about salvation by works. It is about a faith that works, as James says (and Paul in Philip. 2:12). This is also the grateful response to God's grace given freely to sinners in the offering of His Son.

2. It is also essential to recognize and repent of failures to live faithfuly, including such injustices as unconscious exploitation of the poor through the purchase of cheap goods and complicity in systemic injustices of many kinds as well as "addiction" to an affluent lifestyle full of "things" (and measuring the quality of life by possessions).

The following prayer of repentance is a useful guide.

From the litany of penitence for Ash Wednesday (BCP, 267-8)

We have not loved you with our whole heart, and mind, and strength. We have not loved our neighbors as ourselves. We have not forgiven others, as we have been forgiven.

We have been deaf to your call to serve, as Christ served us.

Our self-indulgent appetites and ways, and our exploitation of other people, we confess to you, Lord.

Our intemperate love of worldly goods and comforts, and our dishonesty in daily life and work, we confess to you, Lord

Accept our repentance, Lord, for the wrongs we have done: for our blindness to human need and suffering, and our indifference to injustice and cruelty; accept our repentance, Lord.

For all false judgments, for uncharitable thoughts toward our neighbors, and for our prejudice and contempt toward those who differ from us, accept our repentance, Lord.

For our waste and pollution of your creation, and our lack of concern for those who come after us, accept our repentance, Lord.

Accomplish in us the work of your salvation, that we may show forth your glory in the world.

3. It is important to make specific and concrete changes in life-style. The motto "live simply that others may simply life" summarizes the goal. It is necessary to change both attitudes and behaviors. This is a personal matter, of course, and the details will vary from person to person. Praying for God's guidance in making changes should lead to first hand, face to face interaction with those who are poor, suffering, marginalized or excluded, or hurting in one way or another. This may very well be God's means of answering prayers of repentance. Such actions as increased giving, involvement in service projects, developing relationships with the needy and those from very different backgrounds and situations, and committing to regular prayer for the poor may be some of the ways of responding.

May the prayer Jesus taught be answered in the lives of his faithful followers: Your kingdom come, your will be done, on earth as it is in heaven. Amen.

---

[1] *TDNT*, III, 402.

[2] *NIDOTTE*, IV, 131.

[3] *TDNT*, III, 406.

[4] Vatican II, *The Church in the Modern World*, quoted pp. 61-62 in *An Advent Sourcebook*.

[5] Soong-Chan Rah, *The Next Evangelicalism* , 141.

[6] *Stranger* translates the Heb. *ge'r*: "the reference is to the landless and therefore economically weak individual" (*NCB Deuteronomy*, p. 124 on Dt. 1:16)

[7] *NIDNTT*, III, 355.

[8] Eichrodt, *Theology of the Old Testament*, I, 1961, 241f. quoted *NIDNTT*, III, 356. For more on this see *TDNT*, II, 185, 190, 195 and especially Karl Barth's eloquent statement of God's mercy for the poor as inseparable from God's righteousness, *CD*, II.1, 386-7.

[9] *TDNT*, II, 185.

[10] *TDNT*, II, 186-7; Jer.23:5,6; 33:15; Zech. 9:9 used as a name for Messiah: Wis. 2:18 et al.

[11] *TDNT*, II, 187; Tanch 10, Str.-B, I, 907; Tg. Hab. 2:4, Str.-B., III, 542.

[12] *TDNT*, II, 195.

---

[13] *TDNT*, II, 195.

[14] *TDNT*, II, 195.

[15] *TDNT*, II, 199.

[16] Oliva, *Praying the Beatitudes*, 52.

[17] For more on the importance of the relationship between peace and righteousness/justice, see. *NIDOTTE,* IV, 132-1322.

[18] Martin Noth, *Exodus: A Commentary*, pp.161-2.

[19] *NIDNTT*, III, 354.

[20] D. Hill, *Greek Words and Hebrew Meanings,*p.94 quoted in *NIDNTT* III, 357.

[21] *AB Psalms II,* 270.

[22] Davies, *Matthew*, I, 291.

[23] Davies, II, 296.

[24] N.T. Wright, *Following Jesus*, ix.

[25] Davies, III, 295.

[26] (III, 295)

[27] (Davies, I, 549)

[28] Davies, I, 627

[29] "What My Teachers Taught Me I Try to Teach My Students"

[30] Fitzmyer, Luke, II. 1107

[31] II, 1129.

[32] *Sayings*, 282, noted by Fitzmyer, II, 1072

[33] (quoted in *Forward Day by Day* for 12/12/2010)

[34] (Barrett, *John*, 438)

[35] (Barrett, *Acts*, I, 169

[36] L.T.Johnson, 339.

[37] (Laws, *James*, 121)

[38] (Smalley, *1,2,3,John,* 196)

[39] (*The Johannine Epistles*182)

[40] (*1,2, 3, John*, 197; other commentaries agree: Schnackenburg, Marshall)

[41] G.E. Ladd (p. 243)

Chapter Three

A Brief History of Evangelical Involvement in Social Justice

James J. Stamoolis

IF WE ARE SERIOUS FOLLOWERS of Christ, we want to be people of the Book, faithful to the teaching of the Bible. Even a cursory reading of Proverbs demonstrates God's concern for justice and the Prophetic writers, especially Amos, Micah, and Habakkuk, decry injustice. A deep seated theme of acting justly towards the poor runs throughout the Bible coupled with warnings of impending punishment, both individual and corporate, of those who abuse the less fortunate.

While there are differing opinions on whether the activity in the Acts of the Apostles is normative, descriptive, or something in-between, the historical precedent of the church's behavior needs to be considered. From the beginning of the Church at Pentecost, evangelism and social welfare went hand in hand. We read in Acts the earliest converts supported each other and "they gave to anyone as he had need" (Acts 2:45).[1] The early church did not require a complete communal life but encouraged acts of charity as believers were moved by the Holy Spirit. The sad, but instructive story of Ananias and Sapphira demonstrates the voluntary nature of the sharing and the consequences, at least in this case, of posturing (Acts 5:1-11).

It is not only in the activity of the first church in Jerusalem that we see social concern demonstrated. In the gospels the ministry of Jesus, with its strong emphasis on healing miracles, showed the compassion of our Lord to the human condition and forged the link between social welfare and the good news of redemption. The early church modeled itself after the ministry of its Lord and Savior with the biblical pattern found in the commissioning of the disciples by the risen Jesus. "As the Father has sent me, I am sending you" (John 20:21). This has been the clarion call of the Church in its mission of compassion. We will see in the course of our examination how social concern was allied with the proclamation of the Good News of God's Kingdom and how it was a visible manifestation of the love of God exhibited through the activity of His redeemed people.

Our task here is not to deal with the biblical witness, which is covered ably in another chapter.[2] Rather, this chapter can be seen as a continuation of the story of the ministry of the Holy Spirit. Just as the Spirit worked through the believers as recorded in the Acts of the Apostles, so also the Spirit has been at work in believers throughout the centuries. It is, of course, easier to discern the ministry of the Spirit in Acts since Luke tells us what the Spirit is doing.[3] Having taught Church history, it is rewarding to see students become excited to see the Holy Spirit continuing to work in social issues through the church.[4] What distinguished the church throughout its history was its imperative to meet the physical and social needs of society as well as the spiritual needs. Indeed in many situations, the first witness was that of attempting to correct social ills before the gospel was preached.

Throughout the history of Christianity there were individuals and groups who worked to change the conditions that caused other humans to live in situations of deprivation. One of the latest manifestations of this concern is demonstrated in endeavors to halt human trafficking. While many Christians work to alleviate the pain this inflicts, there are others who seek to challenge the societal and governmental structures which make trafficking possible and profitable.

This is an appropriate juncture to speak about terminology. I am defining social justice as seeking to redress the ills of a society or nation with its widest possible application being to create a just world. This is not a new phenomenon; it can be argued that those of the Clapham Sect who opposed slavery saw it as a world problem because of its impact on four continents; Africa, Europe and the Americas. But not all issues of social justice are global. For example, in India William Carey, the English missionary, worked to eradicate *Sati*, the practice of burning a widow on her husband's funeral pyre. This was a particular problem in Hindu culture that did not have the approval of all Hindus, some of whom became Carey's allies in seeking its abolition. As we will see below, Christians throughout church history have demonstrated a concern for social justice.

Social concern, which is closely connected with the issues of inequality and oppression that are at the core of social justice, is the ministry of ministering to the physical needs of others as a part of the gospel presentation. Again, this has been a feature of the church from its inception in the book of Acts. There needs to be a distinction made between social justice and social concern, primarily because of the rise of what is known as the social gospel. At the end of the nineteenth and the beginning of the twentieth centuries, the working conditions endured by the lower economic classes had become so appalling that a theology, with a base in theological liberalism, was developed which spoke against the evils of the industrial age. These conditions had given rise earlier to amazing acts of social concern which brought the gospel to those "enslaved" by the emerging industries as well as giving material aid to those termed "less fortunate."

This note on definitions is necessary because we need to be precise in describing what has transpired in the past and as a guide to what should be the call to action in the future. While there has been debate in the past over which should have priority, evangelism or social concern,[5] I maintain that these are not the right discussion points. There have been few, if any, missionary enterprises that did not include social concern in what they were doing, whether expressed in medical work, educational ministries, or more direct aid to a particular people group to improve their circumstances.[6] Where the debate lies is over the issues of pressing for cultural and societal change that would move toward social justice.[7] Here there was and is a dividing line, especially noticeable at the beginning of the twentieth century because evangelicals shied away from pressing on social justice issues in reaction to the message of the liberal theologians who were the architects of the social gospel. The evangelicals' lack was in part addressed in political action movements in the second half of the twentieth century.

The terminology will become clearer as we embark on our examination of the history of how the church has moved beyond social concern to include issues of social justice.

The Sub-Apostolic Age

At first glance, it may not be apparent that in an era marked by persecution of the church, however sporadic and at times localized, there would be any mention of social justice.[8] Following the example of the church as described in Acts and with references scattered through the epistles, we would expect to find social concern and welfare; but appeals for justice? Yet if we consider that social justice is not limited to advocating for others but also includes seeking justice for one's own group, then the concept can be seen in the work of the apologists. Justin Martyr, in his apology to the Emperor Titus, appealed for a fair hearing.[9] "We ask that the charges against us be investigated…it is for you, as reason demands, to give a hearing and show yourselves good judges."[10] What follows is an explanation of the Christian faith for which this text is usually cited, but the appeal to fairness is at the heart of any discussion of social justice. While we mine Justin's

39

document for information on the faith and life of the church, a totally appropriate task, it arose out of a plea for just treatment.

Another early apologist, Athenagoras, of whom little is known, addressed the Emperor Marcus Aurelius.[11] His treatise starts out by noting that in the Roman Empire all manner of gods are worshipped. "…different peoples observe different laws and customs; and no one is hindered by law or fear of punishment from devotion to his ancestral ways, even if they are ridiculous."[12] As he describes some of these customs, the modern reader is struck by the diversity represented. Apparently anything was permitted by the Emperor because as Athenagoras noted, "For you think it impious and wicked to believe in no god at all; and you hold it necessary for everyone to worship the gods he pleases, so that they may be kept from wrongdoing by fear of the divine."[13]

But this toleration did not extend to Christians and Athenagoras wanted justice.

> But you have not cared for us who are called Christians in this way. [i.e., with toleration] Although we do no wrong, but, as we shall show, are of all men most religiously and rightly disposed toward God and your empire, you allow us to be harassed, plundered, and persecuted, the mob making war on us only because of our name. We venture, therefore, to state our case before you. From what we have to say you will gather that we suffer unjustly and contrary to all law and reason. Hence, we ask you to devise some measures to prevent our being the victims of false accusers.[14]

The strength of Athenagoras' appeal is that the Christians are good citizens and are a benefit to the empire. This appeal to fairness, even from those who do not, as yet, share the religious convictions of those making the appeal is at the heart of the issue.[15] Like Justin Martyr, Athenagoras goes on to explain the Christian faith. My point here is that impartiality and justice are not always granted by rulers since we know that periodic persecution of Christians continued, even under a ruler like Marcus Aurelius. Whatever the outcome, a defense of the faith is at the heart of social justice. Will our age, with its focus on pluralism and diversity and at the same time a distain for Christians, call forth another Athenagoras to defend the rights of Christians?

The Constantinian Era

Everything changed when Constantine first removed the prohibition against Christianity and then adopted the faith for his own.[16] Much has been written and even more speculated on how Constantine's action "ruined" the church by creating

40

Christendom rather than Christians. Much of this is twaddle, well meaning to be sure, but twaddle nevertheless. To regard the creation of Christendom as a mistake is to claim special knowledge of the workings of the Holy Spirit or that the Holy Spirit was not able to affect the course of human history.[17]

The Constantinian Era, vestiges of which are still with us, was a boon for the church.[18] There were tangible benefits granted to Christians such as exempting Christian clergy from serving as decurions which was really a tax on the wealthy. He also made grants to support poor children thereby undermining the exposure (and thus death) of unwanted children.[19] It is true that Constantine used force to unify the church, as in his suppression of the Donatist Movement.[20] He took an active part in the Council of Nicaea in 325 which settled the Arian dispute about the person of Christ, setting a precedent for imperial involvement in determining doctrine. For his pivotal role in establishing Christianity he is commemorated in the liturgy of the Eastern Orthodox Church as *Isapostolos,* equal to the Apostles.

While it can be argued that justice was not equally applied during this era (just ask the Donatists), it was applied. Throughout the succeeding centuries, the use and abuse of clerical power as supported by the state produces mixed reviews. But there was at least the opportunity to appeal for Christian social justice because of the legitimacy of the faith.

But even in situations where the ruler was hostile to Christians, the witness of Christian social concern was a powerful force. Take, for example, the last of Constantine's descendants to sit on the throne, Julian, known in history as Julian the Apostate. Julian had an excellent classical education and was of the conviction that the return to the ancient ways would preserve the Roman Empire. He reversed the legal and financial privileges of Christians and even persecuted Christians. His reforms included reestablishing paganism in all Imperial Schools and did all he could to restore the old ways. Yet his complaint was that in spite of all his efforts, the Christians were still behaving better than his renewed pagans.

> Atheism [i.e. Christian faith] has been specially advanced through the loving service rendered to strangers, and through their care for the burial of the dead. It is a scandal that there is not a single Jew who is a beggar, and that the godless Galilaeans care not only for their own poor but for ours as well; while those who belong to us look in vain for the help that we should render them.[21]

The Medieval Church

We generally think of the early monastic period as a movement of social protest against the low level of church life in Christendom, when those who wanted to express their spiritual devotion fled to the sanctuary of remote places. While this characterization is true, it is also a fact that some monasteries became centers of both spiritual and societal renewal. Towns grew up around the monasteries as monks raised the living conditions of those dwelling near them. It is also true that monks were the medieval missionaries.[22] Am I stretching the definition of social justice to include a reference to the monastic movement? I think not, because preserving learning and biblical materials, teaching some of the peasants to read, and presenting the gospel as an alternative to bondage to primitive superstitions and fears ranks as a freeing proclamation.[23] Below we will see the work of Luther not only in terms of correcting doctrine but of righting injustice. His monastic predecessors also labored to alleviate humans from inhumane conditions.

Mention must here be made of St. Francis of Assisi's efforts to evangelize the Saracens. While his first attempt to preach the gospel (1212) was cut short by shipwreck, Francis succeeded in preaching to the Sultan of Egypt in 1219. His biographers note that there was little outward effect though the sultan did promise to treat Christian captives more humanely. Again we see the interconnectedness of the evangelistic mission with social justice concerns.[24]

Byzantium

The removal of the imperial throne to Constantinople (330) and the subsequent power vacuum in the West gave rise to the political power of the Papacy. This was not the case, however, in the Eastern half of the Roman Empire with the alliance between the state and the church continuing until the Fall of Constantinople in 1453.[25] The tradition of the Eastern Church in the area of what was termed Philanthropy extends beyond our common definition of philanthropy. As Demetrios Constantelos explained "Philanthropia in Byzantium was not what we understand today as philanthropy and charity...philanthropia assumed a theological meaning which is not easy to translate in any single modern English term."[26] He goes on to devote his volume to how this term is worked out not only in works of charity by individuals and organizations (including the state) but as a characteristic of those in power. In the chapter "Philanthropia as an Imperial Virtue" Constantelos makes the direct link between the expanded concept he has been describing and the role of the ruler. He cites several examples of philanthropia to demonstrate its connection to social justice. The practice of philanthropia was even described by one author "as the most characteristic of all royal virtues."[27]

The link between the church and the state in Byzantium, so often decried as an example of unwarranted state interference in the ecclesiastical areas, was a two edged sword. It gave the church through its spokespeople the right to advise and advocate for social justice, which was a duty of the emperor whose authority to rule came from God. Constantelos points out that philanthropy was alluded to in diplomatic exchanges as the appropriate way for nations to act toward each other. This meaning goes beyond our definition of philanthropy, though not perhaps beyond its actual expression in foreign policy. To cite one of Constantelos' examples:

> There must be a common understanding between the Byzantine emperor and a non-Christian ruler because both receive their authority from God. In a letter to the leader of the Saracens, perhaps to Al-Muktadir, Calif of Bagdad, Nicolas Mysticos appealed for peace on that basis.[28]

One wonders how far a similar appeal would get today. In the West and increasingly around the world, the authority to govern is granted by the people, in spite of what the leaders believe. The age of rulers claiming divine authority is restricted to a few religious dictatorships, none of which claim to be Christian.

I cannot leave this section without one more citation demonstrating this link between rulers and social justice. Lest this seems to be piling on of citations (it is), it also sets the historical stage for later arguing for the necessity of social justice to be delivered by governments. Constantelos goes on:

> If one were to point to a single source which incorporates the Byzantine concept of social justice and philanthropia as an imperial virtue, one would undoubtedly point to two works attributed to an eleventh century author known as Cecaumenos...The first treatise...incorporates much of the mentality and Graeco-Christian tradition before the eleventh century. It is clear that God places a king on the imperial throne to rule and makes him a terrestrial god ...His example must be one of prudence, truth, justice, and impartiality toward all, as befits the earthly representative of the heavenly prototype.
>
> In the Strategicon...the king is urged to restore social justice and to be impartial in his benefactions to all.[29]

When we look around us, we can see that these injunctions from a thousand years ago are not being followed today. Rulers and ruling classes are being deposed because they have not practiced social justice, as the recent unrest in North Africa and the Middle East clearly demonstrates.

The Reformation as a Social Justice Movement

We rightly see the work of the Reformers as a restoration of the gospel emphasis that was obscured by the growth of a hierarchical church administration.

The latter dispensed, in its worse forms, salvation as a commodity to be earned, either by good works or by purchasing the equivalent of good works with cold, hard cash.[30] Therefore when Luther discovered the truth of the gospel of grace, he was moved to protest the selling of indulgences as an abuse of spiritual power. His ninety-five theses were an invitation to debate the injustice of treating salvation as something that could be sold, when Jesus Christ came to set humankind free from the power of sin. Certainly this is a religious issue, but we miss the importance of the nationalistic feeling that accompanied the religious sentiment. It is not remiss to see the social justice elements in the Reformation, which saw its captivity to forces outside of the German principalities.[31] Luther captured some of this sentiment in his treatise "On the Babylonian Captivity of the Church" which sets forth his views on indulgences and the sacraments. One of his opponents, Thomas Murner, a Franciscan, translated the document into German thinking that it would turn the people against Luther. The reverse was true and Murner was responsible for helping to spread Luther's view across the German speaking principalities. While it would be comforting to think that this was because the readers saw the truth of God in Luther's writings as indeed many did, it was also true that injustices suffered at the hands of the Pope's emissaries fanned the revolt.

As Luther stated in thesis 82:

> They ask, e.g.: Why does not the pope liberate everyone from purgatory for the sake of love (a most holy thing) and because of the supreme necessity of their souls? This would be morally the best of all reasons. Meanwhile he redeems innumerable souls for money, a most perishable thing, with which to build St. Peter's church, a very minor purpose.[32]

Luther goes on to discuss the need for the pope to act justly. He should be willing to sell St. Peter's, for which the money was being raised, and return the money, supplemented by his own personal wealth, to right these wrongs.[33] It seems hard to argue against a social justice component in the Ninety-Five Theses and other of Luther's writings.[34]

The Radical Reformation

We know the story doesn't end with what we call the Magisterial Reformation, as some believed the Reformers did not go far enough to separate the church and the state. The Anabaptists opposed both Catholic and Protestant governments which demanded religious conformity to the sanctioned Christian practice. Consequently Anabaptists were persecuted by both Catholic and Protestant powers. Their main crime was to call for the allowance of personal freedom in deciding how to worship God. Like the early Christians, with whom some of the Anabaptists identified, they insisted that worship had to be free from state coercion. And as we saw in the post-apostolic age, the Anabaptists asked for justice from the authorities, though they did not court martyrdom as did some of the early Christians. But court it or not, they received martyrdom aplenty.[35]

My reason for including the Anabaptists in this survey is to note that eventually their reasoning won out and even in European countries where there is still a state church, there is freedom of religion. This freedom is really a social justice issue that is by no means universal. Even in countries which have religious freedom in their constitution, there is often persecution and repression of the non-majority religions. How we think about this is important, for there are many nations where Christians are a persecuted minority. In countries like the United States, do we use our religious freedom to speak out both for a relationship to the one true God and also to stand against religious persecution of our fellow believers in other lands? → *There is persecution now of Christian beliefs*

But there are limits to religious expression. What are our criteria for supporting the right of other religions to be tolerated? This is a live issue in the case of religious extremists of all stripes justifying acts of violence in the name of God. What do we do when we observe or are made aware of behavior that denies religious freedom? For example, presumably all other religious expressions, not just Christians, would censor a sect that had among its rites human sacrifice. As a social justice issue, we need to think about, what, if any, are the limits of religious freedom. Are honor killings to be allowed in non-Islamic societies? Or is this something we protest, not necessarily as Christians but as citizens of a world order that calls for the respect of personal freedom? The issues of social justice need to be taken down to an individual level, even in societies where the basic unit is not the individual, but the family or clan.

Now I strongly identify with the Anabaptists and chose to belong to a church which requires a credible profession of faith by the person as the basis for admission into membership.[36] But I can understand the concern of both the Magisterial Reformers and the Roman Catholic authorities for the perceived fracture of the unity of society by having these voluntary associations. However, I cannot for a moment condone the methods of punishment used against the Anabaptists like burning at the stake or the administration of "baptism" by tying them to a pole and drowning them. Of some were only thrown into prison until they would recant of their heresy. This is a strong lesson we need to take to heart. The power of the gospel must stand on its own right, apart from any attempt, by force or inducement, to sway others to accept the Christianity. Above I referred to the "twaddle" written about the Constantinian era, how this accommodation ruined the church.

45

The truth is there is nothing else that could have been done at that period of history. The coercion was wrong, but understandable in an attempt to have a unified expression of Christianity. The Christological and Trinitarian controversies fought at the Ecumenical Councils hammered out what I believe to be the true faith. A spirit of toleration would not have led to the discovery of truth which we now confess. We must never forget that in some cases, justice was not done to well- meaning and perhaps misunderstood people. My plea here is that we understand truth, however pure, is sometimes bought at the price of unjust acts, with the Anabaptists a case in point.

Where is the wisdom in this particular example? The lesson to be learned is that as the gospel was incarnated in a particular time and place and that incarnation is repeated across the centuries and in all the cultures of the world, so we must learn to understand the particular cultural limitations associated with each epoch, including our own. We may need to advocate for social justice for the other, even if the other has not accepted Christ, while not abandoning the central truth of the gospel that Jesus Christ came to redeem a lost humanity and to give new life.

I think the Anabaptists were right and history has proven them so. But I also think they were creatures of their time and not everything even the good Anabaptists did was right.[37] We need to learn from history how to apply justice, even if our instruction comes from teachers who applied it badly or not at all.

The Age of Exploration and Mission

Since this is a chapter on Evangelical involvement in social justice, I should by all rights skip over the mission activities associated with the Counter Reformation. After all, I imagine some readers would forbear my excursions before the Reformation into the post-apostolic age and even the Constantinian era, but would wonder why I drag into the discussion the Medieval Church and Byzantium. But since the Reformation launched the evangelical movement, the paths should diverge at this point. However, if we define "evangelical" as pertaining to the gospel and the true meaning of the gospel; then notice should be taken of those, whatever their ecclesiastical stripe, who demonstrate their commitment to social justice. We do so if for no other reason than it is useful to note their examples for the instruction of Protestant Evangelicals.

Therefore mention must be made of Bartholomew de Las Casas, a Roman Catholic missionary and champion of social justice. Arriving in the Americas in 1502, he lived a life of ease even as a priest until he underwent a conversion experience. This led him to see how unjustly the Indians had been treated and resulted in his devoting the next fifty years of his life to seeking their well-being by changing the laws that governed the Spanish colonies. Opposed by the colonists and even other clergy and scholars, Las Casas labored for better treatment of the indigenous people. Perhaps guilty of a too simplistic view of human nature as manifested by those he would defend and certainly guilty of reducing all the various tribes to one homogeneous and harmonious type, Las Casas nevertheless is a model to us in his concern for social justice.[38]

Protestants nations were late in getting into the colonial age, but once in made deep inroads in Africa, India and the Far East. In our concern to find models of pioneers for social justice, we can do no better than two of the most famous missionaries from the British Isles, the Englishman William Carey and Scotsman David Livingstone. Carey went to India to preach the gospel but was so appalled by *Sati* where the wife was burned on the funeral pyre of her husband that he worked to end the practice. To achieve this goal he cooperated with Hindus like Raja Ram Mohan Roy who also sought to have *Sati* outlawed. Their efforts were successful when the British colonial government made it illegal in 1829. Carey's work in translation, especially the Bible in several languages, earns him just recognition. But for his work for social reform and other improvements he introduced in India the Indian Government honored his memory with a commemorative postage stamp on the bicentennial anniversary of his arrival in India.[39]

Seven years after Carey's death in India (1834), David Livingstone arrived in South Africa. Famous for his travels across the continent, he is remembered by some as an explorer. But first of all, he was a missionary whose concern was with the betterment of the indigenous people. As Stephen Neill put it, "His cause was the cause of the Gospel, and to that alone he looked for the transformation of the African peoples."[40] He witnessed the desolation caused by the slave trade and this "had burned into his mind the conviction that the righting of this wrong was the greatest duty laid on Europe and on the Churches."[41] His famous phrase delivered at the University of Cambridge that there should be "an open path for commerce and Christianity" needs to be understood in light of his conviction that only a viable non-slave trading economy could overturn the economic benefits to the Africans who were engaged in selling other Africans.

We can fault Livingstone on many fronts, not the least that he neglected his own family, but again we need to focus on what we can learn from his quest for social justice. Livingstone confronted the issue of day and attempted to do something about it. The lesson for each age is to ask what issues need to be confronted today.

The Revivalists

Brief mention must be made here of the interest of the Wesleys and George Whitefield in improving the lot of their hearers. Holding a holistic view of salvation, their concern was not only for souls but for persons, including their social environment. While most of their work involved what we have defined as social concern, Wesley fought against the slave trade and was active in prison reform. What is striking is the evangelistic fervor of these men combined with dramatic social concern and activity. We do well to ask if the same involvement has departed from our evangelistic endeavors. The social needs are as great in many areas, yet there seems to be a greater reliance on government to meet needs that voluntary associations met before.

Under this heading we can include ministries like the Salvation Army which under the leadership of its founder, William Booth, ministered to both the spiritual and physical poverty of people. The nineteenth century was an era of vast expansion of evangelical agencies to assist the needy. Working conditions in the industrial age produced a great deal of misery. We shall note below the work of politicians in redressing some of these conditions but there was a plethora of organizations to meet physical needs.

As Kathleen Heasman points out: "Such a vast number of voluntary charities could never have come into existence had there not been the money available to invest in them. Much of this money was derived from the profits of industry and trade..."[42] There is a weird sense of justice in how these organizations were funded. The excess profits came at the expense of decent wages or wages that matched the productivity of the workers. Then some portion of the profits was allocated to redress the wrongs of the system!

Political Reformers

Chronologically, we take a step back to look at a pioneer of social justice whose name is associated with the abolishment of the slave trade in British possessions, William Wilberforce (1759-1833), a long-time member of Britain's Parliament. His quest for social justice not only concerned the abolishment of slavery, effected by the Emancipation Act of 1833, but also included his support of Catholic Emancipation. The latter removed restrictions on Roman Catholics that included the right to hold landed property and to openly worship. Wilberforce, a convinced and active evangelical, believed strongly in social justice.[43] As we have seen above, social justice requires us to speak out for justice in all circumstances even for other religious expressions.

But Wilberforce was not alone in seeking social justice. Others of strong evangelical conviction used their positions to change what they regarded as intolerable conditions. The Seventh Earl of Shaftesbury (1801-85) used his position in Parliament to ameliorate the conditions of working classes. Legislation reducing the hours of work was seen as a means of reducing the exploitation that accompanied the Industrial Age. He, like Wilberforce, supported the Catholic Emancipation Act.[44]

What do we make of these two examples of political activism? Are they forerunners of the Moral Majority, which sought to affect legislation in late twentieth century America? Are all the big causes, like slavery, finished? Human trafficking continues. According the British Anti Slavery Society, while slavery is illegal, there are an estimated 27 million people, mostly women and children, who are in conditions of slavery.[45] Do national interests hinder governments from taking concerted effort to relieve these conditions? It is a tragedy that there appears to be more slavery now than in the days of Wilberforce. Many organizations of social concern have been formed and this is commendable and necessary as a means of rescuing those in bondage. The global nature of the problem, however, demands a solution that replaces the profit made from trading in humans with more just economic structures, which will eliminate the necessity for families to engage in human trafficking.[46] The sin of slavery will not be eliminated by economic change, but the conditions in which it thrives will be reduced.

While not a politician, Jonathan Blanchard, first president of Wheaton College (Illinois), was a staunch abolitionist.[47] Blanchard came to the college in 1860 and under his presidency it continued to be a hotbed of abolitionist activity. Wheaton had already been a stop on the Underground Railroad. Escaped slaves felt free to move openly in the college. A comment by a Wheaton College student in 1861 sums up the situation.

> So strong was public sentiment that runaway slaves were perfectly safe in the College building, even when no attempt was made to conceal their presence, which was well known to the United States Marshal stationed there. With hundreds of others, I have seen and talked with such fugitives in the college chapel. Of course, they soon took a night train, well-guarded to the next station of the U.G.R.R.[48]

Wheaton was by no means the only abolitionist college; Knox College was also a station on the Underground Railroad. These examples could be multiplied, but the point here is that evangelicals acted on their convictions and worked for social justice. Jonathan Blanchard, who was noted for the list of sinful activities he denounced,[49] did not see himself "as *against* sin as *for* social reform."[50] This is

49

what distinguished activists of the 19th century from their theological heirs in the 20th century. The passion for opposing sin remained among evangelicals in the 20th century but the conviction that their predecessors had about the ability to change society faded.[51]

A Heritage Abandoned, a Legacy Betrayed

What happened to the godly heritage of the evangelicals? How did social justice issues fare in the early twentieth century at the hands of evangelicals? In a word, they were abandoned. Not because they ceased to believe in them, but because the goals had been championed by those whose liberal theology tainted the social justice enterprise.

The Social Gospel, as proclaimed by Washington Gladden and Walter Rauschenbusch, defended the rights of the working class in a time of labor strife.[52] They and others in the movement found their spiritual home in the liberal theology of the day.[53] While the theology of the proponents was never homogeneous, the main elements were sufficiently odious to evangelicals, who decried the movement while admitting the need for social concern. An example of the evangelical response is found in one of the chapters of *The Fundamentals* entitled "The Church and Socialism" by Charles R. Erdman, a professor at Princeton Theological Seminary. We need to remember the situation the authors of *The Fundamentals* were up against. Liberal theology was making great inroads in the churches; the doctrine of progress was sweeping all before it. It appeared that humankind was at the dawn of a golden age of peace and prosperity. Humankind would achieve a type of Promised Land or perhaps, according to the theology of some, usher in the millennium. It was against this backdrop of thinking that evangelical theologians struggled.[54] The enemy of the Social Gospel was the corrupt use of capital and the exploitation of the working classes. Against this, Erdman writes:

> The sudden rise of Socialism is the most surprising and significant movement of the age...With this great movement the Christian Church is deeply concerned; first, because of the endeavor which many are making to identify Socialism with Christianity; and. secondly, because, on the other extreme, popular Socialism is suggested as a substitute for religion and is antagonistic to Christianity; and thirdly, because the strength of Socialism consists largely in its protest against existing social wrongs to which the Church is likewise opposed but which can be finally righted only by the universal rule of Christ.[55]

Note that Erdman admits the Church's opposition to the same social ills but adds the caveat that things won't be made right until Christ's return.[56] The main thrust of his argument is that the state is responsible for alleviating social ills because "the state is quite as purely a divine institution as is the Church...When the Church assumes functions belonging to the state, she involves herself in needless difficulties and places herself in a false position before the world."[57] This is an application of the "two swords" theory where the two swords, the spiritual and the secular, represent the different functions of the Church and the State.[58]

While there is ample biblical teaching on the Christian's duty to obey authority, the issue arises when spiritual and secular clash. The Roman Catholic Church solved this question by asserting that the spiritual authority delegates to the secular authority its role, but maintains that the church is over both swords.[59] Certainly the New Testament is clear that all authority comes from God (e.g., Roman 13:1ff) but that human authority, religious or civil can be disobeyed if those authorities are demanding an obedience that goes contrary to the revealed purposes of God. Perhaps the best examples are found in the Book of Acts where the Apostles disobey the religious authorities to obey God. "Whether it is right in the sight of God to give heed to you rather than to God, you be the judge; but we cannot stop speaking what we have seen and heard." (Acts 4:19-20) This is an example of defiance of both secular and religious authority. The theory of the two swords, then, has limitations. Christians have felt free to disobey both state and church authorities when they believed their consciences were being violated. This disobedience ranged from protest demonstrations to outright defiance of laws, including attempts to overthrow authorities.

In defense of his position, Professor Erdman goes on to define Socialism as an economic theory and defends the communal sharing of the Church in the Book of Acts as "local, voluntary, occasional, temporary."[60] He goes to great length to dissociate the Church from the practice of socialism. He gives the example of the public school system and the postal system as "instances of the application of Socialistic principles. Government ownership might be extended to the railroads, mines, public utilities, factories; this would not involve questions of religion, but of expediency and political wisdom, with which problems the Church has nothing to do."[61]

One of the reasons for the success of this viewpoint has to do with the demographics of American society in the early twentieth century. Basically it was a worldview compatible with the prevailing worldview held by Christians of the time. A detailed analysis would take us too far afield of our subject, but for our purposes it is sufficient to note that the church felt comfortable with allowing the state to run the examples that Erdman lists. It takes little reflection to see some of his presuppositions, for example on public schools, would find less traction today among conservative Christians, both fundamentalists and evangelicals. The growth of the Christian School movement as well as the home schooling phenomenon demonstrates that Erdman's view on schooling is not held by his linear doctrinal descendants.

The rejection of theological liberalism and the causes championed by liberals was the major factor in theological conservatives avoiding social justice issues. The turning point was the publication in 1947 of Carl Henry's *The Uneasy Conscience of Modern Fundamentalism.* While rejecting the liberal theology of the Social Gospel, Henry berated the disengagement of the Fundamentalists from societal concerns. His work started a movement of engagement in social issues. Calling attention to a neglected heritage, Henry attempted to turn the tide back to engagement by evangelicals with the whole gospel.

> Today Protestant Fundamentalism, although heir-apparent to the supernatural gospel of the biblical and Reformation minds, is a stranger, in its predominant spirit, to the vigorous social interest of its ideological forbears. Modern Fundamentalism does not explicitly sketch the social implications of its message for the non-Christian world; it does not challenge the injustices of the totalitarianisms, the secularisms of modern education, the evils of racial hatred, the wrongs of current labor-management relations, the inadequate bases of international dealings. It has ceased to challenge Caesar and Rome, as though in futile resignation and submission to the triumphant Renaissance mood. The apostolic Gospel stands divorced from a passion to right the world. The Christian social imperative is today in the hands of those who understand it in sub-Christian terms.[62]

Carl Henry continued writing on this theme throughout his long and productive career. His influence is difficult to measure, but his strong involvement in evangelical causes allowed for the social concern aspect to have some prominence. In this era, the major social justice issue in the United States was the treatment of racial minorities, in particular the Jim Crow laws which mandated racial segregation in public facilities.[63] In 1966, *Christianity Today* and the Billy Graham Evangelistic Association jointly sponsored "One Race, One Gospel, One Task: The World Congress on Evangelism" which was held in Berlin. The prominence of the "one race" in the title gives an indication of how the organizers felt about racial disharmony. The statement issued by the World Congress makes this clear:

We recognize the failure of many of us in the recent past to speak with sufficient clarity and force upon the biblical unity of the human race...We reject the notion that men are unequal because of distinction of race or color. In the name of Scripture and of Jesus Christ we condemn racialism wherever it appears.[64]

In that in the past, Bible-believing Christians had in places been staunch supporters of racial segregation, the statement broke new ground. Under the part of the congress that was entitled "Strategy for the Future," Paul S. Ress gave a paper on "Evangelism and Social Concern." Rees condemned racism as a hindrance to evangelism around the world and gave three examples of how racism hindered the proclamation of the gospel. He went on to say that "Race is not the only area of social concern to which we Christians should be sensitive."[65] He spoke of the abuses of power and the structures of power which hinder the gospel.

Valuable as the Berlin Congress was, one is tempted to say that one of its greatest gifts was in setting the stage for the International Congress on World Evangelization held in Lausanne, Switzerland in July, 1974.[66] Here speakers from the Two-Thirds World were again prominently featured. Samuel Escobar's presentation on "Evangelism and Man's Search for Freedom, Justice, and Fulfillment" was a call for engagement with the great economic disparities that rack the world. Escobar quotes extensively from several papers given at the Berlin Congress that spoke about the problems of social injustice. He issued a challenge to work for change.

The evangelical community in the Anglo-Saxon countries has money, influence, and numbers that could really make it a decisive force for the reform of their society. By creating a false and anti-biblical dichotomy between evangelism and social action, by closing their eyes to the example of evangelicals in England in the nineteenth century, and by spiritualizing the Gospel to heretical extremes, they have let secularism take the initiative in education, politics, the media, and international relations. Christians in the Third World, who contemplate the so-called West, expect from their brethren a word of identification with the demands for justice in international trade, for a modification of the patterns of affluence and waste that are made possible because of unjust and exploitative trade systems, for a criticism of corruption in the arms race and in the almost omnipotent maneuverings of international intelligence agencies.[67]

Concern for social justice issues was prominently featured in the Lausanne Covenant, the statement approved by delegates that has formed a manifesto of sorts for evangelicals. Article 5, "Christian Social Responsibility," which clearly

53

rejects the equation of political liberation with salvation, also states, "we affirm that evangelism and sociopolitical involvement are both part of our Christian duty."[68] Article 13, "Freedom and Persecution," affirms the duty of governments to uphold The Universal Declaration of Human Rights and goes on to express solidarity with the persecuted church in countries where those rights are denied. The article ends with a call to action. "God helping us, we too will seek to stand against injustice and to remain faithful to the Gospel, whatever the cost."[69]

The Lausanne Covenant changed the debate with this broader understanding of the gospel. Actually, it was not a new departure or innovation but a return to an older evangelical understanding of the necessity to oppose evil structures as well as to proclaim the good news. It echoes the call for justice that we saw in the early Christian apologists who were willing to die for their faith in Christ, but who also were willing to call for fair treatment in a pagan environment.

The Lausanne movement has held two more world congresses.[70] The last one, The Third Lausanne Congress on World Evangelization was in Cape Town in October of 2010. In the conference statement entitled "The Cape Town Commitment: A Confession of Faith and a Call to Action" social concern appears in several places as do calls for justice. The document encourages "the promotion of justice, including solidarity and advocacy on behalf of the marginalized and oppressed."[71] In the section on "Truth and the public arenas" the document states:

> The interlocking arenas of Government, Business, and Academia have a strong influence on the values of each nation and, in human terms, define the freedom of the Church. We encourage Christ-followers to be actively engaged in these spheres, both in public service or private enterprise, in order to shape societal values and influence public debate.[72]

The latter half of the twentieth century and the beginning decade of the twenty-first century have seen a proliferation of organizations both of social concern and social justice. Ron Sider's *Rich Christians in an Age of Hunger* (1977) was a clear call for Christians to champion the cause of the poor. While not all would agree with Sider's economic proposal, the healthy discussion it caused and the general acknowledgement of the biblical obligation to work for social justice still make it mandatory reading.[73]

The engagement with social justice issues spawned several periodicals and many books. *The Other Side* was published for forty years as a spur to radical racial justice.[74] It in turn was part of the impetus behind the *Post-American*, which developed into Sojourner Fellowship and *Sojourners Magazine*.[75] Both of these journals espoused a variant of the social gospel.[76] A series of articles by Donald

Dayton on the history of evangelical social engagement was published in the *Post-American* under the title "Recovering a Heritage." These articles appeared in revised form as *Discovering an Evangelical Heritage* and form an excellent introduction to 19th century evangelical social justice thought.[77]

The list of evangelicals who have spoken against injustice in the United States and in other countries grew longer in the latter half of the 20th century. "Godless" communists were often a target of conservative Christians and the organizations devoted to assisting the victims of communism multiplied. While the issues of injustice came to be seen more clearly under oppressive regimes where the rich get richer at the expense of the poor, the true prophet also addresses the sins of his own people. Such a prophet was Joseph Bayly who wrote profoundly about the failing of Christian America. Bayly wrote a monthly column for *Eternity* magazine in which he took on a number of controversial subjects. For example, long a champion of the poor and a staunch opponent of racial inequality; he deplored the inaction of government to address social inequities. But he was a true prophet as seen in the following:

> For a number of years, speaking writing, and editing, I have espoused the cause of Negroes. I have not merely accepted, but have been thankful for court decisions in the area of equal civil rights for Negroes. I have repeatedly told my white Christian friends, including those who live in the South, that God will judge us if we are content to enjoy the advantages at the expense of others, and the sooner the situation is changed, the better...It is easy for me to sympathize with Negroes and rationalize Negro crime and immorality. But there is one thing I can't rationalize. That is the almost complete silence of Negro leaders, including church leaders, about the situation...So, I look for a prophet, a Negro prophet, who will scorn personal advantage, who will warn his people of sin and judgment, and preach Jesus Christ according to the Scriptures. God give us a thousand such men.[78]

Bayly pointed out in other essays how the great bogeyman of the 50s and 60s was Russian Communism, but that the United States had adopted the "evils" which prevailed under that system. "When I was growing up, I remember, we were impressed by our elders with the evil results of Communist doctrine in Russia."[79] He goes on to show how what was deplored, the breakup of marriage, the banning of the Bible in schools, the compulsory education of children at a young age all were found in US society.

Another prophet of the 20th century was Francis Schaffer who, while best known as an apologist, also commented on the social ills affecting society. His *A Christian Manifesto* is a call for Christians to change the course of history by returning to Biblical truth. He dedicated the book "To all those who have said: 'Here I stand' facing oppressive civil and church power."[80] The book is a discussion of the erosion of the Christian worldview and the dominance of secular humanism in society. The particulars of his argument are cohesive, but of interest for this essay on social justice is his conclusion on civil disobedience. I have cited Schaeffer because his credentials in the evangelical camp are beyond reproach.

> There does come a time when force, even physical force, is appropriate…If there is no final place for civil disobedience, then the government has been made autonomous, and as such, it has been put in place of the Living God…because then you are to obey it even when it tells you in its own way at that time to worship Caesar. And that point is exactly where the early Christians performed their acts of civil disobedience even when it cost them their lives.[81]

Conclusion

In the past, believers have disagreed on how social justice issues should be approached. That will no doubt continue and in part the disagreement is healthy. The issue is not a concern for the well being of people; that has been demonstrated throughout the history of the church. Even among missionary enterprises that placed an absolute priority on the preaching of the gospel, social concern was a natural outflow of the missionaries love for those to whom they had been sent. However, issues of eschatology and the role of government have kept more theologically conservative groups from engaging in issues of social justice. As we have seen above, the "two swords" theory has prevented some from opposing the government.

One of the benefits of the post Christian context that has engulfed Europe and North America is the realization among conservative Christians, fundamentalists and evangelicals alike, that government is not always a friendly force. For some, it is a sign of the end times;[82] however, for others, it has become a rallying call to either return to a Christian past, especially here in the United States, or to call for justice and repentance from our leaders. Eschatology is not as powerful as a motivating force as is the call for social justice, even if the social justice is directed toward finding relief for the believing community. This was part of the reason for the material above on the pre-Constantinian era. The apologists were legitimately seeking justice for their community of faith. Twenty-first century apologists are also seeking justice for believers. This is a major area of agreement between all sides of the social justice issue.

Modern communication has made it possible for Christians in the United States to pray for and at times to lobby for freedoms for fellow believers who are being persecuted in other countries. This is a welcome development in promoting the spiritual unity of believers around the world. The World Evangelical Alliance is able to call attention to mistreatment of Christians, wherever they live. Other worldwide fellowships and organizations have raised the awareness of the global church. There seems to be no obstacle to concern for the church in distant lands. The difference lies in how social justice issues should be applied to other communities, especially those of other faith traditions. What is the role of Christians in promoting social justice in general? Certain issues, e.g. human trafficking or the exploitation of children in manufacturing to name but two, are issues that all can agree must be opposed in the strongest possible manner.

There are differences in tactics, just as in a previous generation the issues of sanctions against the Apartheid government of South Africa divided evangelicals. Some believed that sanctions would hurt the poorer people and opposed the imposition of trade sanctions. Others, equally concerned to end injustice, promoted sanctions as a way of ending what they saw as an evil regime.

The crucial thing is for dialogue to occur among Christians on the issues of social injustice. Some among us need to inform and enlighten the rest of us on the scope of the problem. There will necessarily be discussion on what should be done. From the dialogue can come action, action that does not replace but complements and furthers the proclamation of the gospel. Social concern has been and continues to be a hallmark of true Christianity. Thankfully the discussion and action have moved beyond social concern to the conviction that Christians are to be involved in promoting social justice.[83]

---

[1] Unless noted, all quotations are from the NIV.

[2] "Toward a Biblical Theology of Social Justice" by Bill Molder.

[3] Any number of verses speak of the guidance or activity of the Holy Spirit. Acts 2:4; 4:31; 5:9; 6:9; 7:55; 11:28; 13:2 to cite a few. The most interesting (to this reader, at least) are the passages where the Spirit forbids Paul and his associates to preach in Phrygia and Galatia. (Acts 16:6) and were prevented from entering Bithynia. (Acts 16:7)

[4] Worth mentioning are two studies on social concern in the early church. Susan R. Holman, ed. *Wealth and Poverty in Early Church and Society,* (Grand Rapids: Baker Academic, 2008) is a collection of essays that were originally presented at a conference of the Patristic Institute of the Holy Cross Greek Orthodox School of Theology in 2005. A study of social concern set in the historical context of the time is found in David Batson, *The Treasure Chest of the Early*

Christians: Faith, Care and Community from the Apostolic Age to Constantine the Great, (Grand Rapids: William B. Eerdmans, 2001).

[5] For example see John Stott , *Christian Mission in the Modern World,* (Downers Grove, IL: Inter Varsity Press, 1976, reprinted 2008) where he argues against seeing evangelism and social concern as opponents but as both necessary for mission.

[6] Under this heading would be any food distribution in times of famine or crop failure, better tools for agriculture (e.g., the introduction of iron tools to a pre-iron culture), better seed for planting or even new foods for cultivation; the list of such assistance goes on and on.

[7] For example, Evangelical missions instructed their missionaries working in Apartheid South Africa to avoid pressing for societal change to redress the evils of the Apartheid system so that they could be free to preach the gospel. However, the missions had medical work among the Africans, and where possible, educational institutions.

[8] We do have the example of the Apostle Paul who was not hesitant to use his rights as a Roman citizen to demand justice. Cf. Acts16:37-38; 22:25-29.

[9] Dated at 155 AD

[10] "The First Apology of Justin, the Martyr," in *Early Christian Fathers,* ed. by Cyril C. Richardson, (Simon and Shuster, New York 1996) p.243.

[11] All that is known of this Athenagoras is that he was a Christian philosopher in Athens who had converted to the Christian faith. His "A Plea Regarding Christians" was written late 176 AD or early 177 AD.

[12] "A Plea Regarding Christians by Athenagoras, the Athenian a Philosopher and a Christian," in *Early Christian Fathers,* p. 300.

[13] *Ibid.* p 301.

[14] *Ibid.* p. 301.

[15] This concept formed the basis of C.S. Lewis' argument in chapter one of *Mere Christianity* (New York, Macmillian, 1952) where he discusses "The Law of Human Nature." In his apology for the Christian faith, originally given as broadcast talks on the BBC during World War II, his first series of talks were under the heading "Right and Wrong as a Clue to the Meaning of the Universe." These were published together with the second series "What Christian Believe," as *The Case for Christianity* (1943). Lewis makes the point that in spite of different cultures, what constitutes moral behavior has been quite similar throughout human history. "I know that some people say ...different civilizations and different ages have had quite different moralities. But this is not true. There have been differences between their moralities, but these have never amounted to anything like a total difference." p. 19.

[16] Even though Constantine delayed baptism until he was on his death bed, late baptism was common as it was seen as the remedy for forgiveness of sins and thus delayed by those whose role would expose them to sinning after their conversion. Constantine's involvement in church affairs reveals how seriously he took his adoption of the faith.

[17] The pendulum may be beginning to shift. Cf. Peter J. Leithart, *Defending Constantine: The Twilight of an Empire and the Dawn of Christendom*, (Downers Grove, IL: Intervarsity Press, 2010). Leithart points out the danger of oversimplifying the issues in Constantine's time as some later thinkers, critical of Constantine, have done.

[18] Lest anyone think that I am a proponent of State Churches, let me categorically state that I am a confirmed Anabaptist who believes strongly in the separation of church and state and who is distrustful of any regulation of the church by any but professed believers. I am also convinced, however, that in particular periods of history, the Holy Spirit guided and permitted types of church government best suited to the social-cultural conditions prevailing. Furthermore, the Spirit continues to work in this manner as the church spreads around the world. Here I part company with other Anabaptists who regard Constantine's interference as a great mistake. I think that to do so is to misunderstand the complex interaction of forces that faced the early church and face it again today.

[19] "Constantine the Great" in *The Oxford Dictionary of the Christian Church*, (Oxford University Press, 1997), p. 405. Think of Constantine's action in terms of a "pro-life" policy.

[20] The Donatists were a purifying movement which did not want to recognize the legitimacy of clergy who had yielded up Scriptures during the time of persecutions. The Donatists, initially a reformist and holiness movement, also had elements of nationalist, i.e., North African, sentiment against control from Rome. See W.H.C. Frend, *The Donatist Church: A Movement of Protest in Roman North Africa*, (Oxford: The Clarendon Press, 1952) for an excellent overview.

[21] Stephen Neill, *A History of Christian Missions*, (New York: Penguin, 1986), pp. 37-38.

[22] Cf. James Thayer Addison, *The Medieval Missionary: A Study of the Conversion of Northern Europe A.D. 500 – 1300* (reprint edition Eugene, OR: Wipf and Stock, 2009). Addison documents the work of missionary monks evangelizing and transforming society.

[23] A study of the social concern of the monastic movement as a whole might be a worthwhile undertaking. As it is, there are studies of various monastic orders which describe the social welfare work and at times involvement in social justice issues of monks and nuns. The beginning of any social revolution or societal change comes with the "education" of the underclass to their social

condition. What comes to mind are the peasant revolutions where the oppressed rose up in rebellion to their overlords. For the most part, these groups were led by educated or at least informed leaders. The work of the church, and in particular the monastery, cannot be overstated. It would take us too far afield to note the influence of Christian teaching on revolutionaries whose training included instruction by or influence from Christians. See, however, Gilbert Markus, ed. *The Radical Tradition: Revolutionary Saints in the Battle for Justice and Human Rights,* (New York: Doubleday, 1993). The book has the life stories of individuals from the fourth century to the eighteenth century.

[24] Cf. the article, "St. Francis of Assisi" in *The Catholic Encyclopedia,* http://www.newadvent.org/cathen/06221a.htm. A useful examination of his life is found in the reprint of Paul Sabatier, *The Road to Assisi,* edited with annotations by Jon M. Sweeney (Brewster, MA: Paraclete Press, n.d.). Sabatier's book was published in 1894 and remains a classic of spiritual biography.

[25] I am, of course, simplifying history by omitting the Latin conquest of Constantinople in 1204 and the reign of the Latins for 57 years (1204 -1261).

[26] Demetrios J. Constantelos, *Byzantine Philanthropy and Social Welfare,* (New Brunswick, New Jersey: Rutgers University Press, 1968), page18.

[27] Constantelos cites Michael Psellos, *Chronographia,* (written 1078), *Ibid.* p. 53. Psellos is setting down the history of the emperors from 975 to 1077.

[28] Ibid.

[29] *Ibid.* pp. 53f.

[30] Some of my readers may rejoice that I am finally getting to the "Evangelical" part of engagement with social action. However my defense for the preceding is that the Reformers themselves viewed the work of some of their predecessors in the faith as evangelical, as should we. The gospel may have been rediscovered in the Reformation, but it most assuredly was not invented in the 16th century. We need to see a definition of evangelical that acknowledges the faithful gospel witness of women and men from earlier centuries. A narrow definition of evangelical impoverishes our own testimony to the truth of the gospel. See below for a further illustration of my principle.

[31] One cannot speak of a German nation at this period of history though there was a German identity among the principalities.

[32] Cited from http://www.spurgeon.org/~phil/history/95theses.htm

[33] Thesis 51, *Ibid.*

[34] Cf. George O'Brien, *An Essay on the Economic Effects of the Reformation,* (reprint of 1923 edition, Norfolk, VA: IHS Press, 2003). See also Carter Lindberg, *Beyond Charity: Reformation Initiatives for the Poor,* (Minneapolis:

Fortress Press, 1993). Of particular interest is Chapter 7, "Social Welfare Legislation" where the original source documents are translated. *Ibid.* pp. 200 ff.

[35] The most accessible history of these martyrdoms is found in the various reprints of *Foxe's Book of Martyrs.* John Foxe (sometimes written Fox, 1517-1587) lived during the Reformation and meticulously documented the histories of those who died for their faith. Every serious Christian needs to read at least some of the accounts contained in this volume. An online edition which was updated to cover the time after Foxe by William Byron Forbush is available on-line at http://www.ccel.org/f/foxe/martyrs/home.html.

[36] I use the phrase "by the person" to differentiate from pedo-baptistic fellowship where another person answers the profession of faith questions on the behalf of the infant being baptized into membership.

[37] For the sake of expediency I have ignored the really radical Radicals, like those who took over Munster, Germany and ruled it as a theocracy.

[38] For a short summary of his life, see Stephen Neill, *A History of Christian Missions*, pp. 146-7. Las Casas also serves as an example of how reductionism, while necessary to make a complex issue plain to those removed from the scene by an ocean, means that his views are open to criticism. It is difficult find a balance in presenting the horrors of injustice while at the same time accurately portraying the human faults of the oppressed. The tendency is to turn the oppressed into saints, which in almost all cases is not a true picture of reality.

[39] Cf. *The Legacy of William Carey* by Vishal and Ruth Mangalwadi, (Wheaton, IL: Crossway Books, 1999).

[40] Neill, p. 266.

[41] *Ibid.*

[42] Kathleen Heasman, *Evangelicals in Action: An Appraisal of Their Social Work in the Victorian Age,* (London: Geoffrey Bles, 1962), p.11. It is worth looking at her book just to see the how many charities were formed during this period. See also Derek Tidball, *Who are the Evangelicals: Tracing the Roots of the Modern Movements,* (London: Marshall Pickering, 1994). Tidball devotes a chapter to this theme entitled: "Tread All the Powers of Darkness Down, Evangelicals and Social Action." (pp.177-195)

[43] Studies of the life and work of William Wilberforce abound. William Hague, *William Wilberforce: The Life of the Great Anti-Slave Trade Campaigner,* (Orlando, FL: Houghton Mifflin Harcourt, 2008); Eric Mextaxas, *Amazing Grace: William Wilberforce and the Heroic Campaign to End Slavery,* (New York: Harper One, 2007) Wilberforce was also a crusader who tried to lift the moral nature of society. See his book where he argues his point. *A Practical View of the Prevailing Religious System of Professed Christians, in the Middle and Higher Classes in this Country, Contrasted with Real Christianity,* (reprint ed.

Peabody, MA: Hendrickson Publishers, 2006). For an interesting discussion on how the abolition of the slave trade was commemorated 200 years later, see James Walvin, "The Slave Trade, Abolition and Public Memory" in *Transactions of the Royal Historical Society, Sixth Series, Vol. XIX,* (Cambridge: The University Press, 2009), pp. 139-149.

[44] For more on his life see, Richard Turnbull, *Shaftesbury: The Great Reformer*, (Oxford: Lion UK , 2010).

[45] Accurate figures are hard to come by, this is the generally accepted number. http://socialistworker.org/2005-1/533/533_12_ModernSlavery.shtml

[46] Or as David Livingston said, "Christianity and Commerce," that is a viable alternative for poor families to have income so that their children will not be sold or enticed into being exploited.

[47] See Clyde S. Kilby, *Minority of One: The Biography of Jonathan Blanchard,* (Grand Rapids: Eerdmans, 1959) for the story of this remarkable and unwavering reformer.

[48] Ezra Cook, "Memories," in Charles M. Clark, ed. *The History of the Thirty-Ninth Regiment, Illinois Volunteer Veteran Infantry in the War of the Rebellion, 1861-1865,* (Chicago, 1889), pp. 490-491 as cited by David E. Maas, *Marching to the Drumbeat of Abolitionism: Wheaton College in the Civil War,* (Wheaton, IL: Wheaton College), p. 17. Maas' book deserves wide circulation as it documents an important era of evangelicalism's involvement with social justice.

[49] For example, Blanchard believed Christmas was a pagan holiday and while president of Knox College held classes on Christmas Day. Kilby, *Minority of One,* p. 152.

[50] Maas, *Marching to the Drumbeat of Abolitionism,* p. 13. Italics are in the original.

[51] Cf. George M. Marsden, *Fundamentalism and American Culture: The Shaping of Twentieth-Century Evangelicalism 1870-1925,* (Oxford: Oxford University Press, 1980), especially pages 80-93.

[52] Informative articles on the movement can be found in *The Oxford Dictionary of the Christian Church;* "Social Gospel," and "Walter Rauschenbusch." *The Christian Century* magazine, considered liberal by Fundamentalists, was reorganized in 1908 as a vehicle for the promotion of the Social Gospel and other themes, like higher criticism of the Bible. The association of the Social Gospel movement with liberal theology is what put evangelicals off from participating.

[53] A useful study is Janet Forsythe Fishburn, *The Fatherhood of God and The Victorian Family: The Social Gospel in America,* (Philadelphia: Fortress Press, 1981). Fishburn describes the social milieu of Walter Rauschenbusch and demonstrates its influence on his writings.

[54] *The Fundamentals* was a widely distributed series of 90 essays issued in 12 volumes from 1910 to 1915. These essays were a defense of classic orthodox Christian doctrine against the assaults of liberal theology. The points defended in these essays formed the basis of the confessional statements of conservative Bible colleges, Christian colleges, and Christian organizations in the twentieth century. The truths defended included the authority of Scripture, the deity and humanity of Christ, the Trinity, the Virgin Birth, and the second coming of Christ. These touchstones of orthodoxy reflect the battle grounds of the early 20th century. Reprint editions abound. It must be understood that the fundamentals presented were not merely the basis for what we term today as Fundamentalists but were the basis of all historically conservative Christian denominations and associations. The writers of this series were defending what could be best described as classic Christian orthodoxy through nineteen centuries of Church history and represented, in its doctrinal orthodoxy all expressions of the Church, Roman Catholic, Protestant and Eastern Orthodox. It should be noted that modern Fundamentalists, while appreciating the call to Biblical truth, do not see these essays as the defining theology of their movement. "Fundamentalist fellowships never used this as a complete statement of their faith, since literalism in prophecy, imminency of the Lord's Coming, and a premillennial stance are not found in them." George W. Dollar, *A History of Fundamentalism in America*, (Greenville, South Carolina: Bob Jones University Press, 1973), p. 175. Dollar may be trying too hard to find separation between his view and that of the authors of *The Fundamentals*. See footnote 58 below where Charles Erdman stresses the imminent coming of Christ.

[55] "The Church and Socialism," in *The Fundamentals: A Testimony to Truth,* (The Bible Institute of Los Angles, 1917, reprinted 2003, Baker Books), p. 97.

[56] Later in the same volume, Erdman contributes the chapter "The Coming of Christ" pp. 301-313. He discusses both the Pre-Millennial and Post-Millennial positions. Erdman stresses the "imminent" coming of Christ as the key.

[57] *Ibid.* p.108.

[58] The idea of two authorities can be found in the New Testament. In Romans 13:1ff, Paul calls on Christians to be subject to the ruling authorities "for there is not authority except from God, and those which exist are established by God...it is a minister of God to you for good...for it does not bear the sword for nothing; it is a minister of God."

[59] The Roman Catholic dogma of the two swords was promulgated in the Papal Bull, *Unam Sanctam* (The One Holy) issued 18 November 1302 by Boniface VIII. This document defined the doctrine of papal supremacy by referring to

the two swords, secular (= state) and spiritual (= church) which according to this document were both under the control of the church.

[60] *Ibid.* p. 99.

[61] *Ibid.* p.100.

[62] *The Uneasy Conscience of Modern Fundamentalism,* (Grand Rapids: William B. Eerdmans, 1947).

p. 45.

[63] "Jim Crow was the name of the racial caste system which operated primarily, but not exclusively in southern and border states, between 1877 and the mid-1960s. Jim Crow was more than a series of rigid anti-Black laws. It was a way of life. Under Jim Crow, African Americans were relegated to the status of second class citizens. Jim Crow represented the legitimization of anti-Black racism. Many Christian ministers and theologians taught that Whites were the Chosen people, Blacks were cursed to be servants, and God supported racial segregation." http://www.ferris.edu/jimcrow/what.htm. It was against this social injustice that evangelicals struggled.

[64] *One Race, One Gospel, One Task: World Congress on Evangelism,* (Minneapolis: World Wide Publications, 1967), Volume I, p. 5.

[65] *Ibid.* 307.

[66] The conference is often referred to simply as Lausanne and the subsequent series of meetings and smaller conferences were called the Lausanne movement. When the second assembly was held in Manila in 1989 it became known as Lausanne II, and the third assembly in Cape Town in 2010, Lausanne III.

[67] *Let the Earth Hear His Voice: International Congress on World Evangelization,* (Minneapolis: World Wide Publications, 1975), p. 316. Just one example of the maneuverings of intelligence agencies that may have been on Escobar's mind was the possible CIA involvement in the overthrow of Chile's first Marxist President, Salvador Allende in 1973. Since this was during the Cold War, documents opened after the Fall of the USSR show that Allende had received financial aid in his campaigns from the KGB.

[68] *Ibid.* p. 5.

[69] *Ibid.* p. 8.

[70] Even though the congresses were not held in Switzerland, the name "Lausanne" has been used for Manila, 1989 and Cape Town, 2010. The organization is the Lausanne movement.

[71] "The Cape Town Commitment: A Confession of Faith and a Call to Action," as printed in *The International Bulletin of Missionary Research,* (April 2011, Vol. 35, No. 2,), p. 65.

[72] *Ibid.* p. 69. C. Rene Padilla makes a trenchant observation: "Close analysis of this wording reflects the dichotomy that influences a large segment of evangelicalism, especially in the West: the dichotomy between evangelism and social responsibility. Because of that dichotomy, closely connected with the dichotomy between the sacred and the secular, the Lausanne movement intends "to strengthen, inspire and equip the Church" with regards to the former, but simply "to exhort Christians" with regards to the latter... engagement in issues of public and social concern ...are a *secondary* duty for which Christians do not need to be strengthened, inspired, or equipped but only exhorted." "The Future of the Lausanne Movement," *Ibid.* p. 87.

[73] Original edition was published in 1977 by Inter Varsity Press. There have been two subsequent revised editions where Sider attempts to answer some of his critics by seeking advice from economists. The third edition, with a foreword by Dr. Kenneth Kantzer, a notable evangelical leader and longtime colleague of Carl Henry was released in 1990 by Word Publishing. His collection of Biblical texts on hunger, justice and the poor, *Cry Justice: The Bible on Hunger and Poverty*, (New York: Paulist Press, 1980) was written as a reader for Bread for the World a lobbying organization which seeks to influence government policies that affect hunger.

[74] Cf. Dee Dee Risher, "A Clarion of Justice: For 40 years, *The Other Side* offered a vision of 'justice rooted in discipleship,'" *Sojourners Magazine*, January 2005. http://www.sojo.net/index.cfm?action=magazine.article&issue= soj0501&article=050121. Ms. Risher was the editor of *The Other Side* when it ceased publication. She correctly notes that: "Because *The Other Side* was ecumenical, over time it drew on the strengths of a number of traditions. From the Baptists and evangelicals, it took seriousness for grappling with scripture and an emphasis on conversion. From the Anabaptists, it drew the importance of lifestyle as a vehicle for Christian witness and the conviction that peacemaking was at the core of Jesus' message. From mainline Protestants, it emphasized the social gospel, and from the Catholic tradition, it built on acts of mercy, attention to spirituality, and a sense of the liturgical seasons in our lives. It was inspired by liberation theology movements and Pentecostal movements alike. The mixture was such that almost any reader would get buttons pushed—and fairly often. And that, after all, was the point."

[75] Since this paper was originally given, in shorten form, at the Mid-West Regional Meeting of the Evangelical Missiological Society held on the campus of Trinity Evangelical Divinity School it is worth mentioning that *The Post-American* was founded on Trinity's campus in 1970. The author was present at one of the protests held by those associated with *The Post American* on Trinity's campus.

[76] Cf. Jim Wallis, *God's Politics: Why the Right Gets It Wrong and the Left Doesn't Get It,* (San Francisco: Harper, 2006) and Jim Wallis, *Living God's Politics: A Guide to Putting Your Faith into Action,* (San Francisco: Harper, 2006).

[77] Donald W. Dayton, *Discovering an Evangelical Heritage,* (Hendrickson Publishers, reprint from 1976 ed., 2000).

[78] "Lord, Raise Up a Negro Prophet," (November 1962), reprinted in Joseph T. Bayly, *Out of My Mind: The Best of Joe Bayly,* (Grand Rapids: Zondervan, 1993), 33-35. The use of the term Negro reflects the terminology current when Bayly wrote. A keen cultural observer, Bayly, were he writing today, would have used different terminology.

[79] "Oh, for the Good Old Days" (August 1966), reprinted in Joseph T. Bayly, *Out of My Mind: The Best of Joe Bayly,* (Grand Rapids: Zondervan, 1993), 70. For those unfamiliar with the writings of Joe Bayly an excellent introduction, including his fiction writing, is found in *A Voice in the Wilderness: The Best of Joseph Bayly,* (Colorado Springs: Victor, 2000). Bayly's fiction cut through evangelical platitudes to illuminate what real Christianity should look like.

[80] Francis A. Schaffer, *A Christian Manifesto*, (Westchester, IL: Crossway Books, 1981), p. 5.

[81] *Ibid.* pp.117, 130.

[82] Classic premillennialists saw a world spiraling deeper and deeper into sin until the church of true believers is raptured before the seven year period of tribulation. Some who have held this position saw themselves as getting as many into the "life boats of salvation" as possible before the great and terrible Day of the Lord. But as I have said, even those who held this position found themselves dispensing social welfare.

[83] A useful resource to see the world problem is Richard Stearns, *The Hole in our Gospel,* (Nashville: Thomas Nelson, 2009). A short primer on our duties as Christian citizens is *Building the Shining City: The Grassroots Lobbying Guide for Christian Activists* (Alexandria, VA: Christian Voice, 2003). A interesting book that is written from a more general perspective on the value of charitable giving is Claire Gaudiani, *The Greater Good: How Philanthropy Drives the American Economy and Can Save Capitalism*, (New York: Henry Holt and Company, 2003).

Chapter Four

The Bible and Human Trafficking: Ramabai's Bible Translation a Liberative Model

Rajkumar Boaz Johnson

I SPENT MY CHILDHOOD IN one of the slums of Delhi. Life in the slum was not easy. My neighbors belonged to the lowest castes of society. They were either the low castes, the Shudras – the dhobis, the bhangis; the chamars; or they were the outcastes. Gandhi called them Harijan, God's people. But, no one treated them like God's people. They were treated like dirt. The slum was outside a major hospital. The doctors, the nurses – regular high caste people would walk at a distance from us. They belonged to the high castes of society – the Brahmins, the priests; the Kshatriyas, the militaristic caste; or the Vyashiyas, the business caste. My people, my neighbors cleaned the latrines for these people. They washed their clothes. They served in their houses, doing dirty tasks. But, my people would never sit with these people. The only luxury the men enjoyed was the *hookah*, the tobacco smoking pipe, when it was really dark.

It would have been okay if life were just the way it was. Unfortunately, we saw kids disappear. They disappeared because their parents were poor and needed to borrow money from the high caste moneylenders. They were poor because the high caste Brahmins, the priests, charged them enormous amounts of money for common things like birth, sickness, marriage and death. They were poor because the police, from the high caste society charged them enormous amount of money just to do common things like get the ration card to by a little food.

Most families were in debt. So they had to give their sons to the *bania* caste people, the businessmen. The *banias* would come to these families and say, "Don't worry, your boys will live well." The truth was the opposite. Boys and girls, my friends, were enslaved in the carpet industry. They were enslaved in the garment industry. They were enslaved in the furniture industry. Pretty girls, as soon as they got their first menstrual cycle were taken to the brothels of Delhi, Mumbai, and Calcutta. Ironically, the red light district into which these 13-14 year old girls were taken was called, Mahatma Gandhi Road.

The truth is that:

India is a source, destination, and transit country for men, women, and children trafficked for the purposes of forced labor and commercial sexual exploitation. Internal forced labor may constitute India's largest trafficking problem; men, women, and children in debt bondage are forced to work in industries such as brick kilns, rice mills, agriculture, and embroidery factories. Although no comprehensive study of forced and bonded labor has been carried out, some NGOs estimate this problem affects tens of millions of Indians. Those from India's most disadvantaged social economic strata are particularly vulnerable to forced or bonded labor and sex trafficking. Women and girls are trafficked within the country for the purposes of commercial sexual exploitation and forced marriage. Children are also subjected to forced labor as factory workers, domestic servants, beggars, and agricultural workers.[1]

Sreyashi Dastur writes in *The Telegraph*, October 16, 2007,

One wishes the circumstances were the same, but they seldom are. How does one equate a girl lured away from a village in Meghalaya to a brothel in Delhi with the one pushed into beedi-binding by her own parents just so there is enough money to feed all the mouths in the family? Or a boy thrown into the laps of pedophiliac foreign tourists in Goa with one who runs away from starvation and poverty at home, to be picked up and employed by a brick-kiln owner who gives him a paltry daily wage and lunch? Which arm of the State — women and child development, labour, police, or home affairs if there is border-crossing — has failed to do its job in each of these cases, and which is responsible for ensuring that the trafficked person gets a livelihood and a respectable life?

This is why trafficking is such a tricky crime in developing countries with their many areas of darkness. In Haryana, for instance, where it is acceptable to destroy female fetuses and kill baby girls, young women are trafficked from Bengal and the Northeast and forced into marriage to keep the family line going. How does one, in the absence of a complaint from the girl or her family, initiate criminal proceedings against those who claim the girl as their daughter-in-law?

Out of the 30 million slaves in the world, perhaps half of them are in India alone.

Unfortunately missions in India has not addressed this issue until very recent times. My quest for a solution to the problem of human trafficking in India led me to realization that no one has really come up with a thorough biblical theological approach to the huge problem of human trafficking in India. However, I saw a glimmer of hope in one person.

In 1985, young graduates of a seminary in India decided to take a trip to Kedgaon- small town about 45 miles out of Pune, India. The head sister of the mission escorted us from one dormitory to the next. With tears in our eyes we saw hundreds of women: older women seventy, sixty, or fifty years old; younger women in their thirties or twenties; teenagers; little girls; and baby girls. Under ordinary circumstances this would not have been such a moving experience, but these were no ordinary women. These were women who had been rescued. They had been rescued from child prostitution, from temple prostitution, from forced child marriage to a man who may have been twenty to thirty years older than the little one. They had been rescued from the pains of *sati*, widow burning. They had been rescued from female infanticide . . . the stories went on and on. It was as if all the woman-refuse of India were gathered in one place. Yet, the foundation stone of Ramabai Mukti Mission, which was laid in 1889, told a different story. It read, "The foundation of this building was laid in Christ . . . that our daughters may be as corner-stones, polished after the similitude of a palace (Psalm 144:12)." These were royalty. It all began with the vision of one woman, Pandita Ramabai.

Ramabai's impact on India was so great that in 1989, a hundred years after the founding of Ramabai Mukti Mission, the government of India, even though led by the Hindu party, could not help but acknowledge her legacy. The government issued a commemorative stamp to honor the life and legacy of Pandita Ramabai. The official brochure with the stamp reads as follows:

> Pandita Ramabai (1858–1920): Pandita Ramabai, the youngest daughter of Anant Shastri, was a social reformer, a champion for the emancipation of women, and a pioneer in education. Left totally alone by the time she was 23, Ramabai acquired a great reputation as a Sanskrit scholar. Deeply impressed by her prowess, the Sanskrit scholars of Calcutta University conferred on her the titles of "Saraswati" and "Pandita." She rebelled against the caste system and married a shudra advocate, but was widowed at 23, having a baby girl. In 1882, she established the Arya Mahila Samaj for the cause of women's education in Pune and different parts of Western India. This led to the formation of the Sharda Sadan in 1889— which school completes a hundred years this year—a school which blossomed into an umbrella organization called Pandita Ramabai Mukti Mission, 40 miles outside Pune. In 1896, during a severe famine Ramabai toured to villages of Maharashtra with a caravan of bullock carts and rescued thousands of outcaste children, child widows, orphans and other destitute women and brought them to the shelter of Mukti and Sharada Sadan. A learned woman knowing seven languages, she translated the

Bible into her mother tongue— Marathi—from the original Hebrew and Greek. Her work continues today, a memorial to her life and path.

The above quote from an official Government of India publication makes it clear that Pandita Ramabai made a very holistic impact on Indian society.

The Context of The Development of Ramabai's Theology

Two issues that Ramabai confronted at a very early age in her life were gender bias against women in Hindu society and racial bias against the *Shudras*, the untouchable caste. These two issues form the background of the development of her biblical theology and her work. Ramabai was born in 1858, the daughter of a Maratha Chitpavan Brahman; a member of the purest of the highest caste. At that time in the history of India people of this caste never associated with people of any other caste. They considered themselves to be the purest of the pure priestly caste. Any association with people from other castes would make them unclean. There was an additional problem though. Ramabai was a girl. Women, even those who came from the highest caste, were regarded as being much lower than men, even men of the lowest castes. Much later in her life, after detailed study of Hindu texts, Ramabai would write,

> There were two things on which all those books, the Dharma Shastras, the sacred epics, the Puranas . . . were agreed: women of high and low caste, as a class, were bad, very bad, worse than demons, and that they could not get Moksha (salvation) as men. The only hope of their getting this much-desired liberation from Karma and its results, that is, countless millions of births and deaths and untold suffering, was the worship of their husbands. The husband is said to be the woman's god; there is no other god for her. This god may be the worst sinner and a great criminal; still HE IS HER GOD, and she must worship him. She can have no hope of getting admission into Svarga, (heaven), the abode of the gods, without his pleasure; and if she pleases him in all things, she will have the privilege of going to Svarga as his slave, there to serve him and be one of his wives among the thousands of the Svarga harlots who are presented to him by the gods in exchange for his wife's merit. . . . The woman is allowed to go into higher existence thus far but to attain Moksha or liberation, she must perform such great religious acts as will obtain for her the merit by which she will be reincarnated as a high caste man, in order to study Vedas and the Vedanta, and thereby get the knowledge of the true Brahma and be amalgamated in it.[2]

Commenting on the important issue of race and caste, she continued,

The same rules are applicable to the Shudras, the untouchables. The Shudras must not study the Veda and must not perform the same religious act, which a Brahman has a right to perform. The Shudra who hears the Veda repeated must be punished by having his ears filled with liquefied lead. . . . His only hope of getting liberation is in serving the three high castes as their lifelong slave.[3]

Most Indian women at her time just succumbed to what society required them to be. Ramabai, however, contrary to the norm, set about the task of studying the Hindu texts. Her father, a rebel of sorts, had initiated her into the study of Sanskrit, the language of Hindu priests. She became a diligent student of the language and later studied the Hindu texts in great detail. In the Hindu texts she found that there really was no hope for women. This led her to the study of ideologies beyond Hinduism. In the course of her search she was exposed to the gospel of Jesus Christ. She wrote that quite accidentally, "I had found a little pamphlet in my library. I do not know how it came there, but I picked it up and began to read it with great interest. It was St. Luke's Gospel in the Bengali language."[4] The story of Jesus' dealings with women in particular grabbed her attention. Throughout the text, whenever women encountered Jesus, he elevated their status. He offered them spiritual salvation. He offered them emotional and social salvation. Of course, this was a great contrast to the place of women in Hindu texts. She started reading the rest of the Bible. In Genesis she came to realize that men and women were created equal in the image of God. The reading of the Bible gave her a completely new understanding of the place of women in society.

Ramabai's solution to the problem of racial and caste discrimination was very bold, yet simple. She just decided to marry a gentleman from the lowest caste, the Shudra caste. This was an unthinkable act with immense ramifications. Ramabai was a woman, but at least she was a woman who belonged to the highest caste. When she married a man from the lowest caste, her stature in society plunged to the lowest level. She was now a "lowest caste woman" in the eyes of Hindu society. She was well aware of the fact that in Hindu society, "They are looked upon as being very like the lower species of animals, such as pigs; their very shadow and the sound of their voices are defiling."[5]

Unfortunately, her husband died of cholera two years into their marriage. Hindu society would have interpreted this as a curse on her, but Ramabai kept on confronting the ills of society. She moved from Calcutta in Eastern India to Poona in Western India, closer to Bombay. The life of a widow in the India of her time was very hard. Most widows had to disassociate themselves from society, lest their curse would descend on people with whom they associated. Most widows just lived lonesome lives on the banks of rivers like the holy Ganges, hoping for some sort of reprieve in their next lives. Ramabai, again contrary to the norm, decided to engage deeply in the study of the Bible and society. She sought to understand the solutions that Jesus offered to Indian society of her time.

Ramabai's Confrontation with Prostitution, Slavery, and Female Infanticide

The next stage in the development of Ramabai's thought took place during a visit to England in 1883. During this time she was exposed to the crucial work of the Sisters of Wantage. These Sisters were deeply involved in the emancipation of prostitutes from slavery to cruel urban gangs. Many of these prostitutes belonged to lower-class families. They were forced to sell themselves into sexual slavery due to class distinction. Ramabai found that the work of the Sisters of Wantage was bathed in the teaching of Jesus regarding women. The work of the Sisters had a deep impact on Ramabai. All the while she was thinking of the complexity of issues, which women faced in India. This work among the orphans, widows, and prostitutes became the model of Ramabai's work and words in India. Of this crucial life-changing experience she wrote,

> The Sisters there took me to see the rescue work carried on by them. I met several of the women who had once been in their Rescue Home, but who had so completely changed, and were so filled with the love of Christ and compassion for suffering humanity. . . . Here for the first time in my life I came to know that something should be done for the so-called fallen women, and that Christians, whom Hindus considered outcastes and cruel, were kind to these unfortunate women, degraded in the eyes of society . . . I had never heard or seen anything of the kind done for this class of women by the Hindus in my own country. I had not heard anyone speaking kindly of them, nor seen any one making any effort to turn them from the evil path they had chosen in their folly. The Hindu Shastras do not deal kindly with these women. The law of the Hindu commands that the king shall cause the fallen women to be eaten by dogs in the outskirts of the town. They are considered the greatest sinners, and not worthy of compassion. After my visit to the Homes at Fulham, where I saw the work of mercy carried on by the Sisters of the Cross, I began to think that there was a real difference between Hinduism and Christianity. I asked the Sisters who instructed me to tell me what it was that made the Christians care for and reclaim the "fallen" women. She read the story of Christ meeting the Samaritan woman, and His wonderful discourse on the nature of true worship, and explained it to me. She spoke of the Infinite Love of Christ for sinners. He did not despise them but came to save them. I had never read or heard anything like this in the religious

books of the Hindus; I realized, after reading the 4th Chapter of St. John's Gospel, that Christ was truly the Divine Saviour He claimed to be, and no one but He could transform and uplift the downtrodden womanhood of India and of every land. Thus my heart was drawn to the religion of Christ. I was intellectually convinced of its truth on reading a book written by Father Nehemiah Goreh and was baptized in the Church of England in the latter part of 1883, while living with the Sisters at Wantage.[6]

Ramabai gained a new vision for her life after her encounter with Christ during these years. In several books and booklets she wrote extensively of her mystical communion with Christ, for example:

I have come to know the Lord Jesus Christ as my personal Saviour and have the joy of sweet communion with Him. My life is full of joy, "For the Lord JEHOVAH is my strength and my song; He also is become my salvation." Now I know what the Prophet means by saying, "Therefore with joy shall ye draw water out of the wells of salvation." I can scarcely contain the joy and keep it to myself. I feel like the Samaritan woman who "left her water pot, and went her way into the city, and saith to the men, Come, see a man, which told me all things that ever I did: is not this the Christ?"[7]

The Mukti Mission

On her return to India Ramabai began the process of developing her biblical theology and her work at Mukti. First, there was the horrible practice of female infanticide. Girls were a great liability among all the castes. Parents had to pay huge sums of money in dowry to get their daughters married. Parents went into immense debt as a result of this practice. Boys, on the contrary, were a great asset. They brought in huge sums of money into the family when they got married. As a result, female infanticide was very common. A second issue was the practice of *Temple Dasis* (or prostitute priestesses). This was an alternative for parents to female infanticide. Girls would be just devoted to certain temples as soon as they got their first menstruation. These *dasis* would become the property of the temple priestly hierarchy. It was a form of spiritual-sexual slavery. An alternative form of this sexual slavery was called *nautch* girls. A third challenge Ramabai faced was forced marriages of little girls to men from the same caste, who could be thirty years older than them. They could be the third or fourth wife of the rich, high caste man. This was a more humane alternative to female infanticide or temple prostitution. They did not have to pay a high dowry. Yet, it was abhorrent nonetheless. The fourth challenge that Ramabai faced was the practice of *Sati*, the practice of a widow being forced to jump into the funeral pyre of her husband during the cremation of his body. Those that refused to jump into the funeral pyre were shamefully ostracized from society.

Ramabai's answer was the Mukti Ashram, the temple of salvation. This became the fertile ground of the development of Ramabai's Indian Christian theology. After the initial intense opposition, slowly but surely, instead of killing their female babies, parents began bringing their female babies and leaving them at the door of Mukti. Instead of giving into pressure and jumping into the funeral pyre of their husbands, young brides, some as young as thirteen years old, began running to Mukti for refuge. Ramabai and her group of sisters began going from one place to another, rescuing young women from temple prostitution and *nautch* slavery. When young women who brought "insufficient" dowry were threatened with death, they fled to Mukti. In the early twentieth century, as a result of Ramabai's work, there was a huge spiritual awakening in western India. Hindus, Muslims, and nominal Christians began experiencing the transforming power of God.

During these years of the Great Awakening in India, in addition to an incredibly busy life, Ramabai did a lot of writing. She translated the Bible from Hebrew, Aramaic, and Greek into Marathi, her native language. She wrote numerous theological and devotional works. She composed some of the most profound devotional songs. This material gives us insight into Ramabai's brilliant theological mind.

Ramabai's Development as a Biblical Theologian

The first stage in her development as a philosopher/theologian may be seen in her first book *Stree Dharma Neeti*, which she wrote in 1882.[8] This was a part of a quest for answers to the problem of women and outcastes in India, but it seems clear that it was an unfulfilled quest. *Stree Dharma Neeti* seeks to establish the "code of conduct" for Hindu women. However, it seems like she could not find the basis of freeing women from suppression and denigration in Hinduism. She came to the conclusion that "education" and "westernization" within Indian boundaries, should form the basis of the modern code of conduct for women.

In the book she developed ten principles, which would empower women in India. These ten principles are steadfastness, endurance, self-control, not committing thefts, cleanliness, prudence, learning, truthfulness, and not getting angry. The "foundation" of this *Stree Dharma Neeti* is "self-reliance." She wrote, "The foundation is self-reliance, that is relying on oneself. Now we [Indian women] must not look to others for our advancement. Every woman must exert herself courageously for her own advancement, as self-reliantly as possible." [9]

The second stage may be seen in her second book, *The High Caste Hindu Woman*, which she published in 1887 and which reveals that she realized that the principles she has developed in 1882 in *Stree Dharma Neeti* were a lost cause.10 These principles were really developed in Hindu texts for men, not for women. *The High Caste Hindu Woman* suggests a note of deep despair in her voice. It begins the next major stage in the development in her thought. She is more incisive about Hindu texts. She realized that as long as Indian women are subjected to the codes of conduct expected of them in the Hindu texts, they will never be free. This began a quest for a text, which would become the grounds of female liberation in India. Secularization of the codes of Manu would not cut it. In my opinion this is what fuelled her biblical theology. It became the heart of her quest for a biblical theology for the Indian woman.

She wrote in *The High Caste Woman*, "A Brahman of a High clan will marry ten, eleven, twenty. . . . The illustrious Brahman need not bother with the care and support of many wives, for the parents pledge themselves to maintain the daughter all her life." [11] She observed regarding female infanticide,

> Opium is generally used to keep the crying child quiet, and a small pill of this drug is sufficient to accomplish the cruel task; a skillful pressure upon the neck, which is known as "putting nail to the throat" answers the purpose. There are several other nameless methods that may be employed in sacrificing the innocents upon the unholy altar of the caste and clan system. [12]

Therefore, she deemed it,

> Of first importance to prepare the way for the spread of the gospel by throwing open the locked doors of Indian *zenanas*, which cannot be done safely without giving suitable education to the women, whereby they will be able to bear the dazzling light of the outer world and the perilous blasts of social persecution . . . millions of heart-rending cries are daily rising from within the stony walls of Indian *zenana*; thousands of child widows are dying annually without a ray of hope to cheer their hearts. . . . will you not, all who read this book, think of these, my countrywomen, and rise by a common impulse to free them from life- long slavery? [13]

The translation of the Bible forms the third stage of her development as an Indian Christian, feminist theologian. This is clear in many writings. In the little book called *My Testimony*, written many years later, she wrote, "I realized, after reading the 4th Chapter of St. John's Gospel, that Christ was truly the Divine Saviour He claimed to be, and no one but He could transform and uplift the downtrodden womanhood of India."[14] It is clear to me that, if Ramabai had had time after the translation work was completed, she would have explored these themes more in her writings. However, she died an untimely death, and one is left with the task of discovering her Indian Christian, proto-feminist theology from her translation of the Bible.

The Basis of Ramabai's Indian Christian Hermeneutics: A Hermeneutic of the Indian Woman and Shudra

A Bible Translation to End the Trafficking of Women.

Ramabai's hermeneutics was far removed from Western methodologies. One text from the Hebrew Bible became the primary motto of Ramabai's life: "The spirit of the Lord GOD is upon me; because the LORD hath anointed me to bring good tidings unto the humble; He hath sent me to bind up the broken-hearted, to proclaim liberty to the captives, and the opening of the eyes to them that are bound" (Isa 61:1). According to Ramabai the gospel for India found its central focus in this text. According to Luke this, of course, was the central theme of the message of Jesus (Luke 4:18).

Ramabai's works at Mukti and as a theologian were all tied to this central theme. She translated the word *cànāwĪm* with the Marathi *dìn*, a term which refers to the *Dalits*. She viewed the Hindu women as the *bharg hirdyacha lokas,* the severely wounded ones who need deep holistic medical treatment. These are the ones who are captives to the laws of Manu and societal captivity. Therefore they needed liberty and healing. Ramabai's biblical interpretation and theological formulation were motivated by the deep desire for personal and social transformation, the transformation of the subaltern—the women, and the outcastes.

Ramabai's biblical interpretation seeks to understand inner-biblical intertextuality and then transfers that intertextuality to the realm of the "new text," i.e., the woman and the shudra in their present situation and in their history. Inner- biblical intertextuality, as it is seen in the works and translation of Ramabai, seeks to express and incorporate the intertextuality, which is contained in the Bible in its own context. This is very different from modernistic post-critical, deconstructionist readings of the Bible. In the latter the *receptor* text obliterates the context and the meaning of the *conceptor* text through the process of deconstruction. The codes and conventions of the *receptor* text destroy the codes and conventions of the *conceptor* text. Consequently the new receptor community must destroy the codes and conventions of the conceptor communities of the biblical text. Ramabai, quite in contrast to this interpretive methodology, sought to affirm the codes and conventions of the conceptor communities of the Bible. It seems very clear that in developing her methodology of biblical translation she clearly saw that the codes and conventions of the conceptor biblical communities were directly proportional to the codes and conventions of women and shudras in India. This forms the grounds for the liberation of the Indian woman and the Shudra.

Ramabai's title for her biblical translation project is a poignant example of this. She entitled her Bible translation *Wonderful Testimonies* (*p˘elã ôt cëdôt*). This became the nuclear theme of her development of a biblical theology. She took Ps 119 to be the formative mega theme for the formulation of a biblical theology for the Indian context. She viewed each event in the Bible as an inner-biblical development, a reinterpretation and reapplication. The exodus event, a wonderful testimony, is reinterpreted in the inner-biblical text of the Hebrew Bible. The Hebrew Bible contains a series of wonderful testimonies (*p˘elã ôt cëdôt*) which take on various shades of meaning. At each step the earlier wonderful testimonies are foreshadows of later ones. The Gospels then take the shape of the Jesus event, another wonderful testimony. Ramabai suggested that this is how her Bible translation must be read. The biblical wonderful testimonies must be seen in continuity with the existential situation of the Indian woman and shudra. When one uses the text of the Bible in this sort of a hermeneutic, then the "liberty" of the Indian woman and outcaste will be seen as a continuation of the wonderful testimonies, the salvation testimonials of the biblical texts. This is indeed why she called her life story *My Testimony, Adi.*

In the thought of Ramabai this method of interpretation results in the formation of a "new text," i.e., a "new identity." This is the Mukti text, the Mukti identity, the Mukti community. The oppressed women and shudras of India are in continuity with the biblical tradition and interpret their current context through the formation of the new text, the Mukti text. It is crucial to underscore that this is not merely a modernistic "reader-oriented" method. Ramabai viewed the original text, the wonderful testimonies, very seriously as formulating the "new text."

This philosophy of hermeneutics may also be seen in the title she gave to her original translation of the Bible into Marathi. She decided to go with the Jewish canonical order *Torah, Nevi'im,* and *Ketuvim.* This is a canonical understanding of hermeneutics, which reminds one of scholars like Brevard Childs. The canonical order of the Bible as present in the Masoretic Text became the basis of her development of the wonderful testimonies. Pandita Ramabai came to the opinion that this canonical order bodes well for the development of an Indian Christian, feminist theology. The worship songs she wrote give a clear example of this progression of these wonderful testimonies. They generally contain the canonical order, moving from the exodus event, to the Prophets, the Psalms, and the Christ event. The refrain was the Mukti event. The Mukti Ashram was a continuation of God's wonderful testimonies. This must be seen as a crucial aspect of Pandita Ramabai's feminist and existential biblical theology.

Ramabai's Bible Translation: A Manifesto for a New Womanhood Based on the Hebrew, Aramaic and Greek Text of the Bible

The primary thesis of this paper is that Ramabai chooses words and phrases very carefully in her translation of the Bible, so that the Indian woman is given a brand new identity. Her translation is based on very faithful exegesis of the Hebrew, Aramaic and Greek text of the Bible. I propose that Ramabai saw Indian women receiving a brand new identity as she encountered the text of the Bible. This is very similar to the brand new identity which Jesus gave to the woman at the well in John 4. I will also seek to show in the following that Ramabai's translation is quite a contrast to a couple of present day English translations, and more importantly, the Hindi and Marathi translations of India.

It is crucial to note that Pandita Ramabai is informed in her theology of womanhood from the canonical perspective of the Hebrew. She calls it the TaNaKH, i.e. the Torah, Nevi'im and the Ketuvim. She also calls it the *Wonderful Testimonies* (*pˇelã ôt cëdôt*). This is an interesting choice of words because her first book *The High Caste Woman* described the place of high caste womanhood in India. In her Bible translation she was seeking a transformed state of womanhood which would eradicate all forms of human trafficking against girls and women. Ramabai sees the code of the Bible transform the women of India. In her estimation she was seeing the stories of the Bible actualized in the lives of Indian society and transform the idea of womanhood.

The crescendo of the biblical idea of womanhood is seen in the final section of the Hebrew Bible. The Ketuvim. The Ketuvim begins with the book of Psalms, followed by the book of Proverbs, which is followed by five books which describe the place of womanhood in the Hebrew Bible: Song of Songs, Ruth, Lamentations Ecclesiastes and Esther. These books are followed by wisdom apocalyptic writings of Daniel and wisdom historical writings of Ezra-Nehemiah and Chronicles.

The picture of the Indian woman is an intellectually, emotionally, physically and spiritually strong woman.

I will begin with the book of Proverbs. The title which she gives to the book of proverbs is the same term which she gave to her first book *Stree Dharma Neeti* , the Path of Wisdom of a Woman. Throughout the book Ramabai's focus is to follow the woman Wisdom, *Gyan*. This is a word which is never associated with women in Hindu society. She makes this very clear both in *Stree Dharma Neeti* and *The High Caste Woman.*This woman of wisdom, *gyan*, is the diametric opposite of the "adulterous woman," as NIV puts it. Ramabai's word, *parstree*, makes it clear that this is not the real woman. This is what Hindu society has made out of the woman, whose only value is satisfy the sexual desires of the High Caste men – both in this life and in the life to come.

Instead, Ramabai urges her readers to become like the woman of Proverbs 31: 10, 26-31. The words which Ramabai uses to describe this woman are very telling. NRSV calls this woman a "capable wife;" NIV calls this woman "a wife of noble character." The Hindi translation calls this person a *bhali patni*, an innocent, coy, wife. Much in contrast to these translations, Ramabai calls this woman a *Saduni Bai*, "an emotionally, physically, mentally and spiritually strong woman." She is primarily not a wife, as the English translations put it. She is primarily a woman in her own right. She is not merely a "capable wife" or a "wife of noble character," or "an innocent coy wife," rather she is a "physically, spiritually, mentally a strong woman." This is the kind of woman Ramabai suggested is the essence of womanhood. From Ramabai's perspective, this is how human trafficking is countered. It is by giving those widows and girls saved from female infanticide, an exceptionally strong, biblical concept of womanhood. It is rather unfortunate that our English and Indian vernacular translations do not give us the intended meaning of the Hebrew words *Eshet Chayil*. Ramabai, in her Bible translation seeks to redress this gaping mistake.

It is crucial to note that in the Hebrew book order which Ramabai followed in the *Wonderful Testimonies,* Proverbs is followed by five examples of *Eshet Chayil Wisdom* which are found in the five books which follow: The books of Song of Songs, Ruth, Lamentations, Ecclesiastes and Esther. Jewish tradition calls these books the Megillot.

It is significant that Ramabai translates that the woman is the essential paradigm of the Book of Proverbs. She is the *bayko Yehvache bhye dharite*, one "who fears the LORD." (Prov. 1:7). She is also the woman who sits at the "*vashit*" (Prov. 31:31). This is the place where only the high caste men go. It is not the place where anyone who is low caste or outcaste would dare to be seen. It is unheard of a woman- whether she belongs to the high caste, low caste or outcaste to be seen anywhere near this place. They would desecrate this place. Ramabai elevates the status of the woman a million fold in translating this place as the *vashit*. The woman reader is given the clear thought that she can rise to those places which were the realms of high caste manhood.

The story of Ruth, which is an illustration of this is a poignant example in Ramabai's translation. The English, Marathi and Hindi translations do not see the finer aspects of what is happening in this narrative, as Ramabai does. In Ruth 1:4, the English text says, that the sons of Elimelech and Naomi "married Moabite women (NIV); "took Moabite wives" (NRSV). The Hindi and the Marathi also give the same sense. "They married Moabite women." Ramabai, in contrast to this, translates the "they forcibly took," *ghetleya,* "Moabite women," *bayko.* It seems to me that this captures the Hebrew text quite squarely. These were women had their own rights. Yet, they were taken as prostitutes, or mistresses. It gives the picture of a dominant male society taking advantage of a subservient female society. This is the picture Ramabai seeks to give in her translation. The Hebrew word used here is not *laqach*, the usual word for "taking" a wife, but rather *nasa'*. It is a word which carries the connotation of the women being lifted into the domain of Temple prostitution. This is the picture which Ramabai seeks to give in her translation. Obviously, this action of the sons of Elimelech was not left unpunished. The two sons die.

In the next phase of this story, Ramabai shows how this woman is transformed from the status of a "foreign prostitute material" in Bethlehem to a woman of honor. In Ruth 2, when Ruth encounters Boaz, she says, "Why have I found favor in your eyes that you notice me a "foreigner?" (NIV, NRSV). The Hindi gives us the same sense. Ruth describes herself as a *pardesi*, a person who comes from another country. It seems clear to me that Ramabai gets the meaning of the Hebrew word *nakri* right. She translates Ruth 2:10, "Am I a *parki*, the other." This is the same word which is used to describe the prostitute in Proverbs 5:10, 20. In her translation, Ruth sees herself as being in a very vulnerable place. She sees herself as the other, *parki*, which is always taken into sexual slavery in India. Ramabai seeks to show how Ruth felt in Moab, and now in Bethlehem. That is how the low caste and outcaste women feel in Hindu India. This, it seems clear to me, is the right intent of the Hebrew text.

In the next scene of this story, when Ruth goes and reports her encounter with Boaz to Naomi, the latter exclaims, "Blessed be the man who took notice of you." (Ruth 2:19, so in NIV, NRSV and Hindi). Ramabai, it seems clear to me, gives the essential sense of the Hebrew, and makes good sense in the context of human trafficking in the days of Judges and today. In Ramabai's translation, Naomi says, "Blessed be the one who took deep knowledge of you and gave you the News (*samachar)*of freedom. It seems clear that Ramabai captures the true intent of the Hebrew word *nakar* (Gen. 42:7, 8; Lam. 4:8; cf. Gal. 3:28). The *nakri* is given a new sense of *nakar* by this honorable person called Boaz. This new sense of elevation transforms the *nakri* (Hebrew), the *parki* (Ramabai)*,* into a *nakar*, a known high status.

The transformation of the other further takes place along filial lines. Naomi and Boaz call Ruth, *Bathi*, "my daughter" (Rut. 2:2, 8, 22; 3:10, 11, 16, 18). Ramabai translates this with the closest of endearing terms which breaks down all caste and racial barriers: *Maiya Muli* (my very own loveable daughter). This is not the average word for a daughter. This is the most intimate word for a daughter which breaks down every barrier. It seems to me that Ramabai's biblical theology here is seeking to address the point that human trafficking can only be broken, when one society would look at the other society in these deep intimate categories. Should a person, especially an older man, look at the young woman of another lower and other society as his own *Maiya Muli*, human trafficking would not be an issue. Ramabai experienced situations like this all the time, where older men from higher castes would take girls, young girls, from lower castes to be their second or third wives- girls who were as old as their own daughters. These girls were severely mistreated by mothers-in-law and men. Many were beaten up severely. Bride burning was a regular event. Ramabai's antidote was the word used by Naomi and Boaz- *maiya muli.*

In the grand finale of the story, Ruth becomes the cause of the transformation of the women of Israel. The English translation of Ruth 4:13 reads, "So Boaz took Ruth and she became his wife" (NIV, NRSV). The English translations do not make any distinction between "Boaz taking Ruth," and sons of Naomi "taking wives." (Ruth 1:4). In Hebrew these are two vastly different words, with vastly different meanings. Here the Hebrew word is *laqakh*. In Ruth 1:4, the word is *nasa'*. Ramabai sees the distinction. Ruth 1:4 is enslavement of women. In Ruth 4:13, Boaz is portrayed as giving Ruth her due honor. Ramabai translates, "He marries her with honor," *vivahun ghatli*, and took her, and she became his "woman," *Baye*.

Ramabai's translation addresses two very crucial issues in her choice of words in this last part of the Ruth story. One, she squarely deals with the problem of Temple prostitution and human trafficking. Those who traffick in women, and especially other, low caste women, would meet the consequences of Elimelech's sons. However, those who do like Boaz did, do the honorable thing. Two, she also seeks to give the right perspective of the place of womanhood in marriage. Women should always be brought into a state of honor in marriage. This perspective deals with the issue of place of women in marriage quite squarely. A Ramabai Mukti young woman, based on this translation would only go into a marital relationship, if she is given a place of honor. This picture stands in contrast to the picture of marriage in India even today.

Ramabai's Bible carries this thesis throughout the text of the Old Testament. In the translation of Song of Songs woman is depicted as one who is pure and strong, and is able to express her sexuality in a way that the Indian woman has never been able to do. The translation of the Book Esther, also gives a very strong picture of a woman who is able to stand up with the rights of her people in against some very despotic forces.

The Dignity of Womanhood in the Torah

The perspective on womanhood found in the above crucial sections of the Wisdom Literature of the Hebrew Bible is seen throughout the text of the Pentateuch and the Prophets. It is interesting to observe that Ramabai sees the *Torah* as a new book of laws, *Niyamshastra*. This word is used intentionally to draw a contrast with the Code of Manu. Her first two books *Stree Dharma Neeti* and *The High Caste Hindu Woman* form the framework against which she develops her theological positions in her translation of the Bible. This is the new liberating *Niyamshastra*, which is the diametric opposite of the laws of Manu.

The High Caste Hindu Woman is full of assertions regarding the state of women, female infants, and widows in the *Manushastra*. These laws became the basis of the state of women in Indian society. Ramabai quoted from the *Manushastra,* "Though destitute of virtue, or seeking pleasure elsewhere, or devoid of good qualities, yet a husband must be constantly worshipped as a God by a faithful wife . . . a faithful wife, who desires to dwell after death with her husband, must never do anything that might displease him who took her hand, whether he be dead or alive" (*Manushastra* V, 147–156).[15] The Code of Vishnu adds, "A woman after the death of her husband should either lead a virtuous life or ascend the funeral pile of her husband" (*Vishnu* xx.2).[16]

Ramabai's choice of the names of God in her translation of the Bible is quite telling. For the name of God in Genesis 1, the word '`elōhīm, she chose the word *Deva*. For the Tetragrammaton, YHWH, she decided to transliterate it as Yehovah. Both of these words have their origin in pre-Aryan, pre-Vedic roots. In an explanatory note she suggested that this word ought to be understood as the description of "Triune God." However, she made it clear that this is not the Trinity in the sense of Brahmobandab Upadhyaya's *Sat Cit Ananda*, nor is it classical Hinduism's *Brahma*, the creator, *Vishnu*, the preserver, and *Shiva*, the destroyer. This is the Triune God of Christianity.[17]

In a letter written and published in *Mukti Prayer Bell* (4.3, November 1909), Ramabai wrote:

> There are many words of this kind which clearly refer to Hindu thought, and not Christian. These words should not be allowed to remain in the vernacular translations of the Bible . . . the words *Ishvar* or *Parameshvar* are proper names of *Mahadeva*, one of the Hindu Triade, and do not denote the Supreme God. The words Jehovah, and Jah revealed by God as His proper names, are translated by the word *Parameshvar* in Marathi; and why the words *Yehovah* and *Yah* were not transliterated instead of allowing a mistranslation to take their place is not explained. The word *Parameshvar* does not express the meaning of the name Jehovah as revealed in Exodus 3:14, Revelation 1:4, namely, "Which is, and Which was, and Which is to come.[18]

It seems quite clear that Ramabai took issue with the use of Hindu terminology made in Indian Christian theologies. Her opinion seems to be that the use of this kind of terminology just makes the narration of biblical theology more complicated to the Indian mind. It gives the Indian mind an unbiblical idea of God. She took similar issue with other theologians who use Hindu names for God. She wrote, "These and other such words as *Bhav, Bhavasagar, Bhagwan, Tribhuvan*, etc. are used by different schools of Hinduism. However, when Indian Christian theologians use them, it destroys the biblical theology of God."[19]

Again it is clear that Ramabai sought to avoid terms of divinity, which were intended to subject women and the untouchables to a very demeaning state. *Ishvar, Parameshvar, Bhav, Bhasagar, Bhagwan*, etc. were Brahamanic terms. The theologies of God which emerged from these names of the divine were completely out of reach for women and shudras. For this reason Ramabai preferred to transliterate the Hebrew names for God. For example, she considered that the name *Yahweh*, the "one who is, who was, and who is to come," would give women and untouchables a great amount of encouragement and power. This God does not change according to the whims and fancies of the brahamanical texts which brought the women and shudras under the subjection of the Brahmins. This God is a being who elevates the status of the subaltern.

Throughout the Old Testament and the New Testament Ramabai chose to translate the word *sāmayim, (heaven)* with the word *Akash*. This is the word she used in Gen 1:1: *Pra-rambhi Devane Akashe Ani Prithvi hi asthithvath anli*. Her translation of Ps 19:1 reads, *Akashe Devacha mehima vernithath*—"the heavens declare the glory of God." The literal translation of Ramabai's Marathi would be the "skies." This translation is in contrast to other Indian translations which use the word *swarg*. She wrote:

> The word *swarg* denotes the abode of the gods where Indra, the king of the Hindu gods is supposed to reign. The place is described to be full of sensual pleasure, where a man goes to enjoy the pleasure brought by *apavarga*, merit. He is supposed to be fortunate, and lives a life of unmixed pleasure, enjoying the company of hundreds and thousands of celestial harlots called *apsaras*. After all this *karma* is spent, he is cast down to the earth, and is reincarnated in some good high-caste family. Where he has all the chances of re-attaining *swarga* by his *apavarga*. (This is also the state of) *Nirvana*, which is attained by the *janana*, knowledge of *Brahaman, Bhagawatgita* 9:20, 21.[20]

It seems clear that Ramabai has again avoided anti-feminine terms. The term *swarg* suggests a man-oriented heaven. Women are denigrated to the role of those who ingratiate the sexual desires and needs of men. This was the kind of situation from which she had rescued the temple prostitutes who became an essential part of the Mukti Ashram. These young ladies were taken by high caste Hindus into the temple precincts, as soon as they got their first menstruation. They were then trained to become temple priestesses, who gave men sexual/spiritual pleasures. This also became the picture of the Hindu *swarga*. Therefore, Ramabai very vigorously sought the disuse of terms like *swarga*. Instead, she sought the simple use of pre- Vedic oriented vernacular, which simply presented the place of afterlife, heaven, as the place of the presence of God.

The Creation of the Woman Text

A classical text as to who is a woman is the creation of the woman narrative. The English Bible translates it in the following: "The LORD God said . . . I will make him a helper suitable for him (NIV); ". . . helper as his partner." (NRSV); "an helpmeet" (KJV). In many senses this translation has defined the attitude regarding womanhood, in western as well as eastern societies. Is a woman merely a suitable helper for men? Or is she something else? Unfortunately, this attitude in the Indian context compounds the attitude against women which is already present in the Hindu society. The Hindi translation puts this in similar words to the English translations of the Bible, "I will make his a helper who will be suitable for him, *us se mel khaye*." The Hebrew phrase which is used here is "*ezer kanegdo*," an *ezer* before him. In the third section of the Hebrew Bible, this word is always used to describe God himself: "you are the helper. *Ezer,* of the orphan" (Ps 10:14); "we wait in hope for the LORD; he is our *ezer,* help." (Ps. 33:20); etc.

In this crucial text, Ramabai seeks to underline the strong sense of womanhood portrayed in the Bible. She moves away from the Hindi, Marathi and English translations. She describes this woman as "a companion in his image, a Creator helper, *misathi tyacha pratirupacha sahay nirman karin.*" It seems very clear that in describing the creation of the woman in such strong categories, Ramabai captures the strong sense of the Hebrew, and conveys it to the Marathi readership. In doing so she gives several generations of the women in India self-worth, which will keep them from being ensnared into human trafficking.

This dignity of womanhood is found right through her translation of the Torah. A good example is her translation of the story of Hagar. Hagar is portrayed as an Egyptian slave of Abraham and Sarah. When Sarah is not able to bear a son, Hagar comes into use. Ramabai's translation is quite unique throughout the story. A telling moment is her translation of the moment when the Angel of the LORD reveals himself to Hagar. Ramabai makes it quite clear that this is no ordinary messenger of the Lord as NIV and NRSV portray it, or as it is portrayed in the Hindi and the Marathi translations of the Bible. In her translation, this is God himself. Ramabai makes this clear by emboldening the text, as she does for all the words for God throughout the Bible.

In the Indian context, this is a powerful message. Hagar is depicted, not as a slave woman who just bears the child for a powerful man. Rather, she is a woman to whom God himself appears. She is a prophetess. She is a Guru. This is an amazing picture for girls and women in India.

In the following verses, most English translations, Hindi and Marathi say, "she named the LORD who spoke to her, "you are El-Roi." Ramabai does not leave it in transliteration form. Rather she translates it with the words, "Your Name is the Seeing/Revealing God, *Pahnashya Dev.*" (Genesis 16:10). She uses a word which is used only of the highest caste Brahmin men. This is never the realm of low caste men. Of course, women – high or low caste could never dream of this kind of an encounter with God.

It seems clear to me that this portrayal of the low caste woman – Hagar would give the low caste and the outcaste women especially much strength and hope. Spiritual leadership, through this translation, becomes possible for the low caste and outcaste women. It is no longer the exclusive realm of high caste Brahmin men alone.

The Meaning of "Righteousness" and the State of Women in Society

Ramabai's Bible translation has a wealth of information which gives poor women – the widows, child widows, the sexually enslaved women – a new freedom. It gives them a new womanhood.

Perhaps, in conclusion it would be good to reiterate another significant aspect of Ramabai's translation of the Bible. I want to underline the word "righteousness." This is indeed the quest of the Prophets. The prophets see injustice against the poor and the downtrodden. Much of this injustice is meted out against the poor, the widows and the orphans. The prophets declare judgment against those people who propagate this kind of systemic form of injustice. Yet, in the future, declare the prophets that there is going to be a Messianic era, when the Messiah would come and eradicate all forms of injustice – especially, those against the poor, the orphans and the widows. The crucial question in the Indian context is, "What shape will this messianic era take?" A good example is the text in Isaiah 11:4. NRSV reads, ". . . with righteousness he shall judge the poor." This text in the Hindi reads, "with Brahamanic religiosity, *dharm* he will judge the destitute." Ramabai, in contrast to both the English and the Hindi translates, ". . . with Justice he will bring justice to the economically, socially, and religiously powerless." Similarly, when describing the city of Jerusalem, which is the center of this Messianic kingdom, in Isaiah 1:26, NRSV reads, ". . . you shall be called the city of righteousness, the faithful city." Hindi and Marathi similarly read, ". . . city of brahmanic religious people, Dharmpuri, and city of Sati, (the city of women who have jumped into the funeral pyre of their dead husbands). Ramabai, much in contrast to English, Hindi and Marathi, translates this futuristic place to be ". . . City full of Justice, Nayayachi Nagri, and City of faithfulness, Vishvasupuri."

Ramabai knew that the low caste and outcaste women were not looking for just another future which was the domain of the repressive high caste men. They were looking for a place free of all forms of oppression and injustice against women and the outcastes. In the New Testament, Ramabai's translation leads them to this Messiah, who in John 4 reaches out to the outcaste woman at the well. He offers her the *Nyayachi Nagri* and the *Vishvaspuri*.

Conclusion

It is clear from this analysis that the heart cry of Ramabai was for the poor widows and orphans, who were subjected to horrible forms of systemic evil and enslavement. Her answer takes shape in complex and phenomenological forms in her translation of the Bible. For Ramabai the answer to human trafficking was the faithful translation of the text to free the people – men, women and children. Unfortunately, missions and translators have employed the "who is who" and the high caste of society who, it seems clear, have blurred the force and the transformational encounter with the text of the Bible. Instead, "the widows, the orphan girls, and the poor" have been given a lukewarm text. When Ramabai confronted the powers that be of the Indian church, during her time, she was met with scorn. Yet, that did not stop her. Ramabai Mukti was able to rescue hundreds and hundreds of girls from human trafficking. She gave them text which frees them. It is the encounter with the text of the Bible, and the God of the Bible, and the Messiah of the Bible that gives true freedom from systemic injustice and slavery. From Ramabai's perspective, this is the answer to modern day human trafficking.

Ramabai called her translation the $P\breve{}ela$ $\hat{o}t$ $\ddot{e}d\hat{o}t$, The Wonderful Testimonies. She saw the Bible as not merely a teaching from the past, or a thing of the past. She saw the $p\breve{}el\tilde{a}$ $\hat{o}t$ $c\ddot{e}d\hat{o}t$ as a present reality. She saw the text as being actualized in the lives of the young women she rescued from human trafficking. That is the power of the Word.

[1]U.S. State Dept Trafficking in Persons Report, June, 2009.

[2]Pandita Ramabai, *A Testimony: of Our Inexhaustible Treasure,* (Kedgaon, MA: Mukti, 1907), p. 6.

[3]Ibid., 7.

[4]Ibid., 9.

[5]Ibid., 8.

[6]Ibid., 10.

[7]Ibid., 12.

[8]Pandita Ramabai, *Stree Dharma Neeti* (Code of Conduct for Women), Poona, 1882.

[9]Meera Kosambi, *Pandita Ramabai's Feminist and Christian Conversions*, p. 65. The third chapter is Kosambi's English translation of *Stree Dharma Neeti*.

[10]Pandita Ramabai, *The High Caste Hindu Woman,* (Philadelphia: Jas Rodgers, 1887).

[11]Ibid., 13.

[12]Ibid., 14.

[13]Ibid., 118-19.

[14]Ibid., 118-19.

[15]Ibid., 33.

[16]Ibid., 41.

[17]*Wonderful Testimonies- The Book of Psalms*, (Kedgaon: Mukti Press, 1910), p. 2.

[18]Ibid., 210.

[19]Ibid., 212.

[20]Ibid., 211.

Chapter Five

Exploitation in the Global Medical Enterprise: Bioethics & Social Injustice

Paige Comstock Cunningham

Michael J. Sleasman

BIOETHICS AND SOCIAL INJUSTICE likely seems an odd couple given the other topics covered in this book. On the surface anyone remotely informed about bioethics would make connections between the abortion and stem cell controversies and the injustices affected against the human embryo through his or her commodification and destruction. At the other end of the lifecycle the dismissal of human dignity through euthanasia and physician-assisted suicide seems obvious. Yet, this neglect goes hand-in-hand with a loss of respect for the special value and dignity of human life in its various embodiments throughout the lifespan. Less obvious to those both inside and outside the bioethical conversation is the profound connection of bioethics to issues of social justice, particularly through the interplay of discrimination and exploitation throughout the global medical enterprise. This essay seeks to traverse some of that terrain to raise awareness of these issues of justice within the realm of medical research, women's health, reproductive medicine, global healthcare, organ transplantation, and bioethics as a whole. Each of these topics is worthy of its own devoted essay. Our aim in this essay is modest: to introduce some of the more scandalous facets of bioethics and social injustice; to assist in bringing together two conversations that are often kept apart. Throughout we will point the interested reader to additional literature to explore these topics at greater depth.

In this edition of the essay we are highlighting four key areas of exploitation in the global medical enterprise. We begin with a brief explanation of our shared assumptions regarding the application of discrimination and exploitation within the context of the global medicine. We then turn to a topical discussion where Michael reviews medical research and patient protections. Next Paige examines concerns over the exploitation of the female body through issues raised by assisted reproductive technologies. Michael then examines the "red market" and the global dilemma of black market organ trafficking. Finally, we conclude this essay with a case study on the emerging practice of medical tourism, demonstrating the moral complexity of social justice in a global context.

Discrimination & Exploitation within the Context of the Global Medical Enterprise

At the risk of being overly simplistic one way to organize the disparate issues that coalesce around bioethics and social injustice is to draw an initial distinction between issues which can be categorized as *discrimination* and those which can be categorized as *exploitation*. While this distinction is problematic inasmuch as many issues of exploitation are at their core issues of discrimination, it is useful for our purposes to express the degree of severity to which social injustice is manifested in a given bioethical arena. In this way they serve more as a continuum than as exclusive categories. For instance, one issue of discriminatory medical practices, whether intentional or not, surrounds the frequent lack of availability of basic prenatal and perinatal care within the context of maternal health. The primary issue here is the availability of or access to maternal care leading up to and surrounding childbirth. In some cases the absence of basic maternal health services is quite simply a result of gender discrimination within a given culture. Here discrimination manifests itself through the denial of access (whether this is active or passive discrimination is irrelevant).

Exploitation, as we use it in this essay, is more aggressive in its manifestation. The exploited individual is often a target of market driven forces. Here the human being that is exploited is effectively commodified, treated as a natural resource, or at the very least a source from which resources can be deployed or harvested. This perception of the human being in question as a commodity may be either implicit or, in its most extreme manifestations, explicit. Examples of human exploitation include the renting of wombs, the purchase of organs from live donors, buying human eggs, and unethical forms of medical research. Ultimately, discrimination and exploitation are similar, despite the varying contexts of bioethics, because they both entail the instrumentalization of human beings. Here at its core is a violation of a basic Christian insight into the nature of human beings. Created in the image of God, human beings are unique within the created order. By virtue of being created in the image of God, human beings have a unique value and dignity. Christians, therefore, should be committed to the value and dignity of human beings at every life stage from conception to death regardless of gender, race, ethnicity, class, or capability.

Patient Protections & Human Subjects Research

Medical research by nature should pursue the goal of improving human health. In late 2010 a shocking series of headlines hit the cable news outlets and newspaper covers.[1] The inflammatory revelation? In the 1940s U.S. government researchers with the permission of the Guatemalan government intentionally infected hundreds of male prisoners and poor women with syphilis and then treated them with penicillin to study the effectiveness of the then relatively new treatment.[2] When the news broke, the National Institutes of Health and U.S. government officials quickly moved to condemn this serious breach of human rights from the nation's past. Sadly this was not the first time U.S. researchers had violated human rights in medical experimentation. One of the lead investigators of the Guatemalan study already had gained infamy through his later participation in the notorious Tuskegee Syphilis Study.[3] Additional archival research performed by the Associated Press in the wake of the Guatemalan revelation further uncovered that U.S. medical research practices during the first half of the 20th century raised numerous human rights abuses.[4]

After the lessons from the flagrant dehumanization of human life perpetrated by the Nazi regime in Germany, the once-revered medical profession was scrutinized under the international human rights microscope. In the wake of the experience of Nazi prisoners, the international community established the Nuremberg Code of Medical Ethics in 1947.[5] The Nuremberg Code prohibited non-therapeutic, non-consensual experimentation and led to further reflections on the responsibility of medical professionals to their patients, greater attention given to patient autonomy and rights, and the importance of informed consent in medical practice. Furthermore, special concern was given to the protection of patients in medical experimentation, which evolved into the contemporary concern for human subjects research ethics.

Although the bitter harvest was reaped by the Third Reich, the poisonous seeds were sown in the U.S. Egregious violations of informed consent and the classic medical maxim to "first do no harm" were made public in the U.S. through the Tuskegee Syphilis Study. Initiated before World War II and thus exempt from at least the formal codification of directives for medical research in its early years, the study nonetheless continued without a correction in method until 1972. When the study had run its course hundreds of African-American men previously infected with syphilis had not been accurately informed of their condition nor had they been treated. Despite clearly violating several directives of the Nuremberg Code after its formal codification regarding informed consent and intentionally exposing the subjects to known harm, the study was not halted even when penicillin became recognized as the standard of care for syphilis.[6] Tuskegee and Guatemala stand as stark reminders illustrating the danger and shame of allowing medical research to get ahead of moral reflection, but they also point to a danger of the instrumental use of human beings through medical discrimination and exploitation.

In response to the staggering revelations of the Tuskegee study, the U.S. federal government instituted the Belmont Report in 1979 which codified basic protections by enshrining three fundamental ethical principles (respect for persons, beneficence, and justice). These three principles along with the addition of nonmaleficence (in other words, "do no harm") have become the hallmark of contemporary bioethical reflection.[7] While flagrant violations of human subjects research protections seem to be well insulated from the general U.S. population, the high pressure stakes which constitute the realities of the global medical enterprise highlight the need for clear guidance and reflection. One area in which this has grown in importance involves drug trials within majority world countries that do not have such robust human subjects protections or regulatory infrastructure.

The 2005 film *The Constant Gardener* depicts a British diplomat investigating the untimely death of his wife. In the process of this investigation the diplomat uncovers a fraudulent drug trail being run in Kenya by a multinational pharmaceutical company. While the plot of *The Constant Gardener* may be adapted from a novel, several instances of alleged wrongdoing in medical and biotechnology research within majority world countries demonstrate that such occurrences are well within the realm of the possible and perhaps even likely. These possibilities point to the need for greater attention to the complex arena of drug trials within the global medical enterprise.[8] A variety of concerns ranging from negligent trials, to the outsourcing of drug trials to avoid strict regulatory rules, to the "rights" of the indigenous population to benefit from information gleaned from a given study, to their access to drugs tested on them, span the gamut of topics that are raised within the growing discussion of contemporary medical research with particular attention on the pharmaceutical industry.

While the issues raised by medical exploitation in human subjects research are likely distant from the experience of the everyday person in the U.S., there are several key lessons to learn. The first is that the modern medical enterprise exists as the legacy of a noble profession, but has competing interests that must be held accountable to the high standards of protections for human subjects in research. Any time medical research outpaces ethical guidelines, there is potential for major affronts to human dignity. The Tuskegee Syphilis Study, one of the most notorious examples in U.S. history of medical research abuse, created only modest awareness of human subjects research within the general U.S. population.[9] While a variety of formal mechanisms have been instituted which make such serious violations in medical research unlikely to be repeated in the U.S., this is not necessarily the case internationally.[10] Individuals advocating international human rights should be aware of the issues presented by human subjects research and the potential for medical exploitation. Furthermore, despite the unlikelihood of such blatant exploitation in U.S. medical practice, a continuing area of concern surrounds the number of health disparities of various socio-economic and ethnic groups, particularly within specific minority populations. Unfortunately, the legacy of such abuses exacerbates perceptions and concerns within minority populations that shape responsiveness to and trust in public health systems, calling for both education and outreach.[11]

Reproductive Tourism and Medical Exploitation of Women

March 8, 2011 marked the centenary of International Women's Day. In a global celebration that was both virtual and local, women celebrated economic, political and social achievements of the past 100 years.[12] Within that broad spectrum, individual nations and organizations are free to choose their own annual theme. One of the most persistent themes is the call to end violence against women and girls. The Millennium Development Goals agreed to by 147 nations in 2000, add specific platforms to the call to end women's inequality. Goal 3 focuses on education as a means to "empower women and promote equality between women and men." Goal 5 calls for a 75 percent "reduction in maternal mortality."[13]

World leaders, women's organizations, and individual women understand that within the context of social justice issues such as discrimination, abuse, exploitation, poverty, healthcare, and lack of education, women and girls are particularly vulnerable. This vulnerability exposes women to dangers of exploitation simply because they *are* women, with bodies that are viewed as a valuable resource. Nowhere is that more stark than in the exploitation of women's unique reproductive capacities. Women can provide through technology both the eggs and the womb needed for baby-making. Assisted reproductive technologies (ART) have opened up both the possibility and impetus for the instrumentalization of both babies and the third parties who are essential to their creation.

What began as an acknowledgement of marital privacy has now morphed into a culture of babies-on-demand. How did this change in social expectations emerge? A necessarily brief survey of the development of reproductive rights policy in the U.S. is instructive.

95

Theological Harbingers

The ancestry of reproductive tourism and exploitation begins culturally with the anemic theology of the Protestant church regarding contraception. The most public evolution took place within the Anglican Church. At its 1920 global conference of bishops, they unequivocally condemned birth control: "We utter an emphatic warning against the use of unnatural means for the avoidance of conception, together with the grave dangers - physical, moral and religious - thereby incurred, and against the evils with which the extension of such use threatens the race."[14] One decade later, the Lambeth conference again reviewed the matter, and reversed its earlier opposition. The bishops resolved that "the conditions of modern life call for a fresh statement from the Christian Church on the subject of sex."[15] After stating that "the primary purpose for which marriage exists is the procreation of children" in Resolution 13, the bishops approved the use of contraception by married couples if there were a "morally sound reason" that abstinence was not possible, but condemned its use for "motives of selfishness, luxury, or mere convenience."[16] The bishops went on to record their "abhorrence of the sinful practice of abortion,"[17] and that extramarital sex "is a grievous sin."[18]

Within one generation, at the 1958 Lambeth Conference, the bishops addressed family planning in the context of conscience, and linked "responsible parenthood" with "wise stewardship of the resources and abilities of the family as well as a thoughtful consideration of the varying population needs and problems of society and the claims of future generations."[19] In 1978, the bishops resolved that diocesan programmes should address "the moral issues inherent in clinical abortion and the possible implications of genetic engineering."[20]

Less than twenty-five years later, in 1982, the Episcopal Church U.S.A. fully embraced artificial contraception "as a means of world population control,"[21] the use of *in vitro* fertilization by a married couple, and rejected resolutions encouraging consultation with a priest before surrogate maternal or paternal parenthood. Each policy line that was drawn was moved without a clear theological justification other than changing times and cultural needs. This remarkable development within the Anglican/Episcopal Church is symptomatic of the absence of any robust theological rigor and consistency within the broader Protestant community.

Legal Policy Development

The theological pattern repeated itself in the legal arena. In 1965, the Supreme Court struck down a law against the distribution of artificial contraception, or the use by married couples of contraceptive devices. In *Griswold v. Connecticut*, the Court stated that the marital right of privacy protected this area against

96

government intrusion.[22] A few years later, the Court decided that access to contraception was not about marital privacy after all. In *Eisenstadt v. Baird*, the Court held that "if the right of privacy means anything, it is the right of the *individual*, married or single, to be free from unwarranted governmental intrusion into matters so fundamentally affecting a person as the decision whether to bear or beget a child."[23] These two cases solidified the legal, constitutional right of individuals *not* to procreate.

One year after the *Eisenstadt* case, the Court spoke again. This time, it dealt with the desire to be free from a pregnancy that had already begun. In *Roe v. Wade*, the Court struck down a Texas statute that prohibited abortion except for the purpose of saving the life of the mother.[24] The Court directed that the case was to be interpreted together with *Doe v. Bolton*, decided the same day as *Roe*.[25] The two cases struck down the abortion laws of all fifty states, including the most liberal ones. Abortion, previously a crime, became a protected constitutional right, available virtually on demand throughout the entire pregnancy.

Liberal abortion policy opened the door for coercion of women. Widespread availability of abortion removed "the one remaining legitimized reason that women have had for refusing sex besides the headache."[26] The assumption was that women wanted sex on equal terms with men, at any time, with any person, and without personal risk or consequences. This amplified an era of unprecedented social change.

Women are subject to genuine risks from legal abortion. These include both physical and psychological harm, as well as premature birth in future pregnancies, placenta previa, alcohol and drug abuse, and breast cancer.[27] Women who have abortions are at higher risk of violence, injury and death, and a higher risk of the termination of their relationship with the baby's father.[28] Abortion policy excludes the baby's father from any role in preventing the abortion. On the other hand, abortion relieves him of child support obligations, allowing him to walk away from the relationship.

Cultural Connections to Reproductive Technologies

Once the right *not* to procreate was firmly established, it was not a great leap to the right *to* procreate. After all, for the "embarrassingly fertile," we have "sex without children" via contraceptive technology. Now, for the "frustratingly infertile,' technology presented us with "children without sex." The right to control the timing and spacing of one's children through contraceptive practices was paralleled by the right to induce children to appear at the desired intervals with assisted reproductive technologies (ART). The right to remove an unwanted pregnancy by abortion, a demand to control the foreseeable consequences of natural processes, was joined to its mirror image: the right to attempt pregnancy by ART, a technological process.

The first ART was relatively simple: artificial insemination by husband, also known as homologous insemination. This led to AID, or artificial insemination with the use of donor sperm. Female infertility could be treated by medicine or surgery, to remove tissue blocking the Fallopian tube, or stimulate oocyte production. In all these ART methods, conception takes place inside the woman's body.

Fertilization outside the body occurs through *in vitro* fertilization, or IVF. After at least eighty unsuccessful pregnancies in other women, the technique was publicly announced with the birth of Louise Brown in 1978. Eggs extracted from her mother were fertilized in a petri dish with sperm donated by her father, then returned to Mrs. Brown's uterus for implantation.

In order to harvest eggs, the woman's ovaries must be chemically induced to ripen and release more eggs than normal. Sometimes more than twenty eggs may be retrieved in one cycle. Egg harvesting carries risks, particularly ovarian hyperstimulation syndrome (OHSS). At least 6 percent of women taking the drugs to ripen multiple eggs are seriously affected by OHSS.[29] OHSS symptoms range from mild pain and nausea to severe pain, rapid weight gain, and rapid heartbeat.

In the early years of IVF attempts, as many as six or even more eggs would be fertilized and transferred to the uterus for possible implantation. If more than two embryos successfully implanted, "selective reduction" would be recommended, that is, the elimination of the "excess" embryos. Thus, the couple who desperately tried to achieve a pregnancy had to reverse course and terminate the life of one or more embryos.

In the late 1980s Cryopreservation techniques were developed to permit freezing in nitrogen of embryos for future use. Thus, only two or three needed to be transferred for a pregnancy attempt. Even so, a dozen or more embryos might be plunged in liquid nitrogen for an indefinite period. No regulations restrict the number of embryos that may be created or frozen, nor are accurate records required. Today, there may be 500,000 or more frozen embryos in the U.S.[30] After giving birth to one or more children, the couple may then be confronted with making a decision about the rest of their frozen embryos. They may have them thawed and destroyed, donated for research (and their inevitable destruction), or donated to another couple for attempted pregnancy and adoption. Decision-making can be a lengthy, difficult, and emotional process.[31] Similar to the woman with "too many embryos" who is pressured to abort one or more of them, the couple with frozen embryos may be forced to dispose of the costly resources they gave so much to acquire.

IVF: The Largest Unregulated Business in the U.S.

The clinical practice surrounding the treatment of infertility is shaped by at least two powerful factors: the intense desire of couples to have a "child of one's own," and the reality that infertility is not a disease but a condition and symptom of the disruption of a normal biological process. Rather than treating the causes of infertility, fertility doctors may urge couples to move directly to ART. The industry is lucrative and relatively independent. Although there are professional guidelines, they are voluntary. Only one in five clinics follows the guidelines of either the Society for Assisted Reproductive Technology or the American Society for Reproductive Medicine, which may limit, for example, the number of embryos transferred. The U.S. has one of the highest rates of multiple births in the world.[32]

The IVF industry is large and powerful. Annual revenues in the U.S. are estimated between $1.7 and $5 *billion*.[33] Proposed regulations, such as those that require informed consent about the risks of egg donation and the genetic risks to the child, are opposed as an interference with privacy and choice. Clinics are subject to general regulations, such as those that apply to laboratories that test semen. They are also directly regulated by federal law which requires them to report their pregnancy success rate, but there is no penalty for non-reporting. The FDA has authority to require clinics to register, set guidelines for screening of gamete donors, and establish "good tissue practices."[34]

Although some bristle at the use of the term "IVF industry," it is not unwarranted. Clinics specializing in fertility treatment issue press releases and market their services. One fertility clinic advertised price reductions due to "harsh economic times," and highlighted their extensive database of egg donors who could meet the needs of couples from countries such as Spain, France, Italy, Germany, Norway, Portugal, South Africa, Brazil, Mexico, Japan and Hong Kong.[35] A quick Internet search would yield dozens of IVF clinic advertisements.

The Temptation for Exploitation: Expansion of ART

The demand for IVF was not limited to producing embryos using a woman's eggs and her husband's sperm. Male infertility is a factor in nearly half of all infertile couples. Thus, there was a demand for donor sperm. The first commercial sperm bank opened in 1972. Sperm donors often were medical students, or occasionally a hubristic infertility doctor (reproductive endocrinologist). There has arisen a generation of donor offspring, children whose genetic father is an anonymous sperm donor, who are struggling with identity issues. Elizabeth Marquardt documents their struggles in *My Daddy's Name Is Donor*.[36]

ART using egg donors was first attempted via artificial insemination in the egg donor's womb, followed by retrieval of the embryo and transfer to the wife's womb for continued pregnancy and childbirth.[37] Egg retrieval—rather than embryo retrieval—quickly became the preferred use of egg donors. With the successful use of donor eggs, fertility clinics began soliciting young college women, prime candidates for selling their eggs. Prices as high as $25,000 or more are advertised for Ivy League women with high SAT scores, athletic skill, mathematic and musical ability, blonde hair, and blue eyes.[38] Few coeds qualify for the promised price, with the average payment nationally around $4,000.[39] Although the marketing appeal is to donate "the gift of life," the donor's motivation is usually to pay off credit card or other debts.

Egg donation comes with risks. As noted earlier the drugs a donor must take to cause one or more dozen eggs to ripen simultaneously carry a 6-10% risk of OHSS, which can be serious, if rarely fatal. There is some evidence of a link with an increased risk of cancers, such as colon, breast, uterine or ovarian cancer. The problem is that these health risks simply have not been studied in detail, or over the long term.[40] These young women cannot give fully informed consent prior to egg donation, as the long-term health risks are unknown, unstudied, and sparsely documented.

The egg donor is not the only woman who risks her health. The subfertile woman who sought egg donation, and is pregnant with the embryo created thereby, faces increased health risks during her pregnancy. A meta-analysis concluded that she is at increased risk of hypertension and placental abnormalities.[41]

Surrogacy: Womb for Rent

For some women, infertility cannot be resolved with egg donation, or the couple prefers not to attempt pregnancy with donor gametes. A woman might not be able to carry a pregnancy to term for a variety of reasons. Her dilemma can be addressed by surrogacy, the use of another woman's womb to gestate the child. Surrogacy has tracked two general paths: altruistic and commercial. Altruistic surrogates are usually known to the couple, often a relative. One well-known case is that of Jaci Dahlenberg, who gave birth to her triplet granddaughters. They do not seek compensation, other than for direct medical costs.

Most surrogacy, although often privately arranged, is conducted along a commercial model. Early surrogates were paid for their time and efforts, and medical costs were covered. Financial transactions were carefully arranged so as not to violate laws against "baby selling." Commercial surrogates may be one of two types: genetic or biological. Genetic surrogates provide the egg, agreeing to be inseminated with donor sperm, usually the contracting intended father. This is also called "traditional" or "straight" surrogacy. These arrangements had a higher incidence of conflict, as some surrogates became attached to the fetus that was also their son or daughter, with half of their DNA coming from the surrogate. The most notorious case was that of Baby M, whose birth mother refused to relinquish her, generating a court battle.[42]

Biological surrogates, also called gestational surrogates or "host" surrogates, do not contribute any genes, but only their womb. This has become the preferred arrangement, particularly when the surrogate is of different ethnicity than the contracting couple. She may be impregnated with an embryo created from the egg and sperm of the contracting couple, the father's sperm and donor egg, the mother's egg and donor sperm, or donor egg and sperm. Thus, the child may have a biological connection to three people.

Baby Battles: The Unintended Consequences of ART

Courts have wrestled with the impact of new reproductive technologies, which may help couples achieve their desired ends, but do not fit within legal categories and established case law. In one case, a girl was declared to have "no legal parent." The contracting couple had acquired an embryo created via anonymous egg and sperm, and contracted with a surrogate to carry the baby. Before birth, the commissioning couple's marriage ended, and both the father and the birth surrogate denied parenthood.

Surrogacy and other ART arrangements raise psychological, social, and legal issues regarding the meaning of family and parent. New labels have been created to describe the various kinds of parent: contracting parent, intended parent, gamete donor, biological parent, gestational surrogate, social parent, and, more recently posthumous parent.[43] Meanwhile, the language used to describe the embryo resembles that of a product, not a person: blast, grade 3, good quality, and high-grade embryo.

International Bargain Hunting: Reproductive Tourism

The ART industry is not confined to U.S. borders. At least three factors have contributed to this expansion. First, there is little diversity in gamete donors and the supply of frozen embryos, so couples have solicited donors outside the traditional "blonde hair/blue-eyes" spectrum. Second, among some ethnic groups, ART is frowned upon, intensifying the desire for privacy, secrecy of using a surrogate, and ethnic matching of donated gametes so that any resulting children will resemble the parents. Third, both IVF attempts and commercial domestic surrogacy are expensive, and surrogacy is not legal in every state. Infertile couples have been presented with a new option: international gamete donors and surrogates. One reporter wrote about the financial devastation of her IVF attempts in the U.S. — $70,000 to date—and her and her husband's decision to fly to South Africa to attempt pregnancy with egg donation. They found a sensitive doctor ("how kind he was, compared with American reproductive endocrinologists"), an altruistic egg donor, and a cost of $9500 vs. $30,000 in the U.S.[44]

Relatively little is known about global ART, compared with the minute regulation of other aspects of international trade. In some countries, it is virtually unregulated, and in others such as the Ukraine, there is legal support for all aspects of ART, including creating embryos for research. When the UK changed its laws to prohibit anonymity or compensation to gamete donors, the supply decreased significantly. In response, British Caucasian women have turned to countries such as the Ukraine, choosing Slavic women whose appearance matches their own.[45]

These egg donors are vulnerable to exploitation. Many are poor or unemployed, and some donate in extreme secrecy, not telling even their husbands. Although the eggs net the broker or clinic nearly $5,000, the women may receive as little as $300. Some donors are flown to Cyprus for egg harvesting, which may be illegal in their country of residence. The egg purchasers live in yet another country, implicating the laws of at least three nations, some of which are often evaded during the transaction.[46] If egg donors are injured during the donation process, they may receive inadequate immediate or follow-up medical care. If they did not produce an abundant harvest of eggs, they have little economic value to the broker. Once they have produced the eggs and if there is permanent injury, there is small incentive for the broker to cover any medical costs. They are, in effect, "damaged goods."

The wealthy women who use these services are told little about how donors are recruited or treated. Perhaps their ignorance is intentional, or perhaps they are grasping at any straw of hope. One reporter traced the process, and was told a different story by each party involved: the UK doctor, the permanently maimed Romanian donor, the Bucharest and Kiev clinics. Posing as an infertile woman, she encountered pressure to proceed immediately, without any serious medical examination.[47]

Egg donors are somewhat free to travel to self-administer daily injections, travel to the clinic and then leave. Coercion of these women is more often implicit, preying on their poverty-driven vulnerability. However, there is another aspect to reproductive tourism that is more blatantly confining and exploitative: the use of gestational surrogates.

Reproductive Trafficking: Nine Months of Confinement

Couples who desire a gestational surrogate may obtain her services at a much lower cost if they look outside U.S. borders. They may travel to another country for the IVF procedure and transfer to the surrogate's womb. In countries such as India, commercial surrogacy is "seen as a business opportunity in many locales where public policy is lax and contract pregnancy comes cheap."[48] Commercial surrogacy in India is estimated to be a $445 billion industry. Other surrogacy destinations include Guatemala, Argentina, Spain, China, and Thailand. The "tourists" who seek these services may be avoiding laws that prohibit these arrangements in their home country. In response, India has proposed regulating their active, market-driven fertility industry by requiring, among other things, that foreigners must prove that surrogacy is legal in their home country.[49] There have been situations where couples ran into significant legal obstacles delaying their return home with their commissioned child.

Ironically, the aspects that appeal to the contracting couple represent the greatest potential for exploitation. The intended parents want to ensure that the woman stays healthy during her pregnancy. Victor Hui-Wee commented after their experience with a surrogate in India, "They control everything and that's so important to us. . . . The surrogates live on site in apartments until the baby is born."[50] Married surrogates are separated from their husbands and children for the entire pregnancy and delivery. The contracting couple is not just relying on the altruistic good will of the surrogate; they are paying for a healthy baby. Whether the surrogate understands what she is being asked to do is less than certain. Some potential birth surrogates sign the contract with a thumbprint, because they cannot read, let alone understand English, the language of the contracts. The socioeconomic and power gap between the intended parents and the surrogate is wide:

> Lack of technological understanding among rural Indians also breeds misconceptions about surrogacy. Many, for example, thought that it would be necessary to sleep with another man in order to conceive. Even the pricing structure of surrogacy perpetuates social inequality: Many religious Indian surrogacy clients would prefer for their child to be birthed by an upper-caste *brahmin*, so high-born surrogates can get paid up to double.[51]

103

Surrogates are not paid until after the birth if the intended parents decide they do not want the child—as happened with one couple whose marriage dissolved before birth—they may deny parental responsibility, or demand that the surrogate have an abortion. In either case, the surrogate is oppressed: abortion may violate her religious beliefs, and her poverty increases if she must accept the child as her own.

In a recent breakup of a surrogate baby ring in Thailand, it was revealed that Vietnamese women were lured to Thailand, confined against their will under 24-hour security, had their passports confiscated, and may have been raped. The company advertised "eugenics surrogate," which meant that the "consignor" would never have contact with the surrogate. The embryos could be sent by "mail-order." The couple would never have to come face to face with their surrogate.[52]

The market-driven ethic of using surrogates does not even demand that the contracting couple is infertile. One city in India offers mail-order surrogates. "Busy childless couples and even singles who cannot afford to take extended leaves are now shipping their children-in-the-making to state clinics to be im-planted in the wombs of surrogates."[53] It is a market exchange. The contracting couple has something the surrogate needs: money. The surrogate has something the contracting couple desperately wants: a womb and a guarantee of a controlled pregnancy. Surrogates often say they are doing this to provide a college education for their daughter, to buy a house, to pay off a husband's drinking debts, or be-cause she is a widowed mother.[54] While commercial surrogacy may help a few women and their families in the short-term, it does not answer the problem of ex-ploitation.

Social Injustice Concerns

It is at this point of injustice that Christians are vulnerable. We cannot hide behind the claim that "we wouldn't do that," or "we're not infertile." The exploita-tion of women for their eggs and their wombs is possible, in part, because there are few barriers. Legal barriers exist in some countries, but they are skirted or sel-dom enforced. There are financial barriers, but international reproductive trade has made ART more accessible to Americans, British, and Japanese couples. There are cultural barriers, such as the need for secrecy among some Muslim and Asian communities, but ethnically-matched egg donation or reproductive tourism (where the wife leaves for an extended period and returns home with a baby) negate that barrier.

Can a poor, illiterate Indian woman make an informed choice? Does she have the freedom to resist the promised payment, when faced with no other appar-

104

ent way out of her poverty? Is this the best we have to offer, to induce women to rent their bodies for nine months for the benefit of strangers? While reproductive tourism and trafficking may financially help a small group of women, they do not resolve the income disparities and poverty of majority world women. Nor do they protect them from the predatory and exploitative "baby brokers."

There is yet another aspect to all this, and that is the eugenic aspect of ART. The commissioning couple naturally desires a healthy baby. They may try to control this through PGD—pre-implantation genetic diagnosis—which can reveal genetically-linked diseases. Embryos that do not meet the standard are discarded and destroyed. Or, they may require that as a condition of surrogacy, the surrogate agrees to terminate if something goes wrong. In either case, a much-desired future child is rejected because he or she did not pass quality control standards.

Children are created to serve parental needs and natural desires. Yet, we know that children are a gift, a reward from the Lord to be received with gratitude, not created out of desperation. While technology may be helpful in resolving certain aspects of infertility, it does not prevent exploitation and injury. Instead, global ART may unintentionally enhance their likelihood.

When great goods—whether children or restoration of health, addressed in the next section—are mingled with great harms, our concern for justice must trump our desire for technological restoration. The sacrifice we Christians are called to make may include the denial of what we most deeply long for: a child of our own. But self-denial is not our only option. We are also called to speak out on behalf of those who have no power to speak on their own behalf. Dignity-affirming solutions to poverty and inequality are our task. More families are lifted out of grinding poverty by the education of their daughters than by the selling of female bodies.[55] A business microloan, for example, may do more to redeem a village than the bounty bestowed on one family who buys a house paid for with the ethically tainted payment for a rented womb.

The Red Market for Human Organ Trafficking

"The Red Market: Inside the Business of Selling Human Body Parts."[56]

Not necessarily a headline to be anticipated from a technology and culture magazine like *Wired*. The cultural awareness of a rapidly expanding market for human body parts appears to be on the rise. It has been public knowledge for some time that the demand of individuals in need of organ transplants far outpaces the supply of available donors. Within the U.S. and in similar Western nations, the shortage of donor organs is due to the ethical principles that available organs be supplied voluntarily and in most cases upon the death of the donor.[57] In lieu of alternatives of for-profit models of organ donation which are limited to only a few countries and come with a variety of concerns,[58] an illegal industry of black market organ trafficking has developed. This "red market," as *Wired* magazine labeled it, thrives in contexts where extreme poverty exists such that individuals are either tempted to sell "spare" organs such as kidneys or parts of their livers, or leads to practices where body parts are stolen from the recently dead without consent or taken violently from the living. In some cases individuals reportedly have been killed for their organs.[59]

Seemingly from the scripts of blockbuster films, tales have emerged of the global red market for organ trafficking.[60] As if a scene from a horror film, "blood thieves" kept prisoners alive for a few years and retrieved blood from them multiple times per week over the course of their captivity.[61] In other cases, death row prisoners and political dissidents are executed just as wealthy organ recipients arrive for their matching organ while visiting the country in question. Stories of individuals waking up in alleys missing kidneys, wombs rented, and rendition-like flights where women in poverty are flown to a destination just to harvest eggs, all seem to strain credulity. Yet sadly, truth is indeed sometimes stranger than fiction in the red market world.

Allegations in recent news headlines range from the exploitation of indebted laborers and poverty stricken immigrants to the execution of prisoners (whether military prisoners or political dissidents) for organs.[62] The details of the cases change depending on the marginalized group exploited for their organs, the geographical locale of the harvesting, and the frequently attendant claims of connections of these incidents to other crimes against humanity. The continuous thread connecting together these disparate headlines from far flung regions of the globe is the exploitation of humans for organs, whether voluntarily through unfulfilled promises of financial bonuses or through more nefarious involuntary means such as abduction and execution.

While estimates vary given the difficulty of tracking illegal activities, organ trafficking has been reported to range from 5-10% of all transplants worldwide.[63] Clearly selling one's body has taken on new meaning and significance with the rapid expansion of the red market. For those accounts of individuals who "voluntarily" chose to donate a kidney for financial reasons, many do not ultimately find financial relief through their actions.[64] According to one study, in many cases the live donors are left worse off than before, often experiencing regret and hopelessness, as well as permanent impairment, increased risk of long-term health consequences, and inability to return to manual labor.[65]

106

While less provocative in the headlines, another angle on organ transplantation surrounds the definition of death and the point at which organ procurement becomes permissible. For organs to be viable, they need to be harvested and transplanted within a specific timeframe that varies for each organ. The window for transplantation is relatively small. Recent cases of hospitals utilizing definitions of "cardiac death" and a very minimal passage of time led to charges of premature harvesting.[66] When mixed with discussions of euthanasia and the potential for involuntary euthanasia (meaning the euthanized individual is not a willing participant in their death), this becomes an even more disturbing prospect.

Organ transplantation from its early days included discussion of such issues as the importance of donation as voluntary and the need for proper informed consent. While initially banned, the use of organs from living donors (particularly the donation of a single kidney or a portion of a lung or liver), came to be accepted. Another issue challenging the ethical boundaries of voluntary donation was the commercialization of donation or selling organs. The classic language of organ transplantation as the "gift of life" has undergone a shift toward commodification as growing acceptance of organ trafficking has gained ground (whether or not it has done so entirely within legal frameworks), particularly through the growing practice of transplant tourism. Wealthy organ recipients travel to five-star accommodation medical treatment centers to receive organs procured through often less than noble means. Considerations of this commercialization of organ trafficking has led to questions of who truly benefits from this practice? Clearly, the organ recipient benefits, as do the brokers, hospitals, and doctors who participate. Does the donor generally benefit from this practice? Who ends up making the money? Who carries the greatest risk and burden? Yet the scarcity of organs and the rising demand that comes with an aging population continues to place pressure on the organ transplantation system to find alternative means of supply. Recent moves in countries such as Pakistan and Egypt, which are pursuing legislative means of curbing such abuses, point to positive trends of protecting human rights in these areas.[67] Unfortunately effective enforcement at an international level remains an elusive goal.

Medical Tourism

> *"Five-star accommodations at a coastal resort in an exotic location to convalesce from a state-of-the-art medical procedure"*

Does this statement sound more like a potential advertisement for that long awaited vacation or the possible description of your next hospital visit for a serious medical procedure? In reality it is a little of both. Medical or health tourism is a rising global phenomenon. Cutting across the sectors of medicine and tourism, it is described as "travel with the aim of improving one's health."[68] Spanning the gamut of medical procedures from elective cosmetic surgery and fertility services to advanced treatments such as heart bypass surgery and even organ transplantations, medical tourism is a growing industry in such countries as India, Malaysia, the Philippines, and Thailand. While medical tourism clearly is not an invention of the 21st century,[69] the decreasing cost of international travel, the proliferation of advanced medical technology, and general trends in globalization have led to the exponential increase in foreign patients engaged in and revenue generated by medical tourism. Alongside the substantial benefits and cost effectiveness[70] for foreign patients receiving care in which these resort medical destinations thrive are indigenous populations in poverty whose basic healthcare are not being met.[71]

We close the chapter with a case study to elicit the complexities of dealing with issues of social justice within the global medical enterprise.

Case Study:

Kevin recently began dialysis for kidney failure. His physician has informed him that he is in need of a kidney transplant and has been placed on the organ transplant waiting list. Unfortunately, he has also been notified that this list is long and the transplant may not be for quite some time, including the possibility that it may not be in time to prevent his death. His insurance company has offered for him to receive a kidney transplant in Thailand. The representative suggests that this will allow him to receive his transplant in a timely manner. The insurance company has offered to pay for the transplant and to cover expenses related to the five-star accommodations and care in a Thai facility described in the brochure as a "boutique" resort clinic. The representative seems to imply that a domestic transplant will be rejected for coverage.

Questions for Consideration:

1) Is continued dialysis an option? If not, how does that complicate this decision?

2) Where would the kidney come from? Would it be donated or purchased? Does the procurement process protect the donor from coercion or unnecessary harm? How should we consider the answers to these questions in assessing the decision?

3) Does Kevin have a "right" to a kidney transplant? From the standpoint of his policy coverage? Does he have a moral right to the transplant?

4) What additional factors need to be considered? Are there broader issues of social justice that need to be taken into consideration?

5) As Christians, how should we respond to this dilemma theologically? Practically?

---

[1] Maggie Fox, "U.S. Apologizes for Syphilis Experiment in Guatemala" *Reuters,* Oct 1, 2010, http://www.reuters.com/article/2010/10/01/us-usa-guatemala-experiment-idU.S.TRE6903RZ20101001?pageNumber=2 (accessed January 17, 2011).

[2] Susan Reverby, "'Normal Exposure' and Inoculation Syphilis: A PHS 'Tuskegee' Doctor in Guatemala, 1946-1948" *The Journal of Policy History* 23(1): 11. For additional information regarding this U.S. Public Health Service research, see http://www.hhs.gov/1946inoculationstudy/.

[3] Reverby, 9.

[4] Mike Stobbe, "AP IMPACT: Past Medical Testing on Humans Revealed" *The Washington Post,* February 27, 2011, http://www.washingtonpost.com/wp-dyn/content/article/2011/02/27/AR2011022700988.html (accessed March 10, 2011). This investigative review by The Associated Press yielded more than forty studies in the U.S. that involved mental patients, prisoners, children, and chronically ill patients.

[5] "The Nuremberg Code" Office of Human Subjects Research, National Institutes of Health, http://ohsr.od.nih.gov/guidelines/nuremberg.html (accessed January 17, 2011).

[6] "The Nuremberg Code." The directives of the Nuremberg Code especially in question are the first, fifth, and tenth. The first directive requires that subjects must be informed of the "nature, duration, and purpose of the experiment" as well as "the methods and means by which it will be conducted" and "the effects upon his health or person which may possibly come from his participation in the experiment." The fifth directive states that experiments should not be embarked upon in which "there is an *a priori* reason to believe that death or disabling injury will occur." The tenth directive places the burden of the ongoing continuation of a study upon the investigator's careful judgment to terminate a study at any point if "the continuation of the experiment is likely to result in injury, disability, or death to the experimental subject."

---

[7] Referred to in shorthand as principlism or also as the Georgetown principles, these four principles have become the standard guidelines of bioethical discourse. The principle of "respect for persons" is often used interchangeably in principlism with the principle of "autonomy." Tom Beauchamp and James Childress, *Principles of Biomedical Ethics* 6th ed (New York: Oxford University Press, 2008).

[8] Gregory Rutecki, "How Much Do We Care When Truth Replaces Fiction? Ethical Conduct and Human Subjects Research in Africa" *The Center for Bioethics & Human Dignity*, October 26, 2007, http://cbhd.org/content/how-much-do-we-care-when-truth-replaces-fiction-ethical-conduct-and-human-subject-research-a (accessed January 17, 2011).

[9] Ralph Katz, et al. "Identifying the Tuskegee Syphilis Study: Implications of Results from Recall and Recognition Questions" *BioMed Central Public Health* December 2009, 9:468. http://www.biomedcentral.com/1471-2458/9/468 (accessed January 17, 2011). Earlier studies had demonstrated wide disparities in awareness along ethic/racial lines. Cf. Ralph Katz, et al. "Awareness of the Tuskegee Syphilis Study and the U.S. Presidential Apology and Their Influence on Minority Participation in Biomedical Research" *American Journal of Public Health* 98(6): 1137-1142.

[10] For an international listing with links to key documents in human research protections see the "2011 Edition of the International Compilation of Human Research Protections" produced by the U.S. Health and Human Services Office of Human Research Protections at http://www.hhs.gov/ohrp/international/intlcompilation/intlcompilation.html (accessed Februrary 10, 2011).

[11] Heather Cormack, Benjamin Bates, Lynn Harter. "Narrative Constructions of Health Care Issues and Policies: The Case of President Clinton's Apology-by-Proxy for the Tuskegee Syphilis Experiment" *The Journal of Medical Humanities* 2008(29): 89-109.

[12] International Women's Day http://www.internationalwomensday.com/theme/ (accessed March 30, 2011).

[13] "Empowering Women: The Key to Achieving Millenium Development Goals" *United Nations*, http://www.un.org/events/women/iwd/2003/background.html (accessed March 30, 2011).

[14] Resolution 68. Problems of Marriage and Sexual Morality. The Lambeth Conference Resolutions from 1920, http://www.lambethconference.org/resolutions/1920/1920-68.cfm (accessed March 8, 2011).

[15] Resolution 9. The Life and Witness of Christian Community—Marriage and Sex. The Lambeth Conference Resolutions from 1930, http://www.lambethconference.org/resolutions/1930/1930-9.cfm (accessed March 8, 2011).

[16] Resolution 15. The Life and Witness of Christian Community—Marriage and Sex. The Lambeth Conference Resolutions from 1930, http://www.lambethconference.org/resolutions/1930/1930-15.cfm (accessed March 8, 2011). Interestingly, this is the only resolution on marriage with a recorded vote, 193-67.

[17] Resolution 16. The Life and Witness of Christian Community—Marriage and Sex. The Lambeth Conference Resolutions from 1930, http://www.lambethconference.org/resolutions/1930/1930-16.cfm (accessed March 8, 2011).

[18] Resolution 18. The Life and Witness of Christian Community—Marriage and Sex. The Lambeth Conference Resolutions from 1930, http://www.lambethconference.org/resolutions/1930/1930-18.cfm (accessed March 8, 2011).

[19] Resolution 115. The Family in Contemporary Society—Marriage. The Lambeth Conference Resolutions from 1958, http://www.lambethconference.org/resolutions/1958/1958-115.cfm (accessed March 8, 2011).

[20] Resolution 10. Human Relationships and Sexuality. The Lambeth Conference Resolutions from 1978, http://www.lambethconference.org/resolutions/1978/1978-10.cfm (accessed March 8, 2011).

[21] Resolution 1982-D016. Reaffirm the Right to the Use of Artificial Conception Control. The Acts of Convention 1976-2006. The Archives of the Episcopal Church, http://www.episcopalarchives.org/cgi-bin/acts/acts_search.pl (accessed March 8, 2011).

[22] *Griswold v. Connecticut*, 381 U.S. 479 (1965).

[23] *Eisenstadt v. Baird*, 405 U.S. 438, 453 (1972).

[24] *Roe v. Wade*, 410 U.S. 113 (1973).

[25] *Doe v. Bolton*, 410 U.S. 179 (1973).

[26] Catharine MacKinnon, "*Roe v. Wade*: A Study in Male Ideology." In Pojman & Beckwith, eds. *The Abortion Controversy: 25 Years After Roe v. Wade.* (Belmont, CA: Wadsworth, 1998), 95-104, 100.

[27] The risk of mental disorders is documented in Natalie Mota, Margaret Burnett and Jitender Sareen, "Associations Between Abortion, Mental Disorders, and Suicidal Behaviour in a Nationally Representative Sample." *The Canadian*

Journal of Psychiatry 55(4): 239-247. For the risk of pre-term birth, see, e.g., Calhoun, Shadigian & Rooney, "Cost Consequences of Induced Abortion as an Attri-Attributable Risk for Preterm Birth and Impact on Informed Consent" *Journal of Reproductive Medicine* 929 (2007): 52 (listing 59 other studies going back to the 1960s). Placenta previa risk is documented at Thorp, Hartmann & Shadigian, "Long-Term Physical and Psychological Health Consequences of Induced Abortion: Review of the Evidence" *Obstetrical & Gynecological Survey* 67(2003), 58. Substance abuse increases after abortion, according to Coleman, "Induced Abortion and Increased Risk of Substance Abuse: A Review of the Evidence" *Current Women's Health Reviews* 21 (2005), 1. The risk of breast cancer increases both as an independent risk, and due to the loss of the protective effective of a first full-term pregnancy. Thorp, Hartmann & Shadigian, "Long-Term Physical and Psychological Health Consequences of Induced Abortion," 58.

[28] Injury and death associated with abortion is reviewed at EM Shadigian & ST Bauer, "Pregnancy-Associated Death: A Qualitative Systematic Review of Homicide and Suicide" *Obstetrical and Gynecological Survey* 183 (2005): 60.

[29] Helen Pearson, "Health Effects of Egg Donation May Take Decades to Emerge." *Nature* 442 (August 10, 2006): 607-608, http://www.nature.com/nature/journal/v442/n7103/full/442607a.html?free=2 (accessed March 8, 2011).

[30]Ron Conte Blog, "Frozen Embryos" *CatholicPlanet.Net* August 24, 2009, http://www.catholicplanet.net/forum/showthread.php?t=3485 (accessed March 8, 2011).

[31] Giuliana Fuscaldo, Sarah Russell, and Lynn Gillam, "How to Facilitate Decisions about Surplus Embryos: Patients' Views," *Human Reproduction* 22 (December 1, 2007): 3129 -3138.

[32] See the longer discussion at Kirsten Riggan, "Regulation (or Lack Thereof) of Assisted Reproductive Technologies in the U.S. and Abroad." *The Center for Bioethics & Human Dignity,* March 5, 2011, http://cbhd.org/content/regulation-or-lack-thereof-assisted-reproductive-technologies-us-and-abroad (accessed March 5, 2011).

[33] Alice Gomstyn, "Winning Fertility: Would-Be Parents Win Free IVF"*ABC News Business Unit,* March 18, 2010, http://abcnews.go.com/Business/WellnessNews/winning-fertility-moms-win-free-ivf/story?id=10118313&page=1 (accessed March 11, 2011).

[34] David Adamson, "Symposium on Assisted Reproductive Technology: Regulation of Assisted Reproductive Technologies in the United States" *ABA Family Law Quarterly* 727 (Fall 2005): 39.

[35] "Extraodinary Conceptions Surrogacy and Egg Donor Agency Announces New Lower Fees" *BigNews.Biz*, March 9, 2011, http://bignews.biz/?id=979981&pg=1&keys= (accessed March 9, 2011).

[36] Elizabeth Marquardt, *My Daddy's Name Is Donor: A New Study of Young Adults Conceived through Sperm Donation* (New York: Institute for American Values, 2010).

[37] Sandra Blakeslee, "Infertile Woman Has Baby through Embryo Transfer" *New York Times*, February 4, 1984 http://query.nytimes.com/gst/fullpage.html?sec=health&res=9404EEDC143BF93 7A35751C0A962948260 (accessed March 31, 2011).

[38] Kari Karsjens, "Boutique Egg Donations: A New Form of Racism and Patriarchy" *DePaul Journal of Health Care Law* 57 (Fall 2001): 5.

[39] Roni Caryn Rabin, "As Demand for Donor Eggs Soars, High Prices Stir Ethical Concerns," *The New York Times*, May 15, 2007, sec. Health, http://www.nytimes.com/2007/05/15/health/15cons.html?_r=2&bl&ex=11793744 00&en=39b5461ce5272679&ei=5087%0A&oref=slogin (accessed March 31, 2011).

[40] Helen Pearson, "Health Effects of Egg Donation May Take Decades to Emerge" *Nature* 442 (August 10, 2006): 607-608, http://www.nature.com/nature/journal/v442/n7103/full/442607a.html?free=2 (accessed March 8, 2011).

[41] M.L.P. van der Hoorn, E.E.L.O. Lashley, D.W. Bianchi, F.J.H. Claas, C.M.C. Schonkeren, and S.A.Scherjon, "Clinical and Immunologic Aspects of Egg Donation Pregnancies: A Systematic Review" *Human Reproduction Update* 16(6): 704-712

[42] Interestingly, Elizabeth Stern, the wife of the sperm donor, was not infertile. She wished to avoid the health risks of a pregnancy that might aggravate her multiple sclerosis.

[43] Harriet Sherwood, "Israeli Couple Seek Right to Use Dead Son's Sperm" *The Guardian*, February 8, 2011, http://www.guardian.co.uk/world/2011/feb/08/israeli-parents-dead-son-sperm (accessed March 8, 2011).

[44] Suz Redfearn, "Pursuing a Baby to the Ends of the Earth" *The Washington Post*, January 14, 2007, http://www.washingtonpost.com/wp-dyn/content/article/2007/01/10/AR2007011001394.html (accessed March 8, 2011).

[45] Antony Barnett and Helena Smith, "Cruel Cost of the Human Egg Trade" *The Observer*, April 30, 2006,

http://www.guardian.co.uk/uk/2006/apr/30/health.healthandwellbeing (accessed March 8, 2011).

[46] Scott Carney, "Importing Egg Donors from Ukraine to Cyprus" *Pulitzer Center on Crisis Reporting*, August 17, 2010, http://pulitzercenter.org/blog/untold-stories/importing-egg-donors-ukraine-cyprus (accessed March 8, 2011).

[47] Fran Abrams, "The Misery behind the Baby Trade" *The Daily Mail*, July 17, 2006, http://www.dailymail.co.uk/femail/article-396220/The-misery-baby-trade.html (accessed March 8, 2011).

[48] Marcy Darnovsky, "Pregnancy without Borders: Reproductive Tourism's Global Reach" *Biopolitical Times*, September 28, 2010, http://www.biopoliticaltimes.org/article.php?id=5393 (accessed March 31, 2011).

[49] Doug Pet. "India Moves toward Regulation of Assisted Reproduction and Surrogacy" *Biopolitical Times*, February 10, 2011, http://www.biopoliticaltimes.org/article.php?id=5591 (accessed February 28, 2011).

[50] Kelle Barr, "Kalamazoo Couples Travels to India for Surrogate Pregnancy" *Kalamazoo Gazette*, July 28, 2010, http://www.mlive.com/living/kalamazoo/index.ssf/2010/07/kalamazoo_couple_travels_to_in.html (accessed March 8, 2011).

[51] Amana Fontanella-Khan, "India, the Rent-a-Womb Capital of the World" *Slate*, August 23, 2010, http://www.slate.com/id/2263136/ (accessed March 8, 2011).

[52] AFP, "Thai Police Free Women from Surrogate Baby Ring" *Yahoo!7News*, February 24, 2011, http://au.news.yahoo.com/entertainment/a/-/entertainment/8903363/thai-police-free-women-from-surrogate-baby-ring/ (accessed February 24, 2011).

[53] Radha Sharma, "Busy Couples Now Courier Embryos to Gujarat Clinics" *The Times of India*, August 29, 2010, http://epaper.timesofindia.com/Repository/getFiles.asp?Style=OliveXLib:LowLevelEntityToPrint_TOINEW&Type=text/html&Locale=english-skin-custom&Path=TOIM/2010/08/29&ID=Ar01503 (accessed March 8, 2011).

[54] See, for example, the video-journalism report of Linda Blake. "Booming Surrogacy Trade Attracts Couples to Mother India" *VJ Movement*, November 5, 2009, http://www.vjmovement.com/truth/416?fq=ttype.video&fq=dshow.all&fq=dorder.hot&fq=tab.list (accessed March 8, 2011).

[55] See, for example, the stories and solutions recounted in Nicholas Kristof and Sheryl WuDunn, *Half the Sky:Turning Oppression into Opportunity for*

Women Worldwide (New York: Vintage Books, 2010), and the movement it spawned. http://www.halftheskymovement.org/get-involved.

[56] Christian Weber, "The Red Market: Inside the Business of Selling Human Body Parts" *Wired* February 2011, 112-119.

[57] The practice of living donors has grown in recent years and raises a variety of ethical considerations unique from donation upon the death of the donor.

[58] Iran among a few other countries has developed legal for-profit models of organ donation. A variety of concerns have been raised with this approach, but primary concerns center on financial coercion and the nature of informed consent. Cf. Anne Griffin, "Iranian Organ Donation: Kidneys on Demand" *British Medical Journal* March 10, 2007(334): 502-505.

[59] Separating fact from fiction in the urban myths and rumors of black market organ trafficking proved somewhat more difficult in its early years. In the mid 1980s a story of children being abducted in Northeast Brazil circulated in the international news, raising awareness of this relatively ignored aspect of the ethics of organ transplantation. Similar stories from a variety of other countries began to be circulated in the international news. The Bellagio Task Force in its 1997 report stated that it could find no evidence to support these rumors. D. Rothman, et al. "The Bellagio Task Force Report on Transplantation, Bodily Integrity, and the International Traffic in Organs" *Transplantation Proceedings* 1997(29):2739-45. Cf. Joint council of Europe/United Nations Study "Trafficking in Organs, Tissues, and Cells and Trafficking in Human beings for the Purpose of the Removal of Organs" *Council of Europe*, October 13, 2009, 60-61, http://www.coe.int/t/dghl/monitoring/trafficking/docs/news/OrganTrafficking_study.pdf (accessed March 20, 2011).

[60] Organ trafficking is defined as "the recruitment, transport, transfer, harboring or receipt of living or deceased persons or their organs by means of the threat or use of force or other forms of coercion, of abduction, of fraud, of deception, of the abuse of power or of a position of vulnerability, or of the giving to, or the receiving by, a third party of payments or benefits to achieve the transfer of control over the potential donor, for the purpose of exploitation by the removal of organs for transplantation." "The Declaration of Istanbul on Organ Trafficking and Transplant Tourism" *Clinical Journal of the American Society of Nephrology* 3(5): 1228, http://cjasn.asnjournals.org/content/3/5/1227.full.pdf+html (accessed February 14, 2011).

[61] Weber, 114.

[62] Doreen Carvajal, "Trafficking Investigations Put Surgeon in Spotlight" *The New York Times*, February 10, 2011, http://www.nytimes.com/2011/02/11/world/europe/11organ.html (accessed February 11, 2011). Cf. Simon Robinson, "India's Black Market Scandal" *Time*,

February 1, 2008, http://www.time.com/time/world/article/0,8599,1709006,00.html (accessed February 11, 2011) and Ana Iltis, "Organ Donation and Global Bioethics" *Journal of Medicine and Philosophy* 35(2): 81-85. An alarming set of allegations coming from Kosovo alleged that one clinic was inviting poor immigrants from Eastern Europe to donate kidneys, while also being accused of ties to an organ trafficking ring that harvested organs from Albanian and Serbian prisoners executed in such a manner to facilitate the organ extraction process. Paul Lewis, "Kosovo Physicians Accused of Illegal Organs Removal Racket" *Guardian*, December 14, 2010, http://www.guardian.co.uk/world/2010/dec/14/illegal-organ-removals-charges-kosovo (accessed February 14, 2011).

[63] D. A. Budiani-Saberi and F. L. Delmonico, "Organ Trafficking and Transplant Tourism: A Commentary on the Global Realities" *American Journal of Transplantation* 8(5): 925-929.

[64] Fahat Moazam, Riffat Moazam Zaman, and Aamir Jafarey, "Conversations with Kidney Vendors in Pakistan: An Ethnographic Study" *Hastings Center Report* May-June 2009: 33, 39-41. This study reported measurable disparities between the amount promised for the kidney and that which was actually paid. The researchers noted that often the organs were sold to cover significant levels of accumulated debt, with more than half the donors/vendors ending up with persistent or re-accumulated debt after the transaction.

[65] Ibid., 33-35.

[66] Gregory Rutecki, "Where Is the Public Outcry? Infants also Have Human Dignity When They Are Dying and Donating Organs!" *The Center for Bioethics & Human Dignity*, October 24, 2008, http://cbhd.org/content/where-public-outcry-infants-also-have-human-dignity-when-they-are-dying-and-donating-organs-0 (accessed January 11, 2011). For a discussion of the complexities in the determination of death, see President's Council on Bioethics, *Controversies on the Determination of Death*, December 2008, http://bioethics.georgetown.edu/pcbe/reports/death/index.html (accessed March 31, 2011).

[67] Luc Nöei and Dominique Martin, "Progress towards National Self-Sufficiency in Organ Transplants" *Bulletin of the World Health Organization* 2009 (87): 647, http://www.who.int/bulletin/volumes/87/9/09-068817/en/ (accessed February 14, 2011).

[68] Milica Bookman and Karla Bookman, *Medical Tourism in Developing Countries* (New York: Palgrave Macmillan: 2007), 1.

[69] Harriet Hutson Gray and Susan Cartier Poland, "Medical Tourism: Crossing Borders to Access Health Care" *Kennedy Institute of Ethics Journal* 18(2): 193.

[70] Estimates range from 5-10% on the low end to 50% of the standard costs of medical services in the U.S. Ibid., 50.

[71] Ibid., 7.

Chapter Six

Granting Freedom to Ethiopia through Education

Yelena Lopuga

THE TSAHWA VILLAGE IN Ethiopia is a small, remote village, home to seventeen Ethiopian girls with big dreams. These girls dream of being doctors or engineers knowing that only through education they can achieve their dreams. In underdeveloped parts of the world, like the sub-Saharan regions of Africa, gender roles are still of great importance. Yet, these socially constructed gender roles prevent girls from obtaining education and changing the outcome of their lives. Girls of large, poor families may never get the chance to attend school because priority is often given to male children. However, if given access to education, girls in Ethiopia will be able to rise out of poverty, thus bettering themselves and their communities. The intent of this chapter is to analyze the current state of education for girls in Ethiopia, identify ways to engage the community in this issue, examine the work done by local government and NGO organizations to improve education. Finally, I will provide ways for churches to get involved in improving education in Ethiopia.

The Case of Education in Ethiopia

According to the United States Agency for International Development (USAID), "Ethiopia remains one of the poorest countries in the world, with one in four Ethiopians living on less than $1 per day."[1] Struck by poverty, disease, war, and drought, the people of Ethiopia struggle daily for their lives. Womankind Worldwide, an NGO organization working to change the lives of women in the poorest and most subversive areas of the world reported:

> With one of the highest maternal mortality rates in the world and among the worst rates of school enrolment for girls in Africa, it is Ethiopia's women who suffer disproportionately. Poverty, illiteracy and lack of access to basic health care combine with strongly patriarchal social attitudes which maintain women's low social status and perpetuate

Traditional Harmful Practices such as Female Genital Mutilation and early marriage.[2]

Since the establishment of formal education by the Ethiopian Orthodox Church, education was made available only to male children, thus neglecting girls. Access to education was limited to male children of high social status and those living in the urban sectors of the country.[3] Prior to 1974, schools were located only in urban areas. The schools were built and run by missionaries, NGO's, and the Ministry of Social Affairs and Development.[4] Although today the government of Ethiopia recognizes the need for expanding availability for education, it faces many challenges toward obtaining that goal. These challenges include, but are not limited to, economic instability of the country, traditional values held by the people, strongly defined gender roles, and weak training programs for local teachers.

Obstacles Facing Girls in Ethiopia

Women in Africa still experience gender discrimination. Often women are not given access to education because cultural opinions on education claim that "educating women would make them too independent; in other words, they would not do what they are expected to do - look after the house, bring up children, and cater to their husband's needs".[5] Sharon LaFraniere, in a *The New York Times* article, documented some of the obstacles Ethiopian girls face while attending school. LaFraniere began her report with a story about a girl in Balizenda who, while overcoming financial burdens to attend school, is facing another challenge, staying enrolled. Fatimah Bamun, a fourteen year old girl, is the only girl in her class of twenty three students. There are only three girls in her school, out of the three girls only Fatimah has completed three grades.[6] While these girls face many challenges in attending school, they often cannot stay enrolled after they reach puberty. LaFraniere wrote:

> In a region where poverty, tradition and ignorance deprive an estimated 24 million girls even of an elementary school education, the lack of school toilets and water is one of many obstacles to girls' attendance, and until recently was considered unfit for discussion. In some rural communities in the region, menstruation itself is so taboo that girls are prohibited from cooking or even banished to the countryside during their periods.[7]

The deficiency in restroom facilities not only affects the attendance of female students, but also the availability of women school teachers. Although female school teachers are in high demand, without access to sanitary facilities the number of available female teachers drops. A fifth-grade teacher at a Balizenda school tells of her struggle with the accessibility to sanitary facilities in an interview, stating "the majority of time I use the open field. There is no privacy. Everybody comes, even the students. So we try to restrict ourselves to urinate before school and at nighttime."[8] Furthermore, she reported that due to the lack of sanitary facilities she has developed a kidney infection. The problem with sanitation is not restricted only to schools, as the United Nations Children's Fund (UNICEF) reports, "lack of proper sanitation contributes to the deaths of thousands of children every day from largely preventable causes, including diarrhoeal diseases."[9]

There is also a positive correlation between the number of female teachers and the number of girls in a school because parents are less resistant to sending their daughters to a school with female teachers. LaFraniere emphasized the role that female teachers carry in affecting the enrollment of female students by stating that,

> [T]he pressure on girls to drop out peaks with the advent of puberty and the problems that accompany maturity, like sexual harassment by male teachers, ever growing responsibilities at home and parental pressure to marry. Female teachers who could act as role models are also in short supply in sub-Saharan Africa.[10]

Parental and Community Involvement in Education

In sub-Saharan regions of Africa, parents are becoming increasingly receptive to schooling opportunities for their children. LaFraniere noted the enthusiastic participation of Mali parents in the education of their children. These parents are realizing the importance of education and are taking matters into their own hands, literally. As LaFraniere reported, these parents are "creating their own school system alongside the official one, hand building classrooms out of caked mud and recruiting teachers, even if their sole qualification is having made it through ninth grade."[11] These Mali parents are being proactive by personally ensuring that their children have the opportunity to go to school. The schools built by communities such as the one in Mali are growing more rapidly than the schools built by the government.

In a similar way, parents in Southern Ethiopia are getting involved in their children's schooling. Children like thirteen year old Gebre Selassie, often have to walk long distances to their school. Gebre walks six miles each day to attend school.[12] Due to the long distances, parents concerned with the safety and well-being of their children decided to build their own school. To get support for the project, they lobbied the Ethiopian Ministry of Education. As a result, a school was built in the community. Because their parents took initiative many children are now able to attend a school close to their home. One of the fathers involved in the process said, "We appreciate the importance of education. We built this school with the ability of the people here. We initiated it by ourselves. Education itself is development for this area."[13]

As has been noted, community involvement in education is beginning to grow in sub-Saharan Africa. Many parents are starting to take pride in their community schools. Consequently, community engagement may be the key to reaching the education goals of many sub-Saharan regions of Africa, including Ethiopia. But the extent of community involvement in education may vary from one district to another. In one instance, the community may partner with the government and share responsibilities in making decisions. At other times, the community may act as the mediator between the school administration and the government, as in Southern Ethiopia where parents advocated on behalf of the local school to the government requesting necessary resources for school staff.[14] The interplay between the community and the government can also include the distribution of labor, such as the government supplying the teachers and the community providing the housing.[15]

Other models of community involvement may display more participation from the community in the management of the school. For example, the community might provide financial support for schools and take care of the school buildings while the government provides proper curriculum.[16] According to Jennifer Swift-Morgan's research published by the *Harvard Educational Review*, in the area of community involvement the most successful business relationship between the community and the government is established when there is a "…balance between community and state ownership of the school with regard to both finance and decision making."[17]

Moreover, community participation is becoming a vital source for solving Ethiopia's sanitation problems. The World Health Organization and UNICEF reported that "only 13 per cent of Ethiopians have access to latrine facilities,"[18] which makes Ethiopia one of the countries with "the lowest levels of sanitation coverage in the world."[19] Project Ethiopia started by Interfaith Community Church in Washington, is working with village elders in Ethiopia to partner with the community in providing adequate sanitary facilities for local school children.[20] By involving the community in these projects they are providing facilities that are easily maintained by the local people. In addition, when "the villagers themselves decide what is best…they have more of an interest in the outcome of the projects."[21] With Project Ethiopia, villages in Ethiopia are becoming cleaner, life expectancy is improving, and "the compost gathered from the pit is being used by the farming community to boost the growth of corn and other crops."[22] Project

Ethiopia has also affected the lives of 1,200 students by building a sanitary latrine facility at their school.

Community involvement in education also motivates the children to do well in school and the interest of parents encourages the school teachers. Also, when the parents become active in their children's education they are able to better see the needs of the schools. Girls especially benefit from such community involvement. For instance, when parents and teachers got together in a school located in Southern Ethiopia, they formed an association to make sure girls could safely get to and from school. Thus they addressed a serious social issue in a region where young girls are abducted for marriage.[23]

More progress needs to be made in involving the community in addressing issues affecting schooling. Although more parents are becoming involved in their children's education, it is often the men and the wealthy that are able to be engaged in their children's education. Thus, improvements can be made in order to get more women and the poor engaged in schooling. Swift-Morgan suggests that can be achieved simply through a change in the scheduling of school meetings. For example, the time for parent meetings can be set up early evening so the women in the community can attend to their household chores while also maintaining an active role in the decision making process in their children's schools. In short, the participation of communities in schooling needs to be protected so the government does not put all of its educational responsibilities on the backs of the parents who are limited in their resources and ability to provide adequate education for their children.

The Advancement of Education by Ethiopia's Government

The Ethiopian government has been slow in developing the right initiatives for reaching universal education. Nevertheless it has taken several steps in order to provide adequate education for the Ethiopian people. Starting in 1979, the Ethiopian government began the National Literacy Campaign Coordinating Committee. This committee worked to boost national literacy rates. As a result, enrollment rose from 2.5 million to 4.9 million.[24] In 1997, the Ethiopian government established the Education Sector Development Program (ESDP) with the goal to reach universal primary enrolment by 2015.[25] The ESDP also includes a non-formal education sector for dropout children and young adults to continue their education. Some of the goals of ESDP focus on increasing admission rates in primary education, increasing the number of female students and teachers, building schools in poor communities, improving student-teacher ratio, and removing school fees for children in primary education.[26] All of the goals of ESDP mentioned above cause an increase in female literacy. Furthermore, the government has devoted its attention to "the advancement of women's life in…areas such as education and training for women, women in power and decision-making, and women and poverty."[27]

To improve sanitation, UNICEF has worked with the Amhara regional health bureau to implement a pilot sanitation project. The success of the project has drawn the interest of other regional health bureaus.[28] In 2009, USAID and the Coca-Cola Africa Foundation provided safe drinking water for more than 46,000 people in Ethiopia.[29] They also improved pit latrines and sanitation in Ethiopia. Furthermore, the Ministry of Water Resources in Ethiopia set up a Universal Access Plan with the goal of achieving proper water and sanitation in Ethiopia by 2012. The director of research and development of the Ministry of Water Resources, Abe Ayenew, believes that the Universal Access Plan will be at 98 percent for water improvement and 100 percent in sanitation by 2012.[30] This project is critical for the improvement of education in Ethiopia where over 250,000 children a year die due to inadequate sanitation and hygiene levels.[31]

Current Needs of Ethiopia's Schoolchildren

Although government and NGO's have made great progress in widening access to education, there are still many things that can be done to improve education in Ethiopia. Progress still needs to be made toward obtaining gender equality. Government involvement is vital in order to ensure that enrolment rates for female students continue to grow. While gender inequality is a deep issue that will take much time and effort to breach, steps can be taken to reduce its occurrence. For instance, the government can eliminate school fees for girls, giving girls of poor families the opportunity to attend school. Some African governments have removed school fees all together. As a result, their enrolment went up. Today in Kenya 1.3 million children and in Tanzania 3.1 million can attend school.[32] Furthermore, the government can also give financial incentives to families who have female children enrolled in school. In addition, local teachers can be mobilized if more schools are built near isolated communities. With access to proper sanitation facilities, female teachers will increase as will the number of parents willing to send their daughters to school.

The quality of education in Ethiopian schools needs to be enhanced. The student to teacher ratio in a sub-Saharan African classroom averages 44 students to 1 teacher.[33] This makes sub-Saharan Africa the world's leading region with the highest student to teacher ratio. To improve the quality of education in Ethiopia, classroom sizes will have to be reduced and more teachers will need to be hired.

In addition to having low percentages of available teachers, Ethiopian schools are also suffering from poorly trained teachers.

How Can We Get Involved

With so many needs still present in Ethiopia's schools there are many ways in which churches can become engaged. As mentioned earlier, Interfaith Community Church located in Washington got involved in this social issue by connecting its resources with the resources of local community leaders in Ethiopia. With Project Ethiopia, Interfaith Community Church has donated $12,000 to improve sanitation for 1,200 people.[34] By utilizing their resources and appealing to the community, Project Ethiopia has been a successful and lasting enterprise.

As yearning for education grows in sub-Saharan Africa, the involvement of Christians in the impoverished areas of this region can give these children the tools they need to rise out of poverty. We can empower these children by providing them with quality education. The needs in Ethiopian schools are many. We can address the financial needs by raising financial support to pay for children's school fees. According to the Tesfa Foundation, $21 a month can give one child the opportunity to attend kindergarten for a year.[35] Furthermore, there is great need for proper classroom and sanitary facilities, which can be acquired if we partner with organizations such as Project Ethiopia. As has been noted, the lack of sanitary facilities keeps many girls out of the classroom. In addition, we can work to advance teacher training and curriculum development.

Why is it important for Christians to participate in expanding opportunities for education in sub-Saharan Africa? As Christians we are called to empower people to live lives that will glorify God. If education can protect people from exploitation and disease, it can also help them learn about the true freedom that comes from a personal relationship with God. It has been said by Epictetus (55-135 AD) that "only the educated are free."[36] Christians can be the ambassadors of this freedom. We can help mothers raise healthy children, we can break down cultural traditions that cause gender inequality, and we can give individuals the power to support their families and give their children a brighter future. Through education we can heal, restore, and give power to the broken.

Scripture is very clear about the benefits of education. It encourages individuals to search for wisdom and knowledge. In fact, Proverbs 2:3-5 remarks, "Cry out for insight, and ask for understanding. Search for them as you would for silver; seek them like hidden treasures. Then you will understand what it means to fear the LORD, and you will gain knowledge of God." Although education in a classroom does not automatically equate to an understanding of God, it does carry the potential of transforming the life of an individual. As Christians we are called to alter lives through God's redemptive work. The ministry of Jesus Christ gives us a model of what it means to set people free from sickness and poverty while giving them eternal salvation as they exercised faith in him.

Conclusion

The need for adequate education for Ethiopian girls is an outcry of the Ethiopian people. Without proper facilities, qualified female teachers, and access to local schools, girls in Ethiopia face a serious disadvantage in attending school. Ethiopian girls have fallen victim to this social injustice. The 2010 Education for All Global Monitoring Report reveals the victims and the oppressors of this injustice:

> Children living in the urban slums and rural villages of the world's poorest countries played no part in the reckless banking practices and regulatory failures that caused the economic crisis. Yet they stand to suffer for the gambling that took place on Wall Street and other financial centers by losing their chance for an education that could lift them out of poverty.[37]

In short, as Christians we have a role to fill. We need to dedicate ourselves in providing opportunities for education worldwide. Our endeavor can start in the impoverished regions of Ethiopia.

---

[1]"Sub-Saharan Africa," *USAID*, July 22, 2010, http://www.usaid.gov /locations/sub-saharan_africa/countries/ethiopia/ (accessed January 22, 2011).

[2]"Ethiopia," *Womankind Worldwide*, http://www.womankind.org.uk/ ethiopia.html (accessed January 22, 2011).

[3]James L. Hoot, Judit Szente, and Belete Mebratu, "Early Education in Ethiopia: Progress and Prospects," *Early Childhood Education Journal* 32, no. 1 (August 1, 2004): 3-8.

[4]Ibid.

[5]Swasti Mitter and Sheila Rowbotham, "Overall Status of Women in Africa," 1995, http://www.unu.edu/unupress/unupbooks/uu37we/uu37we0t.htm (accessed May 1, 2010).

[6]Sharon LaFraniere, "Another School Barrier for African Girls: No Toilet," *wehaitians.com*, December 23, 2005, http://www.wehaitians.com/another %20school%20barrier%20for%20girls%20in%20sub%20saharan%20africa%20n o%20toilet.html (accessed May 1, 2010).

---

[7]Ibid.

[8]Ibid.

[9]Kerida Mcdonald, Indrias Getachew, and Wossen Mulatu, "UNICEF Calls for Action to Achieve Universal Access to Sanitation in Ethiopia" (UNICEF, March 22, 2008), http://www.unicef.org/ethiopia/ET_PR_08_WWD.pdf.

[10]Ibid.

[11]Sharon LaFraniere, "Education blossoms in sub-Saharan Africa - Africa & Middle East - International Herald Tribune," *The New York Times*, December 29, 2006, http://www.nytimes.com/2006/12/29/world/africa/29iht-mali.4051275.html (accessed May 6, 2010).

[12]"Ethiopia - Education," *A Glimmer of Hope Foundation*, http://www.aglimmerofhope.org/why_ethiopia/education.html (accessed May 8, 2010).

[13]Jennifer Swift-Morgan, "What Community Participation in Schooling Means: Insights from Southern Ethiopia," *Harvard Educational Review* 76, no. 3 (September 1, 2006): 339-368.

[14]Ibid.

[15]Ibid.

[16]Ibid.

[17]Ibid.

[18]Indrias Getachew, "Creating a Healthy Environment by Building Latrines in Ethiopia's Amhara Region," *UNICEF*, October 17, 2007, http://www.unicef.org/infobycountry/ethiopia_41247.html (accessed May 8, 2010).

[19]Ibid.

[20]"Sanitary Facilities," *Project Ethiopia*, 2010, http://projectethiopia.com/Sanitary-Facilities.php (accessed May 8, 2010).

[21]Ibid.

[22]Ibid.

[23]Swift-Morgan, "What Community Participation in Schooling Means: Insights from Southern Ethiopia."

[24]Cecile Nguyen, Marissa Moses, and Victoria Gabroy, "Education in Ethiopia: Are Children Getting What They Deserve?" 1998, http://www.tulane.edu/~rouxbee/kids98/ethiopia2.html (accessed May 8, 2010).

[25]Johanna Lasonen, Raija Kemppainen, and Kolawole Raheem, "Education and Training in Ethiopia: An Evaluation of Approaching EFA Goals"

(Institute for Educational Research University of Jyvaskyla, 2005), http://ktl.jyu.fi/arkisto/verkkojulkaisuja/TP_23_Lasonen.pdf (accessed May 8, 2010).

[26]Ibid.

[27]Ibid.

[28]Getachew, "Creating a Healthy Environment by Building Latrines in Ethiopia's Amhara Region."

[29]"Partnership Improves Water, Sanitation, and Hygiene in Ethiopia," *Embassy of the United States: Addis Ababa-Ethiopia*, October 24, 2009, http://ethiopia.usembassy.gov/pr40010.html (accessed May 9, 2010).

[30]Heinz Greijn, "Water Access and Sanitation in Ethiopia," *Capacity.org*, 2010, http://www.capacity.org/en/journal/interview/water_access_and_sanitation_in_ethiopia (accessed May 9, 2010).

[31]Ibid.

[32]"Education in sub-Saharan Africa," *ONE*, http://www.one.org/c/us/progressreport/776/ (accessed May 6, 2010).

[33]LaFraniere, "Education blossoms in sub-Saharan Africa - Africa & Middle East."

[34]"Sanitary Facilities."

[35]The Tesfa Foundation, "The hope of a community is the mind of a child," *Tesfa*, 2010, http://www.tesfa.org (accessed May 8, 2010).

[36]"The Quotations Page," http://www.quotationspage.com/quotes/ (accessed April 7, 2010).

[37]"Education at Risk: The Impact of the Financial Crisis" (Education for All Global Monitoring Report 2010, 2010), http://www.unesco.org/fileadmin/MULTIMEDIA/HQ/ED/GMR/pdf/gmr2010/gmr2010-ch1.pdf (accessed May 9, 2010).

Chapter Seven

Orphans: Caring Well For Haitian Children

Sarah Bushman

ON A RECENT TRIP TO the Northern region of Haiti, I witnessed firsthand the operation of a Haitian orphanage. Currently, fourteen children reside in the orphanage operated and funded by Vision of Hope Ministries. The orphanage began when Henoc Lucien, Haitian pastor supported by VOHM, rescued eleven children from a flooded orphanage in Gonaives, Haiti in late 2008 when a hurricane devastated the small island country. With Gonaives in ruins after extreme flooding, Pastor Henoc and VOHM decided to continue caring for the eleven children. Only a few months ago, three more children were taken into the VOHM orphanage. These children were found in their Cap Haitien home with their deceased mother. After days alone in their home, the children were rescued by Pastor Henoc. The children's father is suspected to have killed the mother and fled the scene.

The Vision of Hope Ministry Orphanage has recently relocated to a newly built building in Berard, Haiti, just outside of Cap Haitian. The new orphan home has a Christian couple living in the home to care for the children, seeking to provide a family atmosphere for the children. The children attend the VOHM school in Cap Haitian, College Susan Schueke. The monthly expense for each of the fourteen children is about $1,500. VOHM continually seeks to raise support for the children to provide them with education, a Christian environment, and daily needs necessary for their development.

***

According to the United Nations Children Fund (UNICEF), an orphan is a vulnerable child who is "deprived of their first line of protection, their parents."[1] Children reach this point of vulnerability after experiencing one or more of the following: temporary or permanent loss of caregiver/guardian; lost contact with caregiver (e.g. street or refugee children); separation from parents (e.g. child abduction or parents detained); placement in alternative care by their caregivers (e.g. children placed in institutions, children with disabilities, or children from poor families); kept in extended hospital care; and detainment in an educational, correctional or penal facility as a result of a judicial decision.[2]

UNICEF further breaks down the orphan categories under single and double orphan. A single orphan is a child who has lost one parent while a double orphan has lost both parents. There are an estimated 145 million children worldwide who have lost one or both of their parents (all causes). However, only about 13 million are double orphans, having lost both parents.[3] UNICEF holds a board view of term "orphan" to include both the double and single orphans because of the contrasting definition of "orphan" between developing and industrious countries.[4]

In this study we will be exploring how to best care for the orphaned children in Haiti. There will be four sections highlighted. First, the crisis will be explained and underscored with statistics which establish a basis for orphan care. Second, it is critical to develop a biblically informed worldview for orphan treatment, focusing on God's love and concern. Third, the traditional orphan care solution will be defined and evaluated. Fourth, an alternative plan for orphan care will be proposed, which is compatible with the established biblical worldview. The method utilized within each section will begin with an examination of the global situation and progress toward a localized Haitian perspective.

The Crisis

UNICEF, created by the United Nations General Assembly in 1946 to focus on children's rights, asserts that children who are living without their primary caregivers are lacking the vital protection and guidance they need. Children without this protection are at a higher risk of becoming victims of violence, exploitation, trafficking, discrimination, and sexual abuse. Living without parental support, orphaned children often experience malnutrition, illness, physical and psychological distress, and impaired development.[5]

Acquired immune deficiency syndrome (AIDS) alone accounted for 17.5 million orphaned children by 2008, according to UNICEF. This number was estimated to reach 25 million by the end of the decade.[6] Although not all orphans are the result of HIV/AIDS, creating orphans has become the most predominate factor HIV/AIDS has had on children.[7] The lack of education in AIDS-affected communities has the potential to create a silent killer which can, and has, orphaned millions. Sexual conduct, breast feeding, and availability of AIDS medications are some of the primary concerns for the staggering numbers of orphans. The many complexities of the AIDS crisis must be considered the when exploring the orphan crisis. In 2008, 4.9 million people age 15-24 were living with HIV.[8]

The presence of conflict situations is another predominant factor that has the potential to increase the number of orphans. Conflict situations produce orphans and/or separate one million children from their families.[9] In the event a child is separated from their family in a conflict situation they will likely live in a refugee camp. It is estimated that between 2-5percent of refugees are orphans or vulnerable children.[10]

A Joint United Nations Programme on HIV/AIDS, USAID and UNICEF publication, *Children on the Brink*, highlights research which reveals the age of orphans: 55percent of orphans are between the ages of 12-17, an additional 33 percent are between the ages of 6-11, and finally 12 percent are 5 or younger.[11] These statistics are surprising to many because we typically think of small children when we consider orphans. However, over half the orphan population is over the age of 12.

The Haitian Orphan Crisis

January 12, 2010: a devastating 7.0 magnitude earthquake occurred in the southern region of Haiti, destroying the capital city, Port-au-Prince, which represented the central setting for commerce, governance, education and trade. The effects of this catastrophic event range from homelessness to hunger to an extensive orphan crisis. *Relevant Magazine* reported recently that 50 percent of the 3.7 million people who were impacted by the earthquake are 20 years old or younger.[12]

Prior to the earthquake, UNICEF estimated that Haiti was home to 380,000 orphans. An UNICEF spokesperson, Christopher de Bono, noted that this estimate was "rough at best."[13] In a country with poor infrastructure, weak government support, and overall deficient communication it is difficult to accurately estimate the number of orphans in the country. Post-earthquake orphan numbers are impossible to confirm at this time. However, a simulation was performed by the United States Agency for International Development (USAID), based on the U.S. Census Bureau's 2005-2006 estimates on Haiti's population and a Demographic and Health survey funded the agency in order to estimate orphan numbers. The study indicated that there are potentially 15,000 new double orphans, children having lost both parents.[14]

In summer 2009, according to a CNN article, the Haitian Adoption Authority calculated that Haiti had about 100 licensed orphanages and 67 crèches, which are orphanages licensed to execute adoptions.[15] It is difficult to know the official number of orphanages in Haiti because many choose not to go through the licensing process. Many religious organizations and privately operated homes are not registered.[16] Prior to the earthquake an estimated 50,000 children were living in institutional orphanages in Haiti, many of whom were thought to have at least one living parent.[17] Consequently, most orphans and/or vulnerable children were not living in orphanages. Of the 380,000 Haitian orphans, an estimated 50,000 are double orphans and the remaining single orphans who have only lost one parent.[18]

Some children also find themselves living on the streets in Haiti. An estimated 4,000 children lived on the streets prior to the January 2010 earthquake.[19] According to UNICEF, as many as 2,000 children were being trafficked into or through the Dominican Republic each year.[20] In total, 1.5 million Haitian children are now predicted to be vulnerable.[21] Orphans and vulnerable children in Haiti are at a particularly high risk of injustice, including sexual violence, trafficking, illegal adoptions, life as a *restavec* (domestic worker), gang participation, urban armed violence, and substance abuse.[22] UNICEF, as well as many non-governmental organizations, has been responding to these needs and many more, prior to and since the earthquake.

At the Heart of God

The Bible clearly depicts God's faithful love, compassion and concern for the helpless. In one of the forty-three occurrences of the Hebrew word commonly translated "orphan" or "fatherless" in the Old Testament, Psalm 68:5 makes a clear statement about who God is: "a father to the fatherless, a defender of widows, is God in his holy dwelling." In God's essence as father he provides a foundation, protection, and sustained support for his children. God promises to provide the orphan and widow with identity, belonging, and a home in him.[23]

Just as God's concern for the helpless is clear, he instructs his people to have the same concern (Ex. 22:22; Dt. 10:18; Is. 1:10-17). God instituted a system, by means of the Mosaic Law, which provided opportunities for the less fortunate to have food while at the same time stifling the greed of the land owner. Deuteronomy 24:17-22 commanded the Israelites to freely leave the excess of their harvest for the alien, orphan and the widow to gather. As the prophet Isaiah communicated God's desire for appropriate fasting, the theme of social responsibility arose. "Is it not to share your food with the hungry and to provide the poor wanderer with shelter-when you see the naked, to clothe him, and not to turn away from your own flesh and blood?"(Is. 58:6-7).

The worshipful act of tithing one's earnings to the Lord had a complementary purpose to provide for the orphan, widow, alien, and the Levites. On every third year, "the year of the tithe," everyone was to bring their tithe into the town so that the widow, alien, fatherless and Levite may be satisfied (Deut. 14:28-29, 26:12-

13). God used these means in order to deliver protection and sustenance to the helpless.

Devotion to caring for the helpless extends into the beginnings of the Christian church. Acts 6:1-7 is an example of how the early Christian church in Jerusalem recognized an inequality of food distribution which neglected the Greek-speaking widows. The issue was addressed through the appointment of seven deacons who were given the responsibility to correct the racial and economic injustice occurring in Jerusalem.[24] The result is captured in Acts 6:7, "So the word of God spread. The number of disciples in Jerusalem increased rapidly."

Orphans are specifically mentioned twice in the New Testament (Jn 14:18; Js 1:27).[25] In what is perhaps the most powerful statement on orphan care in the Bible, James 1:27 asserts: "Religion that God our Father accepts as pure and faultless is this: to look after orphans and widows in their distress and to keep oneself from being polluted by the world."[26] James's audience was a group of people who were familiar with the commands of the Old Testament Law and those of Jesus which directed them to care for the less fortunate. However, they neglected to act. The orphan, widow and foreigner represent social classes which are particularly vulnerable to exploitation.[27] As Douglas Moo comments on James' writings, he explains that "Christians whose religion is pure will imitate their Father by intervening to help the helpless."[28]

The care for orphans showed by early church leaders reflects the attitude of Jesus, who used children as an example and recognized their value in spite of the prevailing view of children in Jewish and Hellenistic cultures (Mk 9:33-37; 10:13-16). Childhood, in these cultures, was viewed as a lesser, insignificant form of existence.[29] Darrell L. Bock highlights Jesus' challenge to the cultural norms of his day in emphasizing that "all people are important, even those whom society suggests are not." Jesus goes as far as equating the acceptance of a child with the acceptance of him, strongly identifying himself with the helpless (Matt. 18:1-6; Mk. 9:33-37).[30] Jesus' compassion for the helpless mirrors the heart of his heavenly Father.

Questioning the Traditional Solution

A traditional solution to the orphan crisis is the institutional orphanage. The institutional style of orphan care is typically described as a large-scale, Western funded, non-profit, and in many situations religiously affiliated. This model has provided a safe haven for children throughout history. There is no doubt that institutional orphanages have had a positive impact on the lives of many individuals. However, it has been argued that this model lacks certain necessities which every child needs throughout their developing years. Hence, it is critical to evaluate this approach to gain perspective as to best practices for caring for vulnerable children worldwide.

Orphan care can be traced throughout history. The Western roots of the orphanage lie in the 4th century church. During the Middle Ages, monasteries worked to discourage the child abandonment that was occurring.[31] The orphanage in early American history, established by James Oglethorpe (1696-1785), was a refuge for children. British Colonies at this same time enforced the English Poor Law of 1601, which provided state assistance of the poor and orphaned. The Colonial response to orphans was to place them in apprentice positions to learn a trade in a Christian family. The Civil War era responded to the growing numbers orphaned due to the war by opening up regional orphanages to care for the children.[32] These early measures of care provided a model that has been perpetuated around the globe.

Adapted from the United States Agency for International Development's (USAID) data, the following are essentials to consider when establishing an orphanage. These items serve as a baseline of orphan care. First, there is a vital human need for adequate access to food and proper nutrition which is necessary for development. Second, children must be protected with shelter, proper clothing, and continual access to clean water. Third, children must be protected against stigma, exploitation, abuse, and neglect. Fourth, proper health care needs to be practiced for each child, including standard immunizations and treatment of illnesses. Fifth, children need care and support from qualified adults to help them achieve success in their education and continually prepare for reintegration into the local community. Sixth, education is a vital component of every child's life which provides them with the tools they need for a successful life.[33] Education includes more than academics; it involves training children about culture and morals. The psychological needs of children must also be addressed. These items are essential for proper child development.

The ability of institutional orphanages to meet the vital needs of children has been challenged. First, it has been argued by proponents of the family/community orphan care model that the Western institutional model typically lacks an indigenous aspect, neglecting the local community and especially the local church.[34] In the context where an orphanage has religious affiliation, children need to have the opportunity to experience the fellowship of Christians, as well as have the opportunity to be active members, while serving, learning and growing in their faith.

Orphanages which are operated under a foreign model have the potential to create an environment which is not compatible with the local culture. The issues arise when ideas, beliefs, and practices collide. Orphanages operated by foreign money and staff can become disassociated with the local culture when there is a lack of understanding due to worldview conflicts. Western style orphanages have the potential to create tension toward those who have come from abroad to take care of "their children." In some cases, orphanages are located outside of the given community, creating a sub-community on the fringe of society.[35] The United Nation's Convention on the Rights of the Child in promoting a safe, family environment notes, "When considering solutions, due regard shall be paid to the desirability of continuity in a child's upbringing and to the child's ethnic, religious, cultural and linguistic background (Part 1, Article 20)."[36]

The aspect of the children's need for community must be addressed alongside the indigenous dilemma. Children presumably experience community living among their peers. They live together, study together, share meals and make friends. However, in some instances they lack contact with the greater community and their extended family.[37] In many developing countries, connection to the community and with extended family is considered to be the "most important social safety net," according to the UNICEF, USAID, and Joint United Nations Programme on HIV/AIDS report on vulnerable children. Limiting this support system increases a child's vulnerability to personal threats, such as child trafficking, abuse and child labor, as well as the increased possibility that they will become involved in dangerous activities.[38] As families tend to promote independence and creative thinking, institutional orphanages create an emphasis on dependency and discourage autonomy.[39]

Children living in an orphanage will eventually need to transition from life in the orphanage to life in their local community. As *Children on the Brink* suggested, orphans living in institutional orphanages will face many obstacles as they adjust to a new life outside the orphan community. These obstacles are due largely to their lack of social contacts within the community.[40] Living within a local community equips children with an understanding of the unique cultural skills which are a vital asset to being functional members of that community. Transitioning from a sheltered orphanage into the community will leave the child without the necessary social and cultural skills they need in order to relate to their indigenous culture.[41]

The second diagnosed criticism of the institutional orphanage is the poor child-caregiver ratios. A joint report by the United Nations Joint Programme on HIV/AIDS (UNAIDS), UNICEF, and USAID stated that, "traditional residential

135

institutions usually have too few caregivers and are therefore limited in their capacity to provide children the affection, attention, personal identity, and social connections that families and communities can offer."[42] Children can easily become lost in the crowd. Their individual needs for love, attention, comfort and guidance are not met within a large-scale orphanage context. It is hard to administer the love a child yearns for in an overcrowded orphanage. Children with disabilities are especially at risk of neglect.[43]

Third, according to the Congressional Coalition on Adoption Institute (CCAI), institutional orphan care has been found to hinder development for children, especially those under the age of five.[44] The Vice President of World Vision commented on this issue saying, "In too many cases, the institutionalization of orphans is a short-term fix with long-term issues, while its counterpart of placing unaccompanied minors in families is deemed difficult on the front end but has been found to provide profound blessings as the child matures."[45] Roger Olson, professor at Truett Theological Seminary, finds that, "children raised in foster families and especially by relatives fare better developmentally than children raised in even the best orphanages."[46] A study in Zimbabwe concluded that "countries – and children – are better served by programs that 'keep children with the community, surrounded by leaders and peers they know and love.'"[47]

Fourth, an orphanage can have adverse effects on a struggling community. Orphanages are sometimes seen as lighthouses to the surrounding area suffering from the effects of poverty. As a result many times orphanages are used by poor parents as an "economic-coping mechanism to secure access to services or better material conditions for their children."[48] This results in an "expensive way to cope with poverty and a continuously growing orphan population."[49] The very system which was created to help the community becomes exploited by some desperate members of the community. In order to fight the exploitation, basic necessities need to be made accessible to families through the support of the church and equipping families to provide for their children.

Lastly, the financial aspect of large-scale orphanages has caused debate. Some use the argument that orphanages are more expensive to manage than placing children in families. What it costs an institutional orphanage to support one child could support many more children in family care.[50] A study published in *The New Democrat* on American institutional orphanages reveals that care per child can easily exceed $30,000 (USD) per year, per child.[51]

Questioning Haiti's Orphan Care

With at least 380,000 orphans (without taking into consideration the post-earthquake numbers), orphan care in Haiti is at a crucial intersection. The CCAI noted that a small proportion of orphans are actually living in licensed orphanages, leaving children to find other ways to provide for themselves.[52] The report noted, "How they were orphaned is clearly understood: extreme poverty, death, and disease."[53] These factors will only be intensified after Haiti's recent catastrophe.

Institutional orphanages have received attention from the U.S. Government, in particular, since the January 12, 2010 earthquake. Currently, 220 orphanages have been assessed by the U.S., these numbers alone prove that many orphanages are not licensed with the Government of Haiti (GoH).[54] It is unknown at this time how many orphanages were affected by the earthquake. Family Health International found in 2002 that many Haitian orphan homes are "not inspected, and many struggle to supply food, education and other necessities to the children they house."[55] It is true that there are good organizations in Haiti caring for orphaned children; however, there is a real threat when orphans are not properly cared for.

Across the globe there are children living in orphan care who have living biological parents and the same is the case in Haiti. Poverty is cited as the reason for this phenomenon. Parents are unable to provide for the needs of their children, forcing them to forfeit parental rights to an orphanage. One needs only to consider the recent attempt by well-meaning Baptists from Utah to remove Haitian children from their families[56]. The UN strongly suggests that poverty-related issues "should never be the only justification for the removal of a child from parental care, but should be seen as a signal for the need to provide appropriate support to the family."[57] This principle is also relevant within the *restavec* issue. Children should not be placed in alternative care when their biological parents are living. However, the reality of poverty in Haiti cannot be ignored. As the poorest nation in the Western Hemisphere with a GDP per capita of $667 (verses $46,000 in the US), many families turn to orphanages or the *restavec* option to help meet their child's needs.

Haitian orphan adoption has been a hot topic in the media in recent months. This topic is beyond the immediate scope of this chapter however, a brief note should be made. *Guiding Principles*, published in January 2010 by the U.N. High Commissioner for Refugees' Child Welfare Working Group, led by UNICEF, is a guide to caring for children during emergencies. It captures an important point for the orphan adoption debate:

Unaccompanied and separated children should be provided with services aimed at reuniting them with their parents or customary caregivers as quickly as possible. Interim care should be consistent with the aim of family reunification, and should ensure children's protection and wellbeing. Experience has shown that most separated children have parents or other family members willing and able to care for them. Long-term care arrangements, including adoption, should therefore not be made during the emergency phase.[58]

Dr. Jane Aronson, Founder of the Worldwide Orphans Foundation, visited Haiti after the earthquake to visit and assess orphanages. As an adoptive parent herself, she strongly discourages adoptions from Haiti at this time. Dr. Aronson noted,

Adoption is not the way to solve absolutely massive, tragic issues of vulnerable children," she says. "An earthquake is a traumatizing event. The best thing for these children is to keep them in their communities, with neighbors and relatives, and with food and shelter and safety.[59]

An Alternative Plan

The UN General Assembly concluded in 2009 that, "the family [is] the fundamental group of society and the natural environment for growth, well-being and protection of children."[60] All children need a positive, supportive family environment. However, some children are deprived of their primary caregivers, their parents, forcing the issue of who will care for these children.

Orphanages have traditionally been the alternative to family. Some child-welfare advocates note, for example, that up to half of all children living in an orphanage in sub-Saharan Africa have family relatives who are willing to take in their orphaned relative. The problem is that the relatives do not always have the means to support additional family members.[61] The most common reasons children are placed in traditional institutional orphan care are death of parents and termination and relinquishment of parental rights due to a multitude of reasons. Many children either have living biological parents or living relatives who are unable to provide the necessary support for the child due to financial restrictions.[62]

There are children who need a family but their extended families are unable to support them without help from the local church. The local church also needs support to be able to minister to the orphans in their community. The cycle is not hopeless; it leaves room for us across the globe, in many cases, to step forward and support the indigenous churches which have first hand interaction with the children. Christians need to respond to the need, respond to the mandate from God

(Js. 1:27) and give to organizations that seek to place orphans with families.[63] Current economic times are grim, affecting families across the globe. Families who are caring for orphaned children need the extra support to assure the basic necessities.

In the event that there are no living or available relatives, which is the first priority for child placement, there are other options. The following four options are arranged in order of priority. First, sometimes a group of siblings may be able to provide for themselves. In this case special attention needs to be paid to these children who are probably being raised by the oldest sibling. Children need to be provided with the information on how to protect the land of their parents and resources about proper documentation and the means for these children to continue attending school. This issue of family land arises when a child's parents have died. Land is a precious item of heritage and value. Children should receive aid on how to keep ownership of their family land and should have the option, if the case allows, to continue living on their family land with their siblings. It is crucial that siblings stay together regardless if they are living in a children's home, or sent to live with relatives. These are their closest relationships after losing their parents.

Second, foster families or families within the community may care for orphans. When extended families are not an option, the local church can then find another family where the child can live. Support is provided for the family to raise the child by paying for school, medical and food assistance. In some instance micro-loans may be given to the family to begin a micro-enterprise to provide employment opportunities. When orphans are placed in families outside their extended family the effort is made to keep the child in their home community.[64] Whether the child's new caregiver is a relative or a new family, protection for the child is a high priority. Every child needs protection from those who want to take advantage of them, and sometimes this abuse comes from a placement family. Non-profit organizations partnering with the local church working to place orphans in families must take extreme precaution not to place a child in a situation where they will be abused or neglected. Screening processes, parenting workshops, and community awareness all help fight for the protection of vulnerable children in alternative family situations.[65]

Programs like *Kwasha Mukwenu* [Help Your Neighbour] project in Lusaka. Zambia created a community-based orphan care system. Kwasha Mukwenu connected orphaned children with families in the community and provided support to help the families sustain their increased family demands. Organizations like these believe that "orphanages were 'alien' to Zambian culture and that these could only care for incredibly small numbers of children as compared to those that were already being cared for by communities."[66]

The third option is sending the child to a small, family-based, community-centered home. In many cases these children's homes are conjoined with a local church. This provides the local indigenous church with the direct responsibility for the care of these children. In the case of the organization Warm Blankets, widows are the primary caregivers in the church-based home. Widows are able to relate to the feelings the orphaned children are facing.

Finally, institutional orphanages are a last resort. In some instances, an orphanage is the only thing standing between a vulnerable child and a life alone on the street. This type of care should only be used to bridge a child to a better care network or in the case of emergency situations when a child needs to be rescued from a harmful situation.

With the number of orphans worldwide at 145 million and growing due to the AIDS crisis and Haiti's devastating earthquake, family-based care needs to be made more available or children will continue to suffer the disadvantages of placement in institutional orphanages. This will happen as nongovernmental organizations (NGO) partner with indigenous churches and communities to provide awareness, promoting the community to provide relief to their own.

A New Approach in Haiti

The orphan care system in Haiti currently relies heavily on institutional orphanages. Orphanages are culturally accepted as a viable solution. However, with research showing the negative effects on children who have grown up in orphanages, a new model should be encouraged in Haiti. One suggestion from USAID is for the U.S. to use its aid funding as an agent of influence. The U.S. can eliminate funding for the building of orphanages and instead support the development of family and community-based orphan care.[67]

Orphans International Worldwide (OIWW) is a positive example of an organization seeking to provide a sustainable family model for orphan care in Haiti. OIWW was founded by Jim Luce in 1999 as a response to the global orphan crisis occurring after a series of natural disasters across the world. OIWW is an interfaith, interracial, international, intergenerational, and internet-connected orphan care organization.[68] The standard model for OIWW consists of small clusters of children in homes with a houseparent. A cluster of homes creates the campus.[69] Their newest model of orphan care is the family care model, introduced in 2008. They realized that enough orphan homes cannot be constructed for the growing orphan population; therefore OIWW works to equip extended families to take care of orphaned children. These foster families are equipped with support, training, and stipends to provide the best care possible for the children. OIWW requires that all children be given "the same love and security that each of our team members would give to their own children."[70]

Another example of positive orphan care is World Orphans. World Orphans is a Christian based organization seeking to promote church-based orphan care. World Orphans believes there are not enough families and community networks to provide for all the orphans. They also do not believe that institutional orphanages provide a positive environment for children. Therefore, World Orphans supports church-based orphan care. Under this model children live in a small-scale setting in the community comprised of 8-12 children per each house parent unit. Each home is connected directly to the local church, where children are supported and integrated into the local Christian community. Orphaned and vulnerable children are able to stay within their home communities and remain connected to their community through school, church and community activities. World Orphans seeks to meet the physical, emotional, educational and spiritual needs of each child through their church-based orphan care model.[71]

The third example of positive orphan care is Warm Blankets Orphan Care International. In an effort to move away from the institutional orphanage, WBOCI's model or orphan care is church-based orphan homes. Under this model, each orphan home is physically connected with the local Christian church. Each home has the potential to house 40 children, which if this potential is met could cause difficulties in meeting the needs of each child. Nevertheless, WBOCI is committed to providing a family atmosphere, filled with love and nurturing care. Orphans are typically cared for by the widows of the community. WBOCI believes that widows can best relate to the pain orphans are experiencing with the loss of their parents. An integral aspect of WBOCI is church planting. They have a firm commitment to planting biblically based churches which will serve the orphans in the community, as well as share the gospel message.[72]

The CCAI has called policymakers to consider the following principles when addressing needs of children in Haiti. First, it is optimal for a child to be raised in a family setting. The UN's document *Convention of the Rights on the Child* reiterates this point in the preamble saying, "Recognizing that the child, for the full and harmonious development of his or her personality, should grow up in a family environment, in an atmosphere of happiness, love and understanding."[73]

Second, CCAI emphasizes, the family unit is the primary social unit in civil society. Third, programs responding to displaced children should first seek reunification to keep children in the families to whom they were born. Fourth, institutional care can impair development in children. Fifth, siblings should be kept together if possible. Sixth, development of a child welfare system should be pursued. Sixth, focus should be on orphans as individuals not as a congregate.[74]

The orphan crisis drastically changed in Haiti on January 12, 2010. UNICEF Acting Chief of Communication in Haiti, Edward Carwardine stated, "UNICEF has said from the beginning that the earthquake was very much a children's emergency."[75] Efforts are no longer solely focused on the better care and treatment of children living in orphanages, on the streets and in exploited situations. Current efforts must include the initial emergency care of children who have been displaced, lost a parent, or lost their home. Efforts must include the following: reunification efforts to unite orphaned, abandoned, or separated children with their immediate or extended family members;[76] identification of children who are alone after the earthquake, including an identification card which will provided by dual efforts of Save the Children and USAID; and children who are alone should be sent to child-friendly spaces and local foster families.[77]

In addition, as Haiti is beginning the initial stages of rebuilding after the earthquake, the following principles, adapted from CCAI, should be promoted: development of a child welfare system focused on serving children in and through the family, not through institutions; policies that reinforce children's rights; seeking sustainability in all alternative orphan care solutions; and well-functioning government institutions which will serve as protection for children.[78]

Aronson proposed "conscripting an army of grannies" who will care for Haiti's orphans. Under this proposed system Haitian women would receive stipends to foster one or two vulnerable children. Her organization, Worldwide Orphans Foundation, is currently recruiting American social workers to lead this unique project in Haiti. Displaced children from the earthquake could easily live with a "granny" until other relatives can be located.[79]

Conclusion: Call to Action

We all know how important having a family was to us when we were children. We relied so heavily on them for guidance, protection, support, and care for our needs. We must acknowledge that many children are growing up without a loving, supportive family. These children are vulnerable in a world where many people would take advantage of them. Throughout the Bible we see the cry of the orphan and God's compassionate, loving response. God takes on the role of father to those who are without. He not only takes personal concern for the lives of each individual orphan, but he also calls his people to be his hands and feet to care for the orphans. God has placed Christians as protectors and defenders, those who would show compassion and love to vulnerable orphaned children.

Haiti is our neighbor, suffering from disaster where 1.5 million children are considered vulnerable. As the poorest country in the Western Hemisphere and recently devastated by a 7.0 magnitude earthquake, cholera outbreak and tropical storm Tomas, Haiti stands in great need for assistance, especially their precious children. The future of Haiti is wrapped up in the lives of its children. These little ones are facing difficult circumstances that they will have to overcome in order to bring Haiti out of the current desperate situation. However, with the faithful assistance of Christians living in accordance with God's compassion, Haiti's future will be in good hands.

Christians, allow this to be a challenge. God demonstrated his love and compassion for the orphans and commands his people to also care for them. Finally, words from Philippians 2:3-4, "Do nothing from selfishness or conceit, but in humility count others better than yourself. Let each of you not only look to his own interest, but also to the interest of the other." It is vital that Christians who are seeking to protect the vulnerable remember the words of Philippians 2:3-4. For those whom we are serving are not lesser persons; they are God's precious children whom we ought to view just as God does.

---

[1]UNICEF, "Children without Prenatal Care," Internet resource available from http://www.unicef.org/protection/index_orphans.html. Accessed: 30 March 2010.

[2]Ibid.

[3]UNICEF, State *of the World's Children Special Edition: Celebrating 20 Years of the Convention on the Rights of a Child* (Geneva: UNICEF, 2009), 24; UNICEF, "Orphans," Internet resource available from http://www.unicef.org/media /media_45279.html. accessed: 30 March 2010.

[4]UNICEF, "Orphans."

[5]UNICEF, "Children without Prenatal Care."

[6]UNICEF, State *of the World's Children Special Edition: Celebrating 20 Years of the Convention on the Rights of a Child, Statistical Tables*, (Geneva, UNICEF, 2009), 23.

---

[7]UNAIDS, UNICEF, WHO, UNFPA, "UNITE for Children, UNITE against AIDS," *Children and AIDS: 4th Stocktaking Report Summary*. (Geneva: UNICEF, 2009), 3.

[8]Ibid., 4.

[9]UNICEF, "Children without Prenatal Care."

[10]Ibid.

[11]*Children on the Brink: A Joint Report on New Orphan Estimates and a Framework for Action* (New York: UNAIDS/UNICEF/USAID, July 2004), 12.

[12]"Haiti: A Work in Progress," *Relevant,* May/June 2010, Issue 45, 22.

[13]Jessica Ravitz, "Haiti's orphans: Why they remain in limbo," *CNN.com*, 1/27/10, Internet resource available from http://www.cnn.com/2010 /LIVING/01/27 /haiti.orphans.overview/index.html. Accessed 1 April 2010.

[14]USAID, "Frequently Asked Questions: Haiti's Orphans and Vulnerable Children," Internet resource available from http://www.usaid.gov/helphaiti /opcfaq.html. Accessed 30 April 2010.

[15]Ravitz, "Haiti's orphans."

[16]Tim Collie, "About orphanages in Haiti," *South Florida Sun-Sentinel* *12*/3/06, Internet resource available from http://www.sun-sentinel.com /news/nationworld/sfl-oorphanages03dec03,0,1592817.story. Accessed 1 April 2010.

[17]"Frequently Asked Questions: Haiti's Orphans and Vulnerable Children."

[18]"Frequently Asked Questions: Haiti's Orphans and Vulnerable Children." The 50,000 double orphans are not meant to correlate with the 50,000 children living in institutional orphanages.

[19]UNICEF, *Children of Haiti: Three Months After the Earthquake*, (UNICEF, April 2010), 29. This statistic seems low due to the overall orphan numbers.

[20]Ravitz, "Haiti's orphans."

[21]UNICEF, *Children of Haiti: Three Months After the Earthquake*, 3.

[22] Children of Haiti, 29.

[23]Edgar, 71-73.

[24]Ronald J. Sider, *The Scandal of the Evangelical Conscience*, (Grand Rapids, Baker, 2005), 36-37.

[25]Roy B. Zuch, *Precious in His Sight: Childhood and Children in the Bible*, (Grand Rapids, Baker, 1996), 174.

[26]All Bible references are NIV unless otherwise noted.

[27]Ralph P. Martin, James, Word Biblical Commentary (Waco, TX: Word, 1988), 52.; David Hutchinson Edgar, *Has God Not Chosen the Poor? The Social Setting of the Epistle of James*, Journal for the Study of the New Testament Supplement Series 206 (Sheffield, England: Sheffield Academic Press, 2001), 166 – Widows and orphans were among a class of people who were socially marginal including the poor. This is a class whose very livelihood was endangered because of their loss of support system.

[28]Douglas J. Moo, *The Letter of James* (Grand Rapids: Eerdmans, 2000), 86.

[29]J. W. Drane, "Family," in New Dictionary of Biblical Tehology, ed. T. Desmond Alexander and Brian S. Rosner (Downers Grove, IL: Inter Varsity, 2000), 495.

[30]Darrell L. Bock, *Jesus according to Scripture*, (Grand Rapids: Baker, 2002), 240.

[31]"Orphanage," Encyclopedia Britannica. 2010. Encyclopedia Britannica Online. Internet resource available from http://www.britannica.com /EBchecked/topic/433159/orphanage. Accessed 8 May 2010.

[32]Paul S. Boyer, "Orphanages," The Oxford Companion to United States History, 2001, *Encyclopedia.com,* Internet resource available from <http://www.encyclopedia.com>. Accessed 3 May 2010.

[33]Patrick Yates, Nathan Swartz, et al., "Orphan Model Template," Internet resource available from http://www.uww.edu/cobe/micro/orphange%20DSS%20 documentation.pdf. Accessed 30 April 2010.

[34]Faith to Action Initiative, "Resources," Internet resource available from http://faithbasedcarefororphans.org/resources/. Accessed 4 February 2011.

[35]World Orphans, "Why the Local Church," Internet resource available from http://www.worldorphans.org/why-local-church.php. Accessed 10 June 2010.

[36]UNICEF, State *of the World's Children Special Edition: Celebrating 20 Years of the Convention on the Rights of a Child,* 77.

[37]Orphans and Vulnerable Children Care Reform Initiative, Ghana, "Why Not Orphanages?" Internet resource available from http://www.ovcghana.org /why_not_orphanages.html. Accessed 1 April 2010.

[38]*Children on the Brink*, 20.

[39]Ibid., 19-20.

[40]Ibid.

[41]Ibid.

[42]Ibid.

[43]World Orphans, "Our Solution," Internet resource available from http://www.worldorphans.org/our-solution.php. Accessed 15 April 2010; Orphans and Vulnerable Children Care Reform Initiative, Ghana, "Why Not Orphanages?"

[44]Congressional Coalition on Adoption Institute, "Position Statements on U.S. and International Response to Needs of Orphans in Haiti," 2. http://www.ccainstitute.org/images/stories/ccai_position_statement_on_haiti.pdf. Accessed 25 April 2010.

[45]Roger E. Olson, "How to Help Orphans," *Christianity Today* (53 no. 1 January 2009), 63.

[46]Ibid., Orphans and Vulnerable Children Care Reform Initiative, Ghana, "Why Not Orphanages?"; this organization has focused on the negatives aspects of institutionalized orphanages, noting that "Children need families to successfully integrate and thrive in the society, as the family is the best context for a child to successfully develop."

[47]*Children on the Brink*, 19-20.

[48]Ibid.

[49]Ibid.

[50]Faith to Action Initiative, "Resources."

[51]Richard B. McKenzie, "The Orphan Option," The New Democrat, (Democrat Leadership Council, 1 January 1999), Internet resource available from http://www.dlc.org/ndol_ci.cfm?kaid=114&subid=142&contentid=1306. Accessed 1 May 2010.

[52]CCAI, 1.

[53]Ibid.

[54]Frequently Asked Questions: Haiti's Orphans and Vulnerable Children.

[55]Collie, "About orphanages in Haiti."

[56]Lee Ferran and Ayana Harry, "Ten Americans Charged With Child Trafficking in Haiti; PM Calls it 'Kidnapping'," *abcnews.com*, Internet resource available from http://abcnews.go.com/WN/HaitiEarthquake/haiti-earthquake-ten-americans-charged-child-trafficking-haiti/story?id=9712436. Accessed 30 May 2010.

[57]United Nations, "Guidelines for the Alternative Care of Children," *United Nations General Assembly*, 2/24/10, 4. Internet resource available from http://www.iss-ssi.org/2009/assets/files/guidelines/guidelines_eng.pdf. Accessed 1 May 2010.

[58]CCAI, 4.

[59]Lisa Belkin, "Adopting a Child From Haiti," *nytimes.com/motherlode*, accessed 5/1/10, (New York Times, 1/25/10), http://parenting.blogs.nytimes.com /2010/01/25/adopting-a-child-from-haiti/

[60]Guidelines for the Alternative Care of Children, 2.

[61]Olson, "How to Help Orphans," 63; Life in Abundance International, "Orphans and Vulnerable Children," Internet resource available from http://www.liaint.org/programs/?st=5539. Accessed 20 May 2010. "LIA and our church partners support vulnerable families through food stipends, medical care, micro enterprise training and support, school fees, and spiritual counsel."

[62]Frank Adoption Center, "Frequently Asked Questions," Internet resource available from http://www.frankadopt.org/faq.html#what%20effects. Accessed 25 May 2010.

[63]Olson, 63.

[64]Life in Abundance International, "Orphans and Vulnerable Children."

[65]Faith to Action, "Resources."

[66]Siame, 4-5.

[67]CCAI, 4.

[68]Orphans International Worldwide, "About Us," Internet resource available from http://www.oiww.org/about-us.html. Accessed 20 April 2010.

[69]Orphans International Worldwide, "Known Standards of OIWW as of May 2005," 12, Internet resource available from http://www.oiww.org/images /stories/OIWW_Global_Standards.pdf, Accessed 30 April 2010.

[70]Orphans International Worldwide, "About Us."

[71]World Orphans, "Our Solution."

[72]Warm Blankets Orphan Care International, "Church Orphan Homes," Internet resource available from http://www.warmblankets.org/homes.asp. Accessed 1 April 2010.

[73]UNICEF, State *of the World's Children Special Edition: Celebrating 20 Years of the Convention on the Rights of a Child,* 74.

[74]CCAI, 2.

[75]Thomas Nybo, "Creating a Haiti for Children, three months after the earthquake," Internet resource available from http://www.unicef.org/infobycountry/haiti_53288.html. Accessed 30 April 2010.

[76]Frequently Asked Questions: Haiti's Orphans and Vulnerable Children.

[77]Children of Haiti, 29-32.

[78]CCAI, 5.

[79]Belkin, "Adopting a Child From Haiti."

Chapter Eight

Literacy in Afghanistan

Teressa Mahl

THE UNITED NATIONS EDUCATION, Scientific and Cultural Organization (UNESCO) currently estimates 796 million adults worldwide lack minimum literacy skills.[1] One in five adults are not literate, with nearly two-thirds being women.[2] Adult literacy rates have increased over the last sixty years—from 56 percent in 1950 to 70 percent in 1980, and 82 percent in 2004.[3] However, since 1990, the gender disparity has remained constant. Globally, eighty-eight adult women are considered literate for every one hundred adult men.[4]

Fundamentally speaking, literacy is understood as the ability to read and write.[5] A widely accepted definition of literacy is somewhat difficult to identify as multiple definitions capture various dimensions of literacy. In 1958, following the launch of the first global survey of adult literacy, UNESCO adopted the following definition of literacy: "A person is literate who can with understanding both read and write a short simple statement on his [or her] everyday life."[6] Over time, academic research, international policy agendas, and national priorities have influenced how literacy has been defined and interpreted.[7] Some define literacy in terms of its function with regard to enabling productivity and overall socio-economic development, while others recognize literacy as "an active process of learning involving social reflection, which can empower individuals and groups to promote social change."[8] UNESCO currently defines functional literacy in the following way:

> A person is functionally literate who can engage in all those activities in which literacy is required for effective functioning of his [or her] group and community and also for enabling him[or her] to continue to use reading, writing and calculation for his [or her] own and the community's development.[9]

At its core, however, literacy involves deriving meaning from print and in turn using print to communicate.[10]

It is commonly understood that literacy plays an important role in social and human development.[11] Many would argue literacy to be a fundamental human right, and identify it as essential to the realization of numerous global developmental goals including the eradication of poverty, achieving gender equality, reducing child mortality and ensuring sustainable development, peace and democracy.[12] Literacy has been found to have numerous benefits – economically, culturally, socially, politically, and personally.[13] For example, literacy improves self esteem and empowers learners (especially women). Greater participation in the political process is seen in those who are literate versus those who are not. Literacy helps to preserve cultural diversity and allows for values to be transmitted through critical reflection. The social benefits of literacy include increased capacity to maintain good health and live longer, to learn throughout life, and to raise and educate healthy children.[14]

Recognizing the need for increased literacy skills worldwide, the United Nations (UN) General Assembly declared a United Nations Literacy Decade (UNLD) from 2003-2012.[15] The decade is intended to "mobilize international agencies and national governments to join forces and dedicate resources to implement successful literary activities."[16] It focuses on the needs of non-literate youth and adults alike, giving special attention to women and girls.[17] Coordination of the UNLD and supporting programs has been undertaken by UNESCO.

In support of the UNLD, UNESCO has implemented the Literacy Initiative for Empowerment (LIFE) which is a targeted strategy for addressing the literacy needs in those countries with a literacy rate of less than 50 percent or with more than one hundred million adults without literacy skills.[18] LIFE identifies its overarching goal as that of "empower[ing] people, especially rural women and girls, who have inadequate literacy skills."[19] This initiative seeks to develop partnerships between national governments, NGOs, civil society, UN agencies, donor countries and the private sector with the goal of strengthening the countries' literacy efforts.[20]

Literacy in Afghanistan

One of the countries being addressed by LIFE is war-torn Afghanistan, where the literacy rate is one of the lowest in the world. As of 2006 in rural areas where roughly 75 percent of the Afghan population lives, 90 percent of women and 63 percent of men could not read or write.[21]

Education in Afghanistan has suffered significant setbacks over the last thirty years as a result of wars and the resulting political instability. Women in particular have been denied access to education throughout Afghanistan's history. The educational progress of the early 1970's was put to an end by the Russian invasion in 1979, which disrupted the national distribution of education. Notorious for their repression of Afghan women, the Taliban government, which held power from 1994-2001, excluded women from participation in education. [22] Since then, restoring educational systems nationwide has been a top priority in Afghanistan's building efforts.[23]

Governmental Initiatives

The country's Minister of Education, Hanif Atmar, recognizes the need and is well aware of the challenges facing his country in their efforts to become a literate nation. According to Atmar,

> Becoming a literate nation is the foundation upon which the hopes of this country will be built. Despite the many difficulties we have faced, in the past and now, the people of Afghanistan have demonstrated that education can be the bridge that transforms an emergency situation into one of hope and promise. However for us to become a literate nation where children, youth and adults become active, healthy, productive participants in our country's development efforts – Afghanistan still has a long difficult journey ahead.[24]

The minister of education is not alone in his efforts to increase literacy in his country. Numerous others have joined the crusade to enact literacy measures in Afghanistan. In addition to expanding the formal education system, home-based schools and accelerated learning programs have been implemented with the help of NGO's and other aid organizations, including the UN.

In 2003 the Government of Afghanistan and UNESCO signed an agreement which launched a major project to boost the country's literacy rates called the Literacy and Non-formal Education Development in Afghanistan (LAND). [25] This program, considered to be a flagship program for the UNLD, focuses on training a network of literacy teachers nationwide in modern non-formal education methods as well as training others in the development and production of teaching materials.[26] The establishment of community learning centers also plays a significant role in the program with the goal of reaching as many people as possible with literacy programs.[27] Lastly the Literacy Resource Centre for Girls and Women makes a special effort to address the literacy needs of Afghan women and girls.[28]

Learning for Life is an example of a LIFE project in Afghanistan which has enrolled over 8,500 Afghan women.[29] In this accelerated health and literacy program women learn literacy and numeracy skills as well as improved health practices.[30] Following the completion of the literacy classes, women are eligible to continue their training through prerequisites for a midwifery program and other healthcare fields.[31] The engaging classroom format draws heavily on student participation in discussion and debates about real-life events. As a result, women learn improved communication skills, and in the process learn how to improve the health of themselves and their families.[32] This nine-month program has seen a 90 percent completion rate.[33]

Another example of an accelerated learning program is the Afghanistan Primary Education Program (APEP). Funded by the United States Agency for International Development (UNAID), this literacy program was in operation from 2003-2007 and offered accelerated elementary education for out-of-school youth between ten and eighteen years of age with a focus on females.[34] It provided accelerated learning programs for over 170,000 youth in over 3,000 villages.[35] Research showed that the APEP program was able to overcome traditional gender disparity for the participating female students through pro-active fostering, mentoring and monitoring. [36] Program evaluators also discovered that time constraints remained a significant hindrance to participation for Afghan women since they were generally expected to continue their family responsibilities.[37] Additionally, the community often remained skeptical as to how education will provide immediate benefits for the student and the family.[38] These are obstacles that must be addressed if women are to participate fully in literacy programs in Afghanistan.

One particularly successful type of literacy initiative in Afghanistan has been community-based or home-based schooling (HBS). These programs have been especially effective in increasing education access for girls because they address some of the primary reasons why girls' access to education has been limited.[39] These barriers include the distance from home to school, the prevalence of male teachers from outside the community, and cultural beliefs that undervalue girls' education and pressure them to stay home and marry young.[40] HBS are located in teachers' homes, compounds or community spaces such as mosques and enroll children who would not otherwise have access to education. Local education committees appoint teachers for the schools, and the community members commit to supporting the teachers financially. Women teachers attract girls from more conservative families, and in some communities families allow their daughters to be taught by men from the community when they are known and trusted.[41] HBS only operate for half the day, so children are still available for work and able to help support their families. Research indicates, "HBS has not only contributed to the re-establishment of formal schooling, especially for girls, but has also promoted genuine learning, fostered student well-being, and encouraged a sense of optimism within communities."[42]

An innovative adult literacy program in Afghanistan gives married couples an opportunity to attend the same class together, while also including various ethnicities in the same classroom.[43] In addition to teaching basic literacy skills, the class also strengthened marriages and helped to remove ethnic tensions. Interviews with the participants revealed, "They felt that their newfound literacy skills had changed their daily lives, their view of themselves and their relationships with spouse, family and community, even nation."[44] Participants identified numerous positive outcomes of their literacy classes including the following: engaging in new activities and work aspirations, the ability to write letters to distant family members, improved spousal relationships, better communication with children and families, and a sense of community within the class despite the diverse ethnicities.[45] Of this sense of community, one participant said, "There are many people in class, many ethnic groups, and we are happy about this. This is not a problem. I'm Pashtun, you are Tajik...it doesn't matter. We are all the same. We're all Afghan, and we are happy we are all studying together."[46] These literacy classes also brought hope, as both men and women said their newfound literacy skills helped them feel more engaged in their communities and more hopeful about their own future as well as that of their country.[47]

The success of the program may have been due in part to the way that it was purposefully sensitive to Afghan culture. The program was first offered to men, and after agreeing to be enrolled, they were told that in order to attend they must bring their wives as well. Those who administered the program believed that it would be more acceptable to husbands to learn with their wives than for the women to learn alone. Many of the male participants later said that the honor of being approached with the idea first, enabled them to see the value of the class for themselves and their families.[48]

The results of this program underscore the value of adult literacy training in terms of personal and social development within communities. According to researchers Andersen and Kooij,

> Arguably, adult literacy forms the backbone of development and perhaps to a degree of peace and security as well. If peace and security depend in part on mutual understanding, then the building blocks of knowledge and learning gained through literacy are likely to be important... [Literacy] can help people flourish and is necessary for social development.[49]

Certainly the results of this program are a testament to the truth of the above statement, and argue for the importance of literacy initiatives in Afghanistan, a country struggling to rebuild itself after years of violence and war.

Non-Governmental Initiatives

The plight of Afghan women has not been lost on women in the west. Two women in particular have made noteworthy strides towards improving the literacy landscape for women in Afghanistan.

The first woman, Susan Bellan, founded Breaking Bread for Afghanistan, a volunteer fundraising project to support education for Afghan woman and girls by holding pot luck dinners across Canada.[50] After becoming aware of the lack of funding for education in Afghanistan, Susan decided if she could find a way to pay teacher salaries, she could make a difference in the lives of Afghan girls. She began by inviting a dozen friends to a potluck dinner and asked each one to contribute $75 towards the cause, with the goal of raising $750—the salary for one teacher for one year in Afghanistan. What began as one potluck dinner in Toronto in 2002 has expanded to over seven hundred dinners across Canada, and resulted in over one million dollars raised. Hundreds of Afghan teachers and thousands of Afghan students benefit from the program each year.[51]

The second woman Connie Duckworth founded ARZU, Inc. in 2004 as an innovative model of social entrepreneurship for the purpose of helping Afghan women gain marketable skills as well as access to education and healthcare. Headquartered in Chicago, Illinois, ARZU contracts with Afghan women to weave artisan rugs which are in turn sold in the United States. Among other things, the contract includes a fair market value for their services as well as incentives for highest quality workmanship. The weavers also agree to send their children to school and to participate in literacy classes themselves. In 2008, ARZU earned international recognition for its exemplary social business practices, as the recipient of the Skoll Foundation Award for scalable social entrepreneurship.[52]

ARZU prides itself on having a holistic approach to sustainable community development by targeting their efforts towards women to provide education, job training, basic healthcare, and clean water. ARZU provides mandatory education classes for the women it employs that cover literacy, numeracy, health, hygiene, nutrition, and human rights. Over seven hundred women and children attend these classes. In addition, ARZU provides vocational training through paid apprenticeship programs which also create employment opportunities in the community. ARZU's healthcare services include weekly visits by their health monitors to employees' homes, help with transportation to clinics, and emergency mobile phone calling systems. The organization has also partnered with the Ministry of Health to provide training for midwives and community healthcare workers. In addition, they have piloted projects to address the need for clean water that have simultaneously provided economic opportunities as well.[53]

World Vision is another organization active with literacy initiatives among women in Afghanistan. In 2007 World Vision established the Women's Economy Literacy and Livelihoods (WELL) program to provide literacy and vocational training to women and girls. The program exists in eight villages in the Badghis Province and serves four hundred impoverished women and girls who would otherwise be forced into early marriage and child bearing. Women receive training in tailoring, embroidery, weaving, along with business and marketing skills.[54]

World Vision has also built or rehabilitated forty-one schools in several provinces in western Afghanistan serving tens of thousands of students.[55] In addition to helping to train teachers for these schools, World Vision is providing basic literacy training for nearly 3,500 women in the rural communities of the Badghis and Ghor Provinces. Included in these literacy classes are basic health and hygiene training as well.[56]Furthermore World Vision has established an educational program for midwives, who upon graduation from the program serve in provincial health care facilities using their education to help reduce infant mortality in their communities.[57]

A Theology of Engagement

As with many other social issues, a Christian theology of engagement must begin with the recognition that all people have been created by God and as such, bear His image (Gen 1:27, NIV). As creatures who bear God's image, all humans are owed a certain dignity and respect. Often those living without literacy skills lack such dignity. Their illiteracy prevents them from fully participating in the society and culture in which they live. These deficiencies often relegate them to lives of poverty, without the ability to better their economic situation. Literacy can provide a means of dignity—both in the acquisition of the skill and in its potential to provide a path out of poverty.

Since illiteracy and poverty often go hand in hand, it is important to consider God's perspective on poverty. In numerous places throughout His Word, God makes clear His heart for the poor and instructs His people to care for the poor. For example, throughout the Old Testament law, he makes provisions for the care of the poor and instructs His people not to harvest portions of their fields and vineyards so that the poor could eat from them (Lev 19:10; 23:22). He also gives

157

explicit directives for being generous to the poor (Deut 15:7-11). One way Christians can care for the poor in today's world is by providing skills which will allow the poor the opportunity to lift themselves out of poverty. Literacy is one such skill since individuals with literacy skills often have better economic opportunities than those who do not. Providing marketable skills, rather than simply monetary relief or aid, creates the possibility for sustainable change and economic growth.

Similarly, literacy skills provide not only a potential economic benefit, but a form of protection as well. Those without basic literacy skills are easily taken advantage of—perhaps cheated out of fair wages, deceived into signing a detrimental contract, or conned into paying more for goods and services. Literacy skills give people a form of defense against unjust practices like these. God identifies himself as a defender of the defenseless (Deut 10:18, Ps 72:4) and He commands His people to do the same (Isa 10:17). Psalm 140:12 says, "… the Lord secures justice for the poor and upholds the cause of the needy." He is moved to protect the needy and the oppressed, according to Psalm 12:5. Christians can reflect the heart of God by helping to secure protection from injustice by providing basic literacy skills.

In addition to reflecting God's heart for the poor and defenseless, a Christian theology of engagement must also recognize the role literacy plays in the Great Commission. God had chosen to reveal Himself to humanity primarily through a written medium, His Word. Those who are not able to read are placed at a significant disadvantage when it comes to knowing God. Certainly, God reveals himself in other ways—through miracles, through dreams, and visions, etc. However, the substance of the gospel and God's redemptive story is communicated in written form through the Holy Scriptures. Those who are unable to read must rely on someone else to communicate the truth found in the Bible, and not only that, they are then unable to verify the accuracy of the information presented.

Even if a non literate person comes to know Christ through the verbal testimony of another person, without the ability to read the Bible for himself, he is limited in his ability to grow as a new believer. Communing with God though His Word is foundational to a vibrant Christian walk. The Old Testament emphasizes the importance of meditating on God's Word (Josh 1:8, Ps 1:2) and Jesus instructs his followers to abide in Him by allowing His words to abide in them (John 15:9). This is one of the reasons Christians should be at the forefront of worldwide literacy efforts. Believers are called to make disciples (Matt 28:19), and without basic literacy skills, a person's ability to become a disciple of Christ is severely hindered. Christians must lead the way in expanding literacy around the world in order to build a foundation for fulfilling their call to make disciples of all nations.

As with any type of human social need, there must be a holistic approach to addressing literacy. Providing literacy skills alone will not necessarily serve to lift people out of poverty, secure necessary protection, or lead them to care for their spiritual health. The church must recognize that literacy training should be a part of a larger effort to address the economic, social, and spiritual needs of a community. For example, teaching members of a community to read simply for the purpose of reading the Bible, while ignoring the economic and social issues that may be present, is a strategy that fails to adequately reflect the heart of Christ for mankind.

Christ's example during his earthly ministry was one that combined care for both spiritual and physical needs. He not only taught people the truth about His Kingdom, He also met countless physical needs. Matthew 9:35 says, "Jesus went through all the towns and villages, teaching in their synagogues, preaching the good news of the kingdom and healing every disease and sickness." Applying this approach to literacy means teaching the skills to read and write, particularly when it comes to Christian disciple-making, must be accompanied by care for material needs as well.

Conclusion

As the global needs for literacy loom large, Christians have a responsibility to lead the way in engaging this issue. The church's engagement must be marked by a respect for the dignity of human life and a reflection of the compassion of God in meeting both physical and spiritual needs.

What does this look like in Afghanistan? Certainly, the initiatives highlighted previously are not exhaustive of the efforts targeted at increasing literacy rates in Afghanistan, and much remains to be done. Where does the church fit into the picture? World Vision seems to have led the way in terms of Christian relief organizations operating in Afghanistan, but many of the other initiatives in existence are government led or administered through other NGO's. Additional Christian presence appears lacking. This deficiency is understandable given the hostility towards Christianity which exists in Afghanistan,[58] and it is quite plausible that there are Christian efforts quietly underway which are not highly publicized.

As previously identified, the Christian response to the issue of literacy should be a holistic one aimed at addressing the social, spiritual and material needs of a community. One possibility would be for the church in Afghanistan to partner with World Vision in its relief efforts. For example, it would be ideal if WELL training could be offered at churches or in the homes of believers in the community. In addition, perhaps spiritual training or education could also be offered through churches as an optional part of the WELL program. Since women are already receiving education on other topics through WELL, it seems natural to also include spiritual education as well. This spiritual education could include basic theology as well as perhaps a counseling or emotional care element.

While not a Christian organization, ARZU stands as an excellent example of holistic engagement on many levels. This type of social entrepreneurial approach done in partnership with a local indigenous church has the potential to create sustainable change within the Afghan society. The aspect of care missing from ARZU's strategy is spiritual care and education. Years of oppression and violence have no doubt left emotional and spiritual scars on the women of Afghanistan and a need for hope and healing. If believers in the West were to partner with indigenous churches in Afghanistan to launch social entrepreneurial ventures like the ARZU, the church would then have a greater platform for championing literacy education and engaging the spiritual needs of the people of Afghanistan by introducing them to the Great Healer. Partnerships with local churches also help ensure that any literacy programs initiated would be culturally sensitive in their approach as well as garner needed community support.

In very few places around the world are literacy needs felt as acutely as in Afghanistan. As such, the church should seize the opportunity to address this need with the heart and mind of Christ. By combining care for the material needs with care for the spiritual needs of people, the church has the opportunity to make an impact on the lives and wellbeing of the Afghan people as well as be a significant contributor to the rebuilding of a country.

---

[1] United Nations Education, Scientific and Cultural Organization (UNESCO), Literacy, http://www.unesco.org/en/literacy/, (accessed March 28, 2010).

[2] Ibid.

[3] UNESCO, "Education for All (EFA) Global Monitoring Report 2006," pg 22, http://www.unesco.org/en/efareport/reports/2006-literacy/, (accessed March 28, 2010).

[4] Ibid.

[5] Literacy Hub: Broader Middle East and North Africa (BMENA), "What is Literacy," http://www.literacyhub.org/English/, (accessed March 27, 2010).

[6] UNESCO, "Education for All (EFA) Global Monitoring Report 2006," pg 14, http://www.unesco.org/en/efareport/reports/2006-literacy/, (accessed March 28, 2010).

---

[7]Ibid.

[8]Ibid.

[9]Ibid., 14.

[10]Literacy Hub, "What is Literacy."

[11]UNESCO, Why is literacy important?" http://www.unesco.org/en/literacy/literacy-important/, (accessed March 28, 2010).

[12]Ibid.

[13]UNESCO, "Education for All Global Monitoring Report 2006," http://www.unesco.org /en/efareport/reports/2006-literacy/, (accessed March 28, 2010).

[14]Ibid.

[15]UNESCO, "United Nations Literacy Decade (2003-2012)," (http://www.unesco.org /uil/en/focus/unliteracy.htm, (accessed March 23, 2010).

[16]Ibid.

[17]Ibid.

[18]UNESCO, "Literacy Initiative for Empowerment (LIFE) (2005-2015)," http://www.unesco.org/uil/en/focus/litinforemp.htm, (accessed March 23, 2010).

[19]Ibid.

[20]Ibid.

[21]Council on Foreign Affairs, Minister of Education Roundtable Series: A New Vision for Education in Afghanistan, Speaker: Hanif Atmar, September 27, 2006, http://www.cfr.org/content/thinktank/cue/visionformoeliteracy.pdf, (accessed March 30, 2010).

[22]Jo Ann Intili, Ed Kissam, Eileen St. George, "Fostering Education for Female, Out-of-School Youth in Afghanistan," *Journal of Education for International Development,* 2:1, (2006), http://www.equip123.net/JEID/articles /2/Afghanistan.pdf, (accessed March 27, 2010).

[23]Ibid.

[24]Ibid.

[25]UNESCO, "UNESCO and the government of Afghanistan launch nationwide literacy project," (2003) http://portal.unesco.org/en/ev.php-URL_ID=9031&URL_DO=DO_TOPIC& URL_SECTION=201.html, (accessed March 27, 2010).

[26]Ibid.

[27]Ibid.

[28]Ibid.

[29]Management Sciences for Heath, Rural Expansion of Afghanistan's Community-based Healthcare (REACH), http://www.msh.org/afghanistan/technical_areas/empowering_women.html, (accessed March 27, 2010).

[30]USAID: Afghanistan, "Involving Women in Afghanistan's Community Health Committees: Some Lessons Learned," June 2006, (accessed March 27, 2010), http://www.msh.org/afghanistan/pdf/CD/Women_shura-e-sehi06.pdf

[31]White House Conference on Global Literacy, September 18, 2006, New York City, http://literacyhub.org/documents/white_house_conference.pdf, (accessed March 23, 2010).

[32]Ibid.

[33]Ibid.

[34]Intili, Kissam, and St. George, "Fostering Education for Female, Out-of-School Youth in Afghanistan," 1.

[35]Ibid.

[36]Ibid., 19.

[37]Ibid.

[38]Ibid.

[39]Jankie Kirk and Rebecca Winthrop, "Meeting EFA: Afghanistan Home-Based Schools," USAID (2005), pg 1, http://literacyhub.org/documents/e2-Afg_IRC_Case_Study.pdf, (accessed March 27, 2010).

[40]Ibid.

[41]Ibid., 2.

[42]Ibid.

[43]Susan M. Andersen, and Christina S. Kooij, "Adult literacy education and human rights: a view from Afghanistan," *Globalisation, Societies & Education* 5, no. 3 (2007): 315-331.

[44]Ibid., 315

[45]Ibid.

[46]Ibid.

[47]Ibid.

[48]Ibid.

[49]Ibid., 317.

[50]Canadian Women for Afghanistan Women, "Breaking Bread," http://www.cw4wafghan.ca/what-we-do/breaking-bread, (accessed April 5, 2010).

[51]Ibid.

[52]ARZU STUDIO HOPE, http://www.arzustudiohope.org/home/story/social-programs.html, (accessed May 8, 2010).

[53]Ibid.

[54]World Vision, "Afghanistan,"http://meero.worldvision.org/about.php, (accessed May 3, 2010).

[55]Ibid.

[56]Ibid.

[57]Ibid.

[58]Blake, Daniel, "Muslim Clerics Warn Afghanistan President Against Christian Missionaries," *Christianity Today*, January 1, 2008, http://www.christiantoday.com/article/muslim.clerics.warn.afghanistan.president.against.missionaries/16004.htm (accessed May 8, 2010).

Chapter Nine

Towards a Theology of Food Production and Land

Alex Shaver

SOME OF MY BEST MEMORIES involve sharing meals with friends and family. Growing up in rural Ohio, a good meal was not hard to come by, as our family was blessed with home-cooked meals on a regular basis. For our family, food was just as much about spending time together as it was about nourishment. What strikes me most about sharing meals with my family is the power that food holds. By this, I mean that sharing a meal together is an intimate experience that brings people together.

Food cannot be divorced from the hands that prepare it. The production process is important in that it is directly tied with the people it provides sustenance for. It is just as much cultural as it is biological. The main purpose of this chapter is to work toward an understanding of how food production is tied directly to the way in which we view and interact with our land. This chapter will draw upon an agrarian perspective, a historical example, and upon principles from the Old Testament.

An Agrarian Perspective

First, experts are convinced that the majority of cultural issues related to food production start with the way in which modern agriculture operates. Among them is Wendell Berry, who has much to say on the topic. One of the crucial cultural issues related to food production is plainly the way it is produced. Berry, while defending the family farm, outlines three assumptions based on industrial values: "1. That value equals price…2. That all relations are mechanical…3. That the sufficient and definitive human motive is competitiveness…"[1] These values, according to Berry, have been embraced by our culture, and are important in understanding the shift from the family farm to large scale factory farming.

165

These three assumptions are intriguing. Berry understands well the value system of our culture. His point is that the current model of agriculture has divorced value and meaning from the land from which food is farmed. He says, "...the value of a farm, for example, is whatever it would bring on sale, because both a place and its price are 'assets.'"[2] The problem here is that there is no distinction between the farm and the factory; both are simply assets to be utilized in order to make money. Berry says it well when he writes, "The industrial mind is a mind without compunction; it simply accepts that people, ultimately, will be treated as things and that things ultimately, will be treated as garbage."[3] When place and people are viewed only as assets for profit, there is no use for either once they have been utilized.

Evidence of these values being embraced can be seen in the fact that Americans have collectively bought the idea that cheaper is better. Sustainability and health are put on the backburners for what is cheapest. Bryan Walsh and Rebecca Kaplan write "According to the USDA, Americans spend less than 10 percent of their incomes on food, down from 18% in 1966."[4] There is no doubt that producing much of our food in factories has made things easier on our collective wallet, unfortunately, there is much more to the equation. What Walsh and Kaplan point out is how much money is spent on the corn industry here in the States. This is evidenced in the amount of high fructose corn syrup Americans consume. "Over the past decade, the Federal Government has poured more than $50 billion into the corn industry, keeping prices for the crop--at least until corn ethanol skewed the market--artificially low."[5]

While so much money is being spent on the corn industry, for the production of corn-based products, there is little money being spent on the production of fruits and vegetables. Simply stated, grain production receives a higher emphasis than that of fruits and vegetables. Walsh and Kaplan continue, "A study in the American Journal of Clinical Nutrition found that a dollar could buy 1,200 calories of potato chips or 875 calories of soda but just 250 calories of vegetables or 170 calories of fresh fruit."[6] Because Americans have (on a large scale) embraced the idea of cheaper being better, it naturally follows that we have become so unhealthy. It is more affordable to eat unhealthy foods.

Another problem with the amount of unhealthy foods produced is the amount of fertilizer that goes into the production of these items. Crops, in large-scale factory farming, are the recipients of heavy fertilization. The efficiency cannot be argued with, and again we see that what is valued is the most efficient system; the more produced the better, regardless of the effect. Walsh and Kaplan noted, "American farmers now produce an astounding 153 bu. of corn per acre, up from

118 as recently as 1990. But the quantity of that fertilizer is flat-out scary: more than 10 million tons for corn alone--and nearly 23 million for all crops."[7]

Perhaps what is most ironic about the "efficiency" of our current agricultural system is that much of the food produced is wasted. Admittedly, some food waste cannot be avoided, though much of food waste is, in fact, the product of our own doing. Clifton Coles noted, "On average, Americans waste 14% of the food they buy, including products still within their expiration date but never opened."[8] We have seen the extraordinary amount of money spent to produce massive amounts of food, but what Coles points out is that there is also a huge amount of money being wasted by Americans every year.

Coles appeals to anthropologist Timothy W. Jones as he continues, "He (Jones) estimates the average family of four tosses out $590 per year in meat, fruits, vegetables, and grain products. That adds up to $43 billion annually, making it a serious economic problem."[9] A truly intriguing aspect of Coles' article is that he draws a connection between the amount of money wasted on food, and the amount of money spent on food production. Again he cites Jones as he writes, "Cutting food waste may also go a long way toward reducing serious environmental problems. Jones estimates that reducing food waste by half could reduce adverse environmental impacts by 25% through reduced landfill use, soil depletion, and applications of fertilizer, pesticides, and herbicides."[10] Seen here is a complex cultural issue that appears to be the result of an improper understanding of the relationship between people and land.

A Historical Example

This value system is not only represented by factory farmers in America, it has been the story for many cultures and people groups over the course of history. One in particular that illustrates this is that of the Miskito Indians off the coast of eastern Nicaragua. James Spradley Late and David McCurdy describe their situation, "The coastal Miskito Indians are very dependent on green sea turtles. Their culture has long been adapted to utilizing the once vast populations that inhabited the largest sea turtle feeding grounds in the Western Hemisphere."[11] While the Miskito Indians were dependent on the sea turtle for sustenance, for a long time, their sustenance was not divorced from the culture. Bernard Nietschmann explained, "As the most important link between livelihood, social interaction, and environment, green turtles were the pivotal resource around which traditional Miskito Indian society revolved."[12] Food for the Miskito Indians was just as much about who they were as a people as it was about their sustenance.

The Miskito Indians operated much like Wendell Berry's ideal family farm. "Miskito society and economy were interdependent. There was no economic activity without a social context and every social act had a reciprocal economic aspect."[13] Nietschmann goes on to explain that the Miskito Indians, during the seventeenth and eighteenth centuries, began to trade with English and French buccaneers. This led to the Miskito viewing turtle meat as much more than sustenance, with a market for turtle meat, things began to change drastically.[14] What is stimulating here is the similarity between the Miskito Indians, specifically the turtle hunters, and the farmer Berry defends.

Turtles, before trade with the French and English, were hunted by only the most skilled "turtlemen."[15] Becoming a skilled turtle hunter took years of training as they were hunted with harpoons; a skill few could master. Spradley and McCurdy comment, "Turtlemen work in partnerships: a 'strikerman' in the bow; the 'captain' in the stern. Together, they make a single unit engaged in the delicate and almost silent pursuit of a wary prey, their movements coordinated by experience and rewarded by proficiency."[16] These men were highly esteemed within the Miskito Indian community because they had the responsibility of bringing back turtle meat for everyone. Most importantly, their job was not divorced from its social context. The hunters were not viewed as a commodity for consumption, nor were the turtles they hunted.

Once trade for turtle meat started, things changed drastically. Turtles began being hunted with nets, and skilled hunters were not needed. "Catching turtles with nets requires little skill; anyone with a canoe can now be a turtleman."[17] As more and more turtles were caught, they became increasingly scarce. The reality of the situation is that the Miskito Indians have become dependent on outside markets, and are not benefiting as they did in the past. "The Miskito presently sell 70 to 90 percent of the turtles they catch; in the near future they will sell even more and eat less."[18] I see significant parallels between this story and that of the American agricultural system. While there may be a few differences, there seems to be a value system that is consistent.

Perhaps what is most consistent with the value system adopted by the Miskito Indians and that of modern agriculture is the way in which we define what it mean to be a "worker." Berry says

> Industrial agriculture has tended to look on the farmer as a "worker"—a sort of obsolete but not yet dispensable machine—acting on the advice of scientists and economists. We have neglected the truth that a *good* farmer is a craftsman of the highest order, a kind of artist. It is the good

work of good farmers—nothing else—that ensures a sufficiency of food over the long term.[19]

The "good farmer" explained by Berry, is strikingly similar to the turtlemen described by Nietschmann. It is fair to say that both Berry's family farmer and the Miskito turtlemen became assets over time, commodities for profit. What can be said for this kind of value system that sees people and land as commodity?

Land in the Old Testament

Second, now that we have discussed some of the cultural issues related to food production, it is worthwhile to look at what scripture says regarding the issue. I have been persuaded to believe that a theology of land, based on scripture, is vital to the discussion on food production. We must view the land from a biblical perspective in order to rightly discern our interaction with it. There is a sense in which the land in scripture is both literal and symbolic. Walter Brueggemann addresses this paradox when he writes, "A symbolic sense of the term affirms that land is never simply physical dirt but is always physical dirt freighted with social meanings derived from historical experience."[20] It is evident in Scripture that the land is something to be sought after. This distinction is a helpful one, because it helps in understanding how important the land is both symbolically and physically. Brueggemann continues, "A literal sense of the term will protect us from excessive spiritualization, so that we recognize that the yearning for land is always a serious historical enterprise concerned with historical power and belonging."[21]

The foundation that Brueggeman is setting here is important in our discussion on land and how we are to view it. He argues that human beings over the course of history have always assigned meaning to land; what then is the appropriate meaning of land as seen in scripture? Land for the Israelites was most definitely a gift from Yahweh. This is Brueggeman's starting point, as he argues for land as gift rather than something obtained and objectified by human effort. We see here both the physical nature of land, as gift, and the symbolic nature, as place. Brueggeman stated, "The land to Israel is a gift. It is a gift from Yahweh and binds Israel in ways to the giver."[22] This distinction is a simple one, yet it is profound in the way it is applied. Anything, when understood as a gift, as opposed to something that is earned or even something deserved, is treated with more care and is cherished. This notion helps to fashion an understanding of how to view the land in any context. Regardless of where the land is located, what should be understood is that God is the ultimate provider, who has blessed His people.

Brueggemann identified a key OT text in Deuteronomy that illustrates well the contrast between the old and new land for the Israelites,

> For the land which you are entering to take possession of it is not like the land of Egypt, from which you have come, where you sowed your seed and watered it with your feet, like a garden of vegetables; but the land which you are going over to posses is a land of hills and valleys, which drinks water by rain from heaven, a land which Yahweh your God cares for; the eyes of Yahweh your God are always upon it from the beginning of the year to the end of the year. (Deuteronomy 11:10-12)

What Brueggemann pointed out in this text that is so vital is that God is making it clear that this new land is a gift, while Egypt was a land of coercion. The old land was a land characterized by slavery, whereas the new land is a land of restoration for Israel. "It is a land where security does not need to be manufactured, where well-being need not come by conjuring and calculation. Here security and well-being are not from the grudging task master, but from the benevolent rain-sender, the same one who was bread-giver."[23] This is a beautiful picture of God's grace both in providing rest for His people, as well as a land of restoration.

The land then for Israel is God's gift. It is something to be cared for and cherished. Now that this has been established, it is necessary to understand the way in which land management operated in Israel. What can be seen in scripture, specifically with the Israelites, is what Brueggemann refered to as a confrontation between prophet and king.[24] To illustrate, he interacts with another OT text, 1 Kings 21, that is so apropos for our current situation in America regarding land management.

The story in Chapter 21 contrasts two very different ideas of how to go about managing the land. The first view is represented by King Ahab, who considers the land to be a tradable commodity, and the second view is represented by Naboth, who understands the land to be an inheritance.[25] The opening verses of Chapter 21 set the stage for the confrontation:

> And after this Ahab said to Naboth, "Give me your vineyard, that I may have it for a vegetable garden, because it is near my house, and I will give you a better vineyard for it; or, if it seems good to you, I will give you its value in money." But Naboth said to Ahab, "The Lord forbid that I should give you the inheritance of my fathers."[26]

The land has meaning to Ahab and Naboth, both of which are rooted in their idea about the purpose the land serves. Ellen Davis observed, "Ahab approaches this as a simple real estate deal: The vineyard is an exchangeable and interchangeable commodity. That is antithetical to Naboth's understanding, and he refuses categorically."[27] Naboth has a communal understanding; the land for Naboth represents the gift passed down from God to his ancestors, it is of the utmost importance. Naboth's is a position that cherishes the land and does not seek to exploit it for selfish reasons. Brueggemann added, "Naboth is responsible for the land, but is not in control over it. It is the case not that the land belongs to him but that he belongs to the land."[28]

What happens next in this story is Jezebel, Ahab's wife, manipulates those in leadership in Naboth's city to ultimately have Naboth killed in order for Ahab to take the vineyard he had wanted. Elijah enters the story and is sent to judge both Jezebel and Ahab for what they had done. Jezebel and Ahab illustrate a misunderstanding at best of what it means to inherit the land. Brueggemann says it best when he says, "In the queen's view, quite in contrast to that of Naboth, land is negotiable, that is, it is a piece of property handled objectively and with detachment and rationality."[29]

First Kings 21 also is used in defense of the local economy. This is seen manifestly by the caving in of the local economy when King Ahab acted on his greed and self interest rather than the interest of the community. This thought is summed up well by Ellen Davis when she wrote, "What this narrative reveals, then, is that when Ahab 'enacts sovereignty' in a way that defeats the local economy, he sets in motion a destructive mechanism that he himself is unable to arrest; eventually it will bring down his royal house."[30] Davis is advocating for the local economy and understands this passage to be in support of it as well. She rightly stated, "it is not possible to subtract the essential economic functions from a community and expect mutual trust, goodwill, and aid among the neighbors to remain."[31] Again it can be seen that our view of the land has everything to do with the community in which we live.

Another passage to consider is Proverbs 25. Throughout the Proverbs, there is a dichotomy between that which is wise and that which is foolish: lady wisdom and lady folly. A life of integrity, wisdom, and character are very important in Proverbs. In fact, these things are of the utmost importance. Proverbs 25 is full of wisdom and beautiful imagery about what it means to be wise. Also present here is practical advice regarding land.

While it may seem obvious and perhaps trite, there is wisdom here regarding human interaction with the land as it relates to food consumption. Verse 16 says,

"If you have found honey, eat only enough for you, lest you have your fill of it and vomit it."[32] The beauty of this Proverb is the simple truth and wisdom it offers. I do not believe it is a stretch to view this Proverb through an agrarian lens. Understood here is that food (honey) is to be consumed, though not exploited or hoarded. There is communal expectation present, and wisdom that has self control enough to eat only what is needed.

This Proverb ends in much the same way, when we read, "It is not good to eat much honey, nor is it glorious to seek one's own glory. A man without self-control is like a city broken into and left without walls."[33] One could argue that the man without self-control is equal to the nation who lacks self-control. We see with King Ahab that God takes very seriously the way in which His people interact with the Land he has given them.

Conclusion and Implications

Through the examination of the current agricultural system in America, a comparison to the Miskito Indians, and several key texts in scripture, I have done my best to try to come to an understanding of how food production is related to land. More specifically, how we are to view the land as a gift from God not to be exploited for selfish reasons or personal gain. Once more I appeal to Walter Brueggemann in an effort to sum up Israel's role as it relates to land.

Brueggemann articulated it well when he wrote, "The fundamental dream of Israel is about land. Israel is a social, theological experiment in alternative land management. The God of Israel is a God who gives land, and Israel is a people that holds land in alternative ways."[34] Brueggemann, in my opinion, hits the proverbial nail on the head as he explained this thought further. He wrote, "Israel's theory of land as inheritance is practically designed to resist monopoly and the corresponding social displacement that is caused by monopoly."[35] This is to say that the people of Israel were to continually understand that their inheritance was from the Lord.

Jeremiah says in chapter 29 "But seek the welfare of the city where I have sent you into exile, and pray to the LORD on its behalf, for in its welfare you will find welfare."[36] Our welfare as the people of God is rooted in the welfare of the land in which we live. The question we must ask ourselves in our current context is what then does it look like for Americans to seek this welfare, or shalom?

After examining an agrarian perspective, a historical example and drawing from Old Testament principles, hopefully we are in a better place to begin to answer this question. The challenge for Christians in our current context is to understand that God has been gracious to us; He has provided for us. This land is a gift. It is not to be exploited, rather it is to be cared for and understood in the grand scheme of God's redemptive plan for His creation. We have been given the great responsibility to care for God's creation, and to love His people. Christians have a responsibility to the land as the Israelites did. We have a responsibility to care for the community God has placed us in and a love for the community as a whole, not only ourselves, which is a call that requires much sacrifice.

---

[1]Wendell Berry, *Bringing It to the Table: On Farming and Food*, Later printing. (Counterpoint, 2009), 37.

[2]Ibid.

[3]Ibid.

[4]Bryan Walsh and Rebecca Kaplan, "America's Food Crisis and How to Fix It. (Cover story)," *Time* 174, no. 8 (2009): 30-37.

[5]Ibid.

[6]Ibid.

[7]Ibid.

[8]Clifton Coles, "America Wastes Half Its Food.," *Futurist* 39, no. 3 (May 2005): 12.

[9]Ibid.

[10]Ibid.

[11]James W. Spradley and David W. McCurdy, *Conformity and Conflict: Readings in Cultural Anthropology*, 13th ed. (Allyn & Bacon, 2008), 115.

[12]Ibid., 116.

[13]Ibid.

[14]Ibid., 117.

[15]Ibid., 119.

[16]Ibid.

[17]Ibid., 120.

[18]Ibid., 121.

[19]Berry, *Bringing It to the Table*, 29.

[20]Walter Brueggemann, *Land Revised Edition*, 2nd ed. (Fortress Press, 2002), 2.

[21]Ibid.

[22]Ibid., 45.

---

[23]Brueggemann, *Land Revised Edition*, 48.

[24]Ibid., 86.

[25]Ibid., 88.

[26]1 Kings 21:2-3, *ESV*.

[27]Ellen F. Davis, *Scripture, Culture, and Agriculture: An Agrarian Reading of the Bible*, 1st ed. (Cambridge University Press, 2008), 111.

[28]Brueggemann, *Land Revised Edition*, 88.

[29]Ibid., 89.

[30]Davis, *Scripture, Culture, and Agriculture*, 114.

[31]Ibid.

[32]Proverbs 25:16, *ESV*.

[33]Proverbs 25:27-28, *ESV*.

[34]Brueggemann, *Land Revised Edition*, 178.

[35]Ibid.

[36]Jeremiah 29:7, *ESV*.

Chapter Ten

Social Justice:
Restoring the Rights of Membership

Stephen Paul Kennedy

HISTORY: THE NEOLOGISTIC couplet *social justice* entered twentieth century religious discourse through churchmen responding to the problems of industrial urbanization: poverty, racial discrimination, crime, unemployment, disease and mental illness, etc. Generally, the phrase expressed their concern that the *systemic* societal roots of these growing problems had been ignored by Christians who advocated an excessively privatized vision of piety. More specifically, the idea *social justice* challenged the rising middle class tendency to blame the poor for their poverty and the racist exclusionism of many fundamentalists. Due to their roots in middle class fundamentalism, evangelicals remain suspicious about giving legitimacy to the idea that social injustices include are often grounded in systemic patterns of oppression. This essay explores the ways individual political liberties can mask injustices of exclusion and violate equally crucial rights of membership possessed by each person.

Apology: A Christian must begin an essay on membership with a confession that the Church has allowed and defended systemic exclusions based on irrelevant and indefensible criteria. We have willingly justified arbitrary cultural, political, and economic exclusions based on race, ethnicity, religion, and language in societies where we have been a dominant presence. We have concocted and maintained systems promoting all the hateful ugliness and oppression of racism, xenophobia, and religious imperialism. We have been complicit in war crimes, crimes against humanity, and genocide on the basis of unjust and arbitrary exclusions. "We have left undone those things which we ought to have done, and we have done those things which we ought not to have done, and there is no health in us."[1] May God forgive us, individually and collectively as we commit ourselves to love neighbors in truth and justice.

Dilemma: Consider the story of Rosa Parks. On the morning of 1 December

175

1955, Rosa Parks awakened with the liberty to wear a red dress or a blue one, to wear black shoes or brown ones, and to eat breakfast cereal or scrambled eggs. She had a wide range of personal liberties, but the State of Alabama could still mandate that white bus drivers move black passengers from the middle to the back, or completely off the bus to make way for white passengers. That is precisely what bus driver James F. Blake did by ordering her to move from the middle to the back of a bus. By this policy black people like Rosa Parks were excluded from enjoying the full rights of citizenship, despite the fact that their taxes were used to build the roads, to finance the operations of the bus system, and to pay the bus driver. She was taxed as a citizen—a *member* of the United States of America, and of the State of Alabama—but she was excluded from enjoying the rights of citizens to ride a bus in the ways white people did because she was black. The demand that Rosa Parks sit in the back of the bus abrogated her *liberty* to sit where she wanted to. However, the deeper injustice was her arbitrary *exclusion* from the full rights of a citizen. By guaranteeing *de minimus* liberties, the "separate but equal" doctrine masked the gross injustices of exclusion.

Argument: The Church little understands the political implications of the doctrine of human sociality. We have accepted uncritically an inadequate understanding of human nature which has led us to adopt the anti-Christian ideologies of the Right and the Left. Blinded by adherence to the core doctrines of political Liberalism, especially as they have developed in modernity, few can think outside the limitations of modern Liberalism. Consequently, Christians have been remarkably uncreative in thought and action to remedy the harms of exclusion. To remedy this great oversight we must restore our grasp of the biblical doctrine of human sociality, critique the inadequacies of political Liberalism, and insist on the rights of membership while putting possessory rights on a firmer foundation.

Human Sociality

> No man is an island, entire of itself; every man is a piece of the continent, a part of the main. If a clod be washed away by the sea, Europe is the less, as well as if a promontory were, as well as if a manor of thy friend's or of thine own were: any man's death diminishes me, because I am involved in mankind, and therefore never send to know for whom the bell tolls; it tolls for thee.[2]

There is belonging and there is *belonging*. Things belong to us such as our shoes and shirts, our bodies and souls. On the other hand, there are groups to which we belong such as families, religious groups, ethnicities, and nations. When my wife uses the possessive adjective—"*my* shoes, *my* husband"—she appropriately refers to what belongs to her. Both belong to her, but in rather different senses—her shoes by purchase, and me by promise. Belonging is one of those *first things* that we apprehend by simple intuition. The things that belong to us we often call our *members*, like our arms and legs, and we are *members of* that to which we belong. *Belonging*, I argue, is the heart of justice.

However, the story about Rosa Parks reveals how modern political theory focuses exclusively on what belongs to us, not on what we belong to. So decisive has been the influence of political *Liberalism* that we have lost sight of how important it is to protect our membership in families, churches, and ethnicities. We need to examine our blindness by reminding ourselves that we are social beings. Most modern people believe a sub-biblical doctrine of human nature that vaunts our individuality, and minimizes our gregariousness. This mistaken anthropology infects the ways we think about our basic relationships, both personal and political.

First Things First

The New Testament insists that everyone belongs to God generally, and that by redemption Christians enter into a special relationship of belonging.[3] We may acknowledge that we belong to God as a creedal statement, but few of us live deeply in that understanding. There is tremendous confusion today among Christians concerning the nature of membership, which is easily explained by a personal illustration. Several years ago our youngest daughter asked why the Bible forbade tattooing in ancient Israel.[4] I had no reasonable answer, but a few days later I read a remarkable book, *Ancient Marks: The Sacred Origins of Tattoos and Body Marking*. Here documentary photographer Chris Rainier illustrates the findings of many anthropologists: that among ancient and contemporary traditional peoples, tattooing and body scarring signify membership in adult society, and most believe that such markings have "sacred origins."[5] Once the initiate completes the initiation rites, the tattoos and/or scars signify that he or she belongs to the group with all the rights and duties of membership.

So, God forbade tattoos because if Israelites wore pagan markings they would have been wrongly identified as belonging to the regional Canaanite idols.[6] Instead, He commanded an initiatory cutting that signified membership in the covenant community of those who belong to the God of Abraham.[7] Circumcision was to be performed on the eighth day after birth on all male infants. Interestingly, circumcision is not an externally visible public sign. Neither was its replacement—baptism—in the new covenant community! Indeed, as soon as the water dries, the sign is invisible, but the membership remains. The point of the sign is membership—belonging to the God who calls out a people who belong to Him. Our identity should reflect the fact that we belong to God.

Metaphors of Membership

The Bible says that mankind is made in God's image.[8] Human sociality mirrors God's sociality. God is a social Being—a Trinity of Persons in a unity of substance—in relationship among Himself and with His creatures. Human beings are a singularity of person in a unity of substance—appropriately fitted by design for personal relations with God and with each other. We are innately social, not a mere collection of isolated individuals related by the will to be related. Sociality and individuality are intrinsic to our nature. 9 Human sociality is part of the image of God, which is not a vague idea, but rather a specific and identifiable ensemble of attributes that mirror God's own image: personality, rationality, spirituality, creativity, morality, affectivity, and authority. These communicable attributes ideally suit human beings to be in relation with God, each other, and the entire creation.

The importance of human *gregariousness* is revealed in the story of Eve's creation. Adam is a meaningful individual, but he is made for relationship. In the biblical account, God says it is "not good" for Adam to be alone. God made Adam to be in relationship. Alone he is incomplete. Human beings are innately social, as God is social, so Adam needs an *other* with whom to enjoy friendship and intimacy and a family. Adam is made both for the vertical relationship with God, and for the horizontal relationship with fellow human beings. Eve is that person.[10]

The importance of human *gregariousness* is also revealed by the metaphors utilized by the New Testament authors to explain the ways people are designed to be in social relationships. Christian social thought envisions people enjoying harmonious relationships that are respectfully mindful of ethnic, religious, linguistic, and cultural variation. The Church is intended to be a model of ideal membership. It can be studied historically or sociologically like any other institution, but its origin is not a human one, and its existence is not arbitrary. The church is created, sustained, nourished, and given its true identity by God. It is God's right to create a people for Himself, and it is God's purpose to bring the Church through whatever ill treatment it may encounter from hostile cultures.[11]

St. Paul

St. Paul's primary metaphor for describing the Church's organic unity is "the body of Christ."

> There are diversities of gifts, but the same Spirit. There are differences of ministries, but the same Lord. And there are diversities of activities, but it is the same God who works all in all. But the manifestation of the Spirit is given to each one for the profit of all: for to one is given the word of wisdom through the Spirit, to another the word of knowledge through the same Spirit, to another faith by the same Spirit, to another gifts of healings by the same Spirit, to another the working of miracles, to another prophecy, to another discerning of spirits, to another different kinds of tongues, to another the interpretation of tongues. But one and the same Spirit works all these things, distributing to each one individually as He wills.

> For as the body is one and has many members, but all the members of that one body, being many, are one body, so also is Christ. For by one Spirit we were all baptized into one body—whether Jews or Greeks, whether slaves or free—and have all been made to drink into one Spirit. For in fact the body is not one member but many.

> If the foot should say, "Because I am not a hand, I am not of the body," is it therefore not of the body? And if the ear should say, "Because I am not an eye, I am not of the body," is it therefore not of the body? If the whole body were an eye, where would be the hearing? If the whole were hearing, where would be the smelling? But now God has set the members, each one of them, in the body just as He pleased. And if they were all one member, where would the body be?

> But now indeed there are many members, yet one body. And the eye cannot say to the hand, "I have no need of you"; nor again the head to the feet, "I have no need of you." No, much rather, those members of the body which seem to be weaker are necessary. And those members of the body which we think to be less honorable, on these we bestow greater honor; and our unpresentable parts have greater modesty, but our presentable parts have no need. But God composed the body, having given greater honor to that part which lacks it, that there should be no schism in the body, but that the members should have the same care for one another. And if one member suffers, all the members suffer with it; or if one member is honored, all the members rejoice with it.

> Now you are the body of Christ, and members individually.[12]

The point of the metaphor is that each part of the body is useful and necessary to all the other parts. Without each of its constituent parts the body dies. This metaphor describes how Christians are *practically useful* to one another.13 They do not lose their uniqueness as individuals when they are grafted into the Church, but the metaphor signifies a real unity of purpose and identity—e.g., authentic membership.[14]

This metaphor exegetes a real belonging: "and you belong to Christ; and Christ belongs to God."[15] Christians represent Christ's presence and on-going ministrations to all the earth's inhabitants. We belong to Him, He belongs to us, and we belong to each other. In many epochs and places throughout the world belonging to the Church has been a life-threatening public identification. There is no foot, eye, or ear that is unrelated to the other parts. Those who authentically belong to Christ really have no existence apart from His body. The ministry of the Holy Spirit is to move individual believers in such a way as to accomplish God's goals for all: the praise of the Son, growth to mature character, and blessing the world through Christ.

St. Peter

St. Peter weaves several Old Testament images into metaphors illustrating Christian identity and membership.

> But you are a chosen race, a royal priesthood, a holy nation, a people for God's own possession, so that you may proclaim the excellencies of Him who has called you out of darkness into His marvelous light; for you once were not a people, but now you are the people of God; you had not received mercy, but now you have received mercy.[16]

A chosen race (*genos* and *genus*), is the root upon which the twentieth century Polish lawyer Raphael Lemkin constructed the neologism *genocide* ,meaning the annihilation or attempted annihilation of an entire *kind* of people. It is a word commonly applied to racial and ethnic groups. Peter pointed insists here that Christian identity transcends racial and ethnic identity. Racial and ethnic identities are real things and form the basis for meaningful attributes of life, but they are subsumed in many ways by membership in Christ's Church as long as they do not assert racial or ethnic superiority over others. The Christian *genos* is formed by God's choice into a holy nation— *ethnos*, which is similar to *genos*—and means: "a body of persons united by kinship, culture, and common traditions, nation, people."[17] Christian identity is rooted in membership in Christ's Church. Other identities, while important and meaningful, are secondary and relative to place and time. We belong to God above all else, subordinating all other allegiances to Him. It is difficult to overestimate how many lives would have been saved if Christians had practiced this doctrine throughout the ages.

St. John

This people who belong to God have a common purpose: "to proclaim the excellencies" of the One who made them, so that others may come to know Him. According to Jesus, this proclamation is to be made known by the love Christians have for each other.

> A new commandment I give to you, that you love one another, even as I have loved you, that you also love one another. By this all men will know that you are My disciples, if you have love for one another.[18]

The three-fold emphasis on love in this passage reveals a profound recognition of human sociality. To be sure, Christians must love all their neighbors as they love themselves;[19] but they are to practice love for their neighbors by learning to love other Christians in the most practical ways, including those from other races, ethnicities, and nations. This is how God's people are intended to participate with Christ to reveal His purposes for the world. Specifically this means that non-Christians have "the *right*" to judge the authenticity of people's faith according to their practice of love for other Christians.[20] And they do make such judgments all the time, as Jesus makes clear in His great Prayer:

> I do not pray for these alone, but also for those who will believe in Me through their word; that they all may be one, as You, Father, are in Me, and I in You; that they also may be one in Us, that the world may believe that You sent Me.[21]

The "world" does judge whether or not God sent Jesus on the basis of His people's love for each another. It is a fearsome thing, and too often it does not end well for the honor and glory of God Himself.

Summary

We have to be mindful that when the New Testament authors address their letters to churches in cities and regions of the ancient world they address individuals *as members*. Not all the Galatians were drifting into a dangerous misunderstanding about the relationship between faith and works, but the drift characterized their church to the extent that St. Paul addressed them as members. Not all Corinthians participated in the immorality and chaos of the local churches there, but St. Paul addresses them as members of that Church. Finally, St. John's proclamations to the seven churches in the first three chapters of the Apocalypse make clear that certain sins (and virtues) characterize groups as well as individuals. The Bible does not hesitate to address us as social beings.

The Church is to be the model of sociality fully realized. Where she fails in this vocation she puts before the world a false and idolatrous understanding of humanity. When Christians fail to reckon with their natural gregariousness they are blind to the structural evil plaguing social institutions. The scriptural metaphors discussed here reveal that human nature is both individual *and* social. Christians have no life—spiritually, rationally, personally, creatively, or morally—outside the Church. Human beings are not mere individuals who associate with others on the basis of rational calculations of self-interest. Biblically conceived, human sociality is beyond human consent—beyond negotiations and bargains. We are made for peaceful harmony with others in loving friendships. When governments oppress and persecute racial, ethnic, religious, or linguistic minorities the Church must respond in truth.

Political Liberalism

Political philosophy influences people and societies in ways that theories about metaphysics and ontology do not. Indeed, coupled since the beginning of the Industrial Revolution with open market capitalism and extraordinary technological dynamism, one can argue that Liberalism is the world's most influential theory since the eighteenth century. Its core doctrines are: liberty is mankind's greatest good, and the State's legitimacy is rooted in maximizing liberty; only individuals are real;[22] people have rights to what they want, all rights are possessory, and people are bound by duties only when they give their consent; and, justice is the product of a negotiation (a social contract) rooted in a *calculation* of self-interest (utility).

Liberty

Ancient and medieval political theory rested on the doctrine that virtue is the highest human good so the purpose and legitimate authority of the State and its laws is derived from rewarding virtue and punishing vice.[23] The foundation of this view is the belief that there is a knowable common human nature which gives expression to a common human *télos* (end, goal, or purpose), and that this *télos* has fitted all people by *nature* to be wise, just, courageous, temperate, displaying faith, hope and love in its fullness, and that where virtue flourishes so societies flourish.[24] This consensus began to collapse under the weight of the interminable wars between European Protestants and Catholics in the sixteenth and seventeenth centuries. Political theorist Thomas Hobbes became skeptical of the teleological basis upon which earlier political unity was based. Slowly, liberal theorists replaced virtue as the highest good with liberty. For Liberalism liberty is the greatest human good, and the purpose and legitimate authority of the State and its laws is to maximize liberty.

Individualism

The doctrine that people are commonly fitted by nature for successful social relations explains that violence is due to vice. When Liberalism jettisoned this doctrine it established a new explanation for violence: Hobbes's invented the idea of the *state of nature*. For most moderns this idea needs no defense—it seems to be empirically obvious and enjoys unquestioned authority in most contemporary moral and political reasoning. The fact that it is an early modern invention of political imagination is now forgotten, and the doctrine serves as the singular explanation for why people fail to get along. It claims that in humanity's *natural* state—the *state of nature*—people are individuals seeking to fulfill their desires. Human society is not constituted by cooperative social beings pursuing their interests harmoniously; rather, the state of nature is characterized by a war of all against all where life is, as Hobbes famously wrote, "solitary, poor, nasty, brutish, and short."[25] As such, society is comprised of individuals who agree to exist in society only to ameliorate the state of nature's intrinsic violence.[26] Sadly, most theologians thought that this explanation of human violence concurred with the Christian doctrine of the ubiquity of sin. However, this idea only explains what life is often like in a fallen world, and not what people are designed for. It was disastrous for the Christian doctrine of human sociality.

Justice

It is a pre-liberal dictum that justice requires that everyone remain in possession of what *belongs* to them.[27] If there is a common human *télos,* justice can be a virtue—a cultivated disposition of the soul. Prudent people are fitted to know what they owe to others. On the other hand, if people pursue their various desires without a common nature or *télos* fitting them for social life, as Liberalism insists, justice can be no more than a contract—a pact to mitigate the violence of the state of nature. Such a contract must be negotiated under the guidance of the State which compels individuals to yield some of their rights in order to keep peace in the war of all against all.[28] Justice, then, is not what people are fitted for, but rather a contractual agreement that is always open to further negotiation for people to get what they want.

Rights and duties

A right is a claim of belonging: a claim that the *properties* of ones being (body and soul) and the property one owns must remain in ones possession.[29] These *possessory* rights protect people's properties and persons from arbitrary State seizure or harm. They are usually claimed against governments so some call them *negative* rights, and they are enshrined in the United States Constitution and Bill of Rights as well as in international human rights covenants and conventions. In the language of these documents rights are declared to be inherent, intrinsic to human nature, unalienable, and universal.

However, in Liberalism there is no common human nature for rights to be inherent in or intrinsic to. Rights are the product of a bargain, so they cannot be beyond all bargains. People claim rights to what they desire, and who is to say what is and is not a legitimate desire? All our desires are open to continuing negotiations for recognition as rights. Thus modern rights treaties specifically, and liberal political discourse generally fails to connect a justificatory theory for rights that are beyond all bargains—e.g., for rights as inherent, intrinsic, and inalienable. The modern theory of natural rights or Liberalism has attempted to replant the old natural law idea of rights in a non-native soil of agnosticism concerning human nature and the relation between desire and right, and that project has failed.

The other major difficulty with this non-native soil is that agnosticism regarding the *summum bonum* offers no guidance to know what people owe to one another. People cannot know their duties to others because all they have in common is the fact that they have various desires.[30] However, most people realize that duties are always the flip-side of rights. If there is a legitimate right, that right imposes duties on others. Put differently, duties are recognized, not consented to. The point of a duty is not that one gives it validity by ones consent, but that it imposes upon all what they should do whether they like it or not. Otherwise it is not a duty at all.

Summary

Modern liberal rights theory does not adequately protect possessory rights—beyond all bargains—as illustrated by abortion-on-demand and eminent domain for "social purposes." The teleological account offers a firmer foundation that puts rights beyond all bargains. Modern liberal rights theory does not adequately bind people to their obligations in justice. The teleological account insists that duties are the flip side of rights so people can know what they owe to others are not merely a matter of consent. A State must do more than desist from arbitrarily taking the lives and property of its citizens without just and legal reasons. Significantly, the genocidal violence of the twentieth- and twenty-first centuries has arisen directly not against people as individuals, but against individuals *as members* of racial, ethnic, religious, and linguistic groups. These patterns of persecution and oppression compel us to recognize that justice must protect our memberships as well as our liberties.

The Difference It Makes

The argument within Protestantism in the early twentieth century was a "family" squabble: both liberal churchmen advocating social justice and fundamentalists arguing for pietistic "separation" from the world had adopted Liberalism's primary doctrines.[31] The Churchmen arguing against social injustice and systemic evil were unable to see Liberalism weaknesses to unmask the racist exclusion at the core of much poverty. Pietists relied on Liberalism's assumptions regarding liberty and consensual duties to maintain racist segregation policies. It should be clear that Christians cannot make peace with Liberalism. Although we have to live in it we are, as always, aliens in the land. The uncritical adoption of Liberalism has led to a theologically untenable embrace of an alien identity, an alien view of law, and an alien view of liberty itself.

Identity

Christians watched on the sidelines while Liberalism became the cornerstone of modern political and jurisprudential theories. It suited the growth of the middle class which most of them helped create. The biblical account of human sociality, well summarized by Philip E. Hughes, was nearly lost:

> Personal being is realized only in relation to the personal being of others. It is because his personal being is intrinsically plural, not singular, that God is self-sufficient in his personality. His oneness is not oneness in isolation. He is not dependent on a relationship with someone other than himself for the fulfillment of his potential as a person. Man, however, on his own is without self-sufficiency. The individual man does not possess personal being in the way in which God does. Man in isolation is without plurality. Nonetheless, man is a personal being, and, as we have seen, he is so by virtue of his having been created in the image of God who is fully and absolutely personal. The stamp of the divine image upon man's constitution means that there is a vital and immediate "built-in" relation-

ship between man and his creator. And this, inevitably, is a personal relationship by which man's being as a person is established and fulfilled.[32]

We do not have relationships—we *are* relationships. Individualism as an ideology has led to a destructive quest for human autonomy (*auto-nomos*, literally, "self-law"). It is destructive because it seeks the self-sufficiency possessed only by God as a Trinity. The human rebellion against God for autonomy is a willful quest for isolation, "a stupid and futile act ... of mutinous self-assertion, because we cannot autonomously be the center of our personhood."[33] The broken autonomous self needs integration back into virtue—Christlikeness—not the mirage of autonomy. The restoration of God's image in us restores our personal relationship with God and with other people.

Law

Many Christians have adopted the popular libertarian assertion that "morality cannot be legislated." It is one of Liberalism's cardinal doctrines due to the State's agnosticism concerning human nature and purposes. However, law is intrinsically moral. It cannot be otherwise because it is a command of the sovereign, and noncompliance invokes punishment. If a law has nothing to do with morality, it has no purpose or authority. Perhaps the gamesmanship of contemporary legal practice is all that is left once practitioners stop thinking that theirs is an intrinsically moral enterprise. Certainly Liberalism has led to the current view that law is not an honorable vocation, crucial to the life and health of a society. Indeed, the calling of the political sphere in any society is to rule through law in justice.

Law must reward virtue and punish vice. Law must protect people from the State and its agents because they are fallen like the rest of us, but unlike the rest of us they have the authority to use violence. Law must keep people from being poisoned by chemicals that are mindlessly pumped into rivers and streams. Law must protect people from the violence and manipulations of vicious behavior—of drugdealers, pimps, and corporate cheats. Liberal theory once assumed that liberty would be maximized by virtuous people. If people are increasingly out for themselves at everyone else's expense, liberty must give way to legal protections. Government regulation is a necessary *sin*-tax.

Liberty

The problem with the idea that liberty is the *summum bonum* is that liberty is not an end—it is a capacity—a means. Liberty is a condition in which we can pursue our desired ends and purposes without interference from the State or other powerful entities. The point of having liberty is to pursue ones purposes, and its value is determined by the quality of those purposes. For those who pursue virtuous ends, liberty is good. For those who seek to cheat people out of their savings, to rob a store, or to blow up innocent people, liberty is bad. Modern Liberalism confuses people by focusing on the means—unimpeded liberty to act—with the goodness of people's actions. Thus Liberalism has become a theory that obfuscates a crucial fact: the moral quality of ones actions determines the extent to which people are treated justly, both individually and in the social institutions they create.

Summary

The roots of Liberalism are in *Nominalism*, which means it had few resources to resist the rise of possessive individualism. Coupled with open capitalist markets and stunning technological innovation, Liberalism developed almost inexorably to its current impasse: how do we think seriously about people's rights without knowing what good those rights accomplish? Obligations have to be part of the solution, but without a common understanding about what is good for human beings, it is difficult to know what people owe each other. Liberalism did not have to develop into radical individualism, but together with market capitalism and its technological system it became the system that "delivers the goods" *par excellence*. What individuals have come to expect from the system that delivers the goods is expanding choice-maximization which dovetails nicely with the modern view of liberty as the right to what one desires. In modern Liberalism, justice is the fruit of a negotiation (social contract) or a calculation (utility) that maximizes individual choices while remaining agnostic about values. This has been a disaster, especially for the peoples whom Europeans enslaved, and for their lands which Europeans wanted for their resources.

Liberty Is Not Enough

The great good achieved by liberal rights theories is that many people ruled by democratic governments have astonishing security of person and property when compared to non-liberal States. Such rights are often entrenched with other accompanying goods such as the rule of law, stable governments demonstrated by peaceful regime change, and a staggering potential for creating wealth.[34] The range of individual liberties is impressive, such as speech liberties to speak openly against State policies, or press liberties which hold public officials accountable for their behavior, etc. Had *classical* Liberalism (natural right theory) developed without jettisoning the common view of human nature, as well as the insistence

187

that the State remain agnostic about human ends it might have avoided its massive failures to protect the rights of minorities.

Tragically, liberal rights theories were unable to protect the peoples in the newly discovered lands of Africa, Asia, the Middle East, and the New World from oppression, persecution, expropriation, and exploitation. As those peoples have been liberated to create their own Liberal political and economic systems and institutions they have sought to do so without replicating the rootlessness, anomie, and alienation endemic to Western societies. They have also sought to avoid replacing meaningful communities with sterile, contractualized relationships. As important as possessory rights are, they do not exhaust the richness of human belonging. Most of us are just as concerned about our memberships as we are about our possessions. Traditional societies do a better job of protecting membership because modern liberal rights theories, of the Left and the Right, cannot account for them.

Perhaps these emerging democracies can balance intimate community relations with protecting possessory rights. They need to preserve the deep obligations of membership while at the same time protecting people's persons and property. All societies—Liberal and otherwise—rely on scapegoating and exclusion in order to maintain social cohesion and control. Perhaps the new democracies can find in the rights of membership new ways to protect social communal goals without sacrificing individual liberty right protections.

The Rights of Membership

Each worldview must offer an account for membership, and the test is that it must truly protect minorities without masking unjust exclusion. It is important in such a regime that States protect both possessory human rights and the rights of membership—the rights that preserve the ways we belong to one another. So thorough has been the collapse of the idea of rights of membership that we scarcely have language to think about it in our time. Interestingly, however, English is the only language that preserves two words that describe the twin aspects of justice I seek to delineate: *liberty* and *freedom*. In his brilliant book by that title, historian David Hackett Fischer explains the variant etymologies of the two words. Liberty is derived from the Latin, *libertas* (Greek *eleutheria*), "which meant unbounded, unrestricted, and released from restraint." The moral and political idea is to be able to act without external impediment, or without someone ordering your movements for you—e.g., one way not to be a slave.

However, there is another way to be a slave, and that is to be *excluded* from social membership.

> Freedom has another origin. It derives from a large family of ancient languages in northern Europe. The English word free is related to the Norse *fri*, the German *frei*, the Dutch *vrij*, the Flemish *vrig*, the Celtic *rheidd*, and the Welsh *rhydd*. These words share an unexpected root. They descend from the Indo-European *priya* or *friya* or *riya*, which meant dear or beloved. The English words freedom or free have the same root as friend, as do their German cousins *frei* and *Freund*. Free meant someone who was joined to a tribe of free people by ties of kinship or belonging.[35]

The moral and political idea in freedom is *to belong*—to be included as a member. Fischer explains how the two rather different ideas behind liberty and freedom actually move in opposite directions: freedom in northern Europe was an inherent right for those born free, whereas liberty in Rome was a right gained or purchased from "a condition of prior restraint."[36]

> In that respect, the original meanings of freedom and liberty were not merely different but opposed. Liberty meant separation. Freedom implied connection. A person with *libertas* in Rome or *eleutheria* in ancient Greece had been granted some degree of autonomy, unlike a slave. A person who had *Freiheit* in northern Europe or *ama-ar-gi* in southern Mesopotamia was united by kinship or affection to a tribe or family of free people, unlike a slave.[37]

Furthermore,

> Freeborn people in northern Europe had possessions that are called rights in English, or *rechte* in German. These words began as adjectives that meant straight, sound, correct, or good. They became nouns for specific entitlements that could be claimed as a matter of obligation, and also for the general idea of entitlement itself: rights as a matter of right. In northern Europe, rights were recognized as belonging to members of a particular folk. The laws of King Canute called them *folchrichts*.[38]

Thus rights actually arise more naturally from the idea of membership than from that of possession. These related but quite different ideas have been collapsed into the idea of liberty, with grave consequences for modern conceptions of justice and rights.[39] Hackett opines:

> It is interesting (and urgently important for us to understand in the modern world) that these ancient traditions of liberty and freedom both entailed obligations and responsibilities. But they did so differently. The

189

gift of *libertas* and *eleutheria* brought with it an obligation to act in a wise and responsible way—not as a libertine. A person with liberty was responsible for his own acts.

A person who was born to freedom in an ancient tribe had a sacred obligation to serve and support the folk, and to keep the customs of a free people, and to respect the rights of others on pain of banishment. In modern America too many people have forgotten this side of our inheritance. They think of liberty as license without responsibility, and freedom as entitlement without obligation. To think this way in the modern world is to remember only half of these ancient traditions.[40]

I am convinced that justice must protect people's memberships as much as their liberty. This idea has developed over many years of interaction with students, as well as through reflection on the sources of Liberalism's inability to protect people. It is especially a response to reflection on the human penchant to stereotype, blame, and scapegoat minorities, and then to oppress, persecute, and exterminate them *as members* of groups. While teaching courses on the law of war, genocide, and the rights of indigenous peoples I came to see how *de minimus* liberties mask the injustices of exclusion. I also came to understand why so many white Americans think that discrimination is nearly at an end, despite the explicitly articulated experience of Native Americans, blacks, Muslims, and other minorities. The widespread and multitudinous harms of minority exclusion in America are hidden by the minimal liberties minorities enjoy.

Natural and Artificial Relations

Membership is not possible in the [post]modern idea that all relationships or group affiliations are consensual productions of artifice: of human making and unmaking—of limitless human invention. Quite obviously, race, ethnicity, birth, religion, and nationality are not human productions.[41] Reflection on human relations and our consequent obligations in justice begin with this fact. Not all social relations entail the kind of memberships that require the protection of rights. Theologically and sociologically we can distinguish between two kinds of human relationships: *natural* and *artificial*. Some relationships are *natural* because they are necessary to our nature, and the means prescribed for fulfilling a natural relationship is not arbitrary—it is intimately related to who we are as created beings. Natural relationships are not human inventions, but are ordained or "established" by God: including marriage and family, tribe (racial or ethnic and linguistic group affiliation), and religion.[42] These relationships are not voluntary—e.g., not governed by consent. The same is true of citizenship—we are necessarily situated in a State and while some aspects of that entity are, as we shall see, arbitrary, being so situated should guarantee protection.

Artificial relationships are based on consent, and their nature is arbitrary. They are products of artifice—the consequence of human inventiveness. They fulfill necessary social purposes, but the means for their fulfillment is arbitrary. God has ordained that we have a government, but its form is a matter of judgment.[43] For millennia government was simply the law of family/tribal elders. As long as a government promotes justice and protects its people, it can be a monarchy, a democracy, or an autocracy. The same is true in ordering economic relations—its form is arbitrary as long as it is just. We may allow large business corporations to form, or we may limit their activities for the sake of justice. Democracy and capitalism are human inventions—they are not written in the stars, or essential to human nature. We allow them as long as we believe that they redound to the common good, but if they fail—say, they only create wealth for a small number of people over time—we may seek other arrangements by which to order more just relations. Social clubs and civic organizations are all useful, but they are expendable and voluntary. As a human invention, artificial relations and their institutional structures have an ambivalent nature.

Human sociality is expressed in both natural and artificial relationships: both are good. Natural relationships are more primary and intimate, but we need artificial ones as well to order people's collective efforts. Most importantly, we must not lose sight of the distinction between the two because artificial relationships *are* arbitrary. In natural relationships we belong to each other in ways that are simply lacking in artificial ones. Natural relationships are not easily abandoned, or at least ought not to be. One may abandon a job as an employee of the Ford Motor Company with moral impunity, but one cannot similarly abandon ones children. Natural relationships—family, ethnicity, religion, and language—are not the product of artifice, negotiation, or calculation.

Exclusion

Exclusion is inevitable. States have a right to define membership because no government can protect and establish justice for every person in the world.[44] Families have a right to define membership for the same reasons—no one can be responsible for all the welfare and needs of all the children of the world. Religions have a right to define their membership and to exclude non-adherents. Race and ethnicity exclude by definition: one cannot be Asian, Cherokee, Celtic, or Awas

Tigni by will or desire.

Exclusion means that there are nonmembers: those who are *foreign*, alien—strangers. Every language defines non-membership. The Greek *xenos* (the adjective means *strange* or *foreign*; the noun means *stranger* or *alien*), from which we derive our word *xenophobia* (which means literally, *fear of aliens*). Also in Greek *paroikos* (*par*, "by" + *oikos*, "house") refers to an alien living among a people who does not enjoy a citizen's rights but does enjoy the community's protection. In most societies, the alien enjoys some protections but not liberties or membership.

Inclusion and exclusion must be based on criteria for determining the nature and scope of membership in relationships: blood (kinship and ethnicity), land (citizenship and nationality), covenant (marriage and family, religion), friendship, or contract (business). Historically, blood and land form ones primary identity, and are grounded in marriage, family, and religion.[45] Christian identity is in Christ and His Church, not blood and land, and over time Christian theologians should have inveighed against social exclusion based on what the Gospel has transcended: "For as many of you as were baptized into Christ have put on Christ. There is neither Jew nor Greek, there is neither slave nor free, there is neither male nor female; for you are all one in Christ Jesus." Putting off identities of blood and land was also mirrored in the early chapters of the Book of Acts, and in the missionary endeavors of the early Church.

Tragically, Christians have failed to root out the xenophobia characteristic of most of the world societies. Christians under the influence of Liberalism have remained blind to the injustices motivated by racial, ethnic, religious, and linguistic hatred. Christians have failed to articulate the rights of membership, actively participating in the mendacity and tenacity of racist exclusionary systems that oppress minorities. The Church should have been at the forefront of curing this mendacity, but it has lagged behind, to our shame. The rights of membership are beyond bargains, negotiations, and calculations. Governments may not withhold the rights of some citizens for arbitrary reasons, such as ethnicity or religion. The great shame of American state and federal governments throughout its history has been legally to uphold and to maintain systems for excluding people from their rights of citizenship. The great shame of the Church has been to participate in those systems.

Exclusion and the Rise of International Law

The twentieth century offers a humiliating record of our failures to protect minority groups from atrocities. Examples abound: when the British handed political control to India and Pakistan at least three million lives were lost due to the lack of protection for the Muslims who remained in India, and for Hindus and Sikhs remaining in the Punjab region of what became Pakistan. Later, three million Muslims lost their lives in Bangladesh when predominantly Bengali East Pakistan separated from West Pakistan. The former was a religious genocide, and the latter was a tribal genocide. The most recent failure was preventing the tribal genocide in Rwanda where one million lives were lost in 100 days. Historically, the international movement to protect human rights was motivated by the need to protect vulnerable minorities.

The Minority Protection Systems

The first international effort to create a system to protect minorities began with the League of Nations after World War I. Minorities were defined as members of racial, ethnic, religious, and linguistic groups. World War I was ignited by ethnic conflict in the Balkans, and the atrocities of World War II, especially the Jewish Holocaust, confirmed that persecuted minorities—racial, ethnic, religious, and linguistic groups—need special protection. Hence the definition of minorities was integrated into the International Convention for the Prevention and Punishment of the Crime of Genocide in 1948, which defines genocide as "the attempt to destroy, in whole or in part, a racial, ethnical, religious … group." Individuals are protected as individuals by human rights law, but when their unalterable group memberships cause rights violations, they need to be protected as members of groups.

Indigenous Peoples

Most nations have minorities of two principal types: those who seek integration into the dominant social life, and those who resist such integration. Marginalization and exclusion is a chief injustice perpetrated against the former, and coercive assimilation is a chief injustice against the latter. Policies that perpetuate these injustices are the consequence of racism, but they arise from different goals: motivated by hatred one seeks to exclude a people from social life by exclusion, or motivated by the desire to possess the land and resources of the other one seeks to eliminate them other by assimilation. Due to their resistance to social homogenization indigenous peoples are especially vulnerable. Indigenous peoples need protection, if for no other reason than that they live much of what we have forgotten: that many obligations are beyond our wishes and desires—beyond our maximized choices. We have much to learn from them about the practices of simplicity, silence, fidelity, generosity, joy, and the eagerness to learn.

The modern movement to protect the rights of indigenous peoples has caused all sorts of problems for liberal theorists. Tribal identities are group identities, so tribes claim *group* rights, for which liberal theory has no basis. Tribal obligations, the heart of their communities, are beyond consent and bargaining. Worse, tribal law is frequently illiberal and it occasionally violates equal protection provisions, etc. Worse still, tribal religious *beliefs* are easy to protect, but their religious *practices* often require the exclusion of non-tribal members from mountains, mountain ranges, or other large tracts of land. The inconvenience of not being limited to an urban or suburban building is compounded by the knowledge that these large tracts of land often have the resources that others want.

Religious Minorities

Religious belief is well protected in most democratic nations, but religious *practice* is less well protected, as noted above. It is not possible in a paper this short to discuss the ways the dominant secular society inhibits the exercise of religious liberties among religious adherents, including larger religious groups such as evangelicals, Roman Catholics, and Eastern Orthodoxy. Some religious groups want to be homogenized into the social mainstream, like newly arrived Buddhists and Muslims, and they want to be able to build temples and mosques. Other long-term citizens want to remain outside the social mainstream, like the Amish, and they want to be left alone by State officials. So far both groups have fared fairly well in such enterprises, but the suspicion of many often threatens their tenuous existence in the United States. In Europe their religious liberties are in greater jeopardy in the self-declared secular States.

Immigrants and Refugees

Stateless people are the most vulnerable people. No one is responsible to protect their lives, properties, and memberships. Most countries have a bewildering assortment of rules governing immigration and asylum that lead to corruption, arbitrariness, and clear injustices, which, in turn, produces cynicism and insecurity in citizens and non-citizens alike. Liberalism has no deep way of understanding the bases for exclusion due to its emotivist theory of rights and duties. What is needed is a system rooted in mercy and compassion grounded in firm, reasonable criteria that are not arbitrarily exclusionary in regard to race, ethnicity, religion, or language. The long practice of mistreating immigrants and immigrant workers and the laxity of dealing with trafficking, coupled with our long history of expropriating people's labor to support the rich (plantation slavery, Jim Crow laws and sharecropping, the theft of indigenous lands, etc.) require a definitive set of policies that make sense for citizens, immigrants, and refugees.

Liberalism's Inadequacy to Protect Minorities

Liberal political theorists worry that the reassertion of membership rights will reawaken tribalism, which threatens the protection of individual liberties, and there is good reason to believe that individual rights are less often protected in traditional societies. However, the destruction of membership does not necessarily correct the problems of tribalism. The international human rights regime, as it is often called, looks primarily to the triumph of secular systems of individual rights protection, thus hoping to minimize tensions aroused by racial, ethnic, religious, and linguistic plurality. However, as minorities assert their rights, the shallow theoretical moorings of the current system are inadequate to protect membership rights. The international human rights systems are making some headway to protect membership rights for indigenous peoples, but not much.

Each worldview needs to offer an account of how to protect people against the harms of arbitrary exclusion, and the Christian account should insist that protecting people's and *peoples'* memberships is profoundly important, in concert with protecting possessory rights. Communities could have protected both possessory rights and membership rights. Political theory, however, is never undertaken in a socio-economic vacuum, and one must suspect that market forces were the primary solvent to community obligations because traditional duties are an economic disincentive to the consumption that drives modern production. Indeed, the modern market requires the death of community for its marketers and propagandists to succeed. In traditional communities people do not have to consume in order to overcome the boredom and alienation of radical individualism. The Church should provide an alternative to Liberalism—not allowing itself to be co-opted by protecting the system that delivers the goods.

Ironically, Christians are a minority in most places, and desperately need the membership protections they helped deny to others. More ironically, the right to practice ones religion—especially to speak in public about the implications of that religion—is a membership right. Christians cannot be content to be "with our own kind."[46] The Church is to be the great social, racial, and ethnic leveler because no Christian who understands what we have been saved from can pretend that race or ethnicity puts us above the rest. Our right to assemble, to worship, and to associate with other Christians is a membership right. What we need is our right to exist *as members*. That is a far more robust right than simply a liberty to believe "as we choose."

195

Why People Exclude Others

> Blessed are you when men hate you, and when they exclude you, and revile you, and cast out your name as evil, For the Son of Man's sake. Lk 6:22

Exclusion typically arises from hatred. Fallen human beings hate others because of pride, envy, jealousy, and anger. Hatred causes exclusion, and exclusion causes *in-juria*—literally: *injustices*. Unjustifiable and arbitrary exclusion is fundamentally unjust, and at some point its harms must be sanctioned.The consequence of not sanctioning exclusion is violence: on the one side, those oppressed by exclusion may revolt and cause violence, or, on the other hand, the oppressors may press their claims further and what follows is mass murder, war crimes, crimes against humanity, and genocide. Hate ultimately seeks the extinction of its object.

Hatred does not usually erupt into violence without further conditions—it is like gasoline awaiting a spark. The usual sparks are envy and blame. All societies have internal tensions, and there are healthy ways to deal with them: regular elections, peaceful changes in power, the rule of law, protections for minorities, etc. The most common way to resolve tensions is to blame a group, usually a minority, for the tensions. This reductionism replaces prudent reasoning with easily digested over-simplifications. Blame the minority and solve the problems.

This process is called *scapegoating*. It begins with a stereotype of the minority group to be blamed, which makes it easy to identify them. Immigrants are typically stereotyped, but indigenous peoples are just as handy. The point is not the identity of the group, but rather their weakness to resist the blame. Once the group has been identified and blamed, persecutions begin with propaganda, exclusion, removal, or outright violence can ensue once a flame has been introduced. This process obviates the need for people to think hard about the tensions in their midst in any deep way. Typically, incivility will have reached a fever-pitch and the scapegoating becomes a quasi-religious quest for social purification.

Scapegoating begins slowly as a group is blamed by another group for social tensions. One party of the dominant group may resist stereotyping and scapegoating for a time, but the inability to resolve the tensions causes more people to join with the majority. As exclusion expands to official, institutionalized *discrimination* the strength of the counter group wanes and violence becomes more of a certainty. Exclusion may begin narrowly, but as the group blaming the victims grows in power. Minorities and immigrants are the typical subjects of scapegoating, which achieves its final purpose when the object of blame is destroyed. Once enough people are convinced that extinction is good for all because it will resolve and reconcile social tensions ("The only good Indian is a dead Indian."), the elimination of the group marked for extinction becomes a merely technical matter to be resolved by technical means. *eg. Holocaust,*

Race/Ethnic/Religious Hatred is Heretical

Hate is forbidden to Christians, who may not hate even their enemies.[47] Civil religion tied historically to a Protestant, Catholic, or Orthodox denomination is heretical if it promotes hatred and contempt for other races, ethnicities, or religions. Hatred and contempt reveal evil character *and* wrong belief. Between the fifteenth and nineteenth centuries European conquerors invented the notion that the indigenous peoples of the Americas, Asia, and Africa comprise a category of being between animal and human. It is an utter fiction. Animals are not morally responsible for their actions. Human beings are. The Europeans should have known better.

Hate-inspired racist social policies—political, economic, or cultural—are forbidden to Christians. Theories of racial or ethnic supremacy are heretical and heterodox. They violate the doctrines of creation, moral accountability, and salvation. Human beings share equal moral possibilities, and an equal potential for a robust relationship with the living God. Just wars cannot be justified by racial, ethnic, or religious hate. If war is necessary, it must be justified by humanitarian concerns to restore justice in a specific time and place, or in self-defense.

All of this may seem so obvious as scarcely to warrant mention, but the most gruesome human rights violations typically arise from racial, ethnic, and religious hatred, and Christians have not lived out these doctrines. There is no legitimate religious basis for violence between Protestants and Catholics in Northern Ireland, or Serbians against Muslims, or Hutus against Tutsis, etc. The so-called doctrinal basis for white supremacy in South Africa and in America was, and is a vicious affront to God's image.

Conclusion: Shaping the Discussion

The international movement to protect human rights proceeds apace. Christians should be part of this process and offer prudent direction. Our unwillingness to participate contributes to the slaughter and enslavement of millions throughout the world, especially where they, including our own brethren, are racial, ethnic, and religious minorities. In this regard two points are emphasized here: first, the Church must be mindful that it is an international, transcultural *body*, so we have duties to *all* people; second, these duties insist that we adapt our political and economic commitments so as to avoid the ideological gridlock that inhibits creating new, more just arrangements that really serve the goal of removing systemic impediments to ensuring justice for everyone.

Most people cherish their own people and land, and their own political, cultural, and economic institutions. God has made us society-builders.[48] Such building is inevitable and good—culture enables people to make sense of the world so they can create and pass on a heritage of meaning to their children. Cultures shape the ways people belong to one another, protect and nourish families and religious belief and practice, educate children, and give expression to artistic creativity. All of this nourishing, educating, and expressing builds the institutions and traditions that constitute culture. Trying to live without culture is like trying to breathe without oxygen.[49] Culture can be good or evil—it is evil when it is ethnically or religiously triumphalist.

While it is our nature to build the political and economic institutions that maintain and govern life they are, however, human inventions. We hold such institutions lightly because they must be just, and must be constantly scrutinized for unjust patterns and behavior due to the propensity of powerful people to take what belongs to the weak, and to exclude those who are thought to be threats. We have to do that building in concert with others who do not share our religious, political, and economic commitments. Fundamentalist movements (Muslim, Hindu, Buddhist, secular-atheistic, or Christian) loathe rival worldviews and, because the task of working together involves compromise and negotiation, they opt for violent engagement or reclusive retreat instead.

Christians should have resisted the temptation to impose Jewish, Roman, or any other ethno-religious social customs or legal codes on others.[50] All societies have unjust political, cultural, and economic features because they are human constructions. Christians must learn to navigate participation in any society by balancing social membership with belonging to Christ. This is the tension of living "in the world, but not of it."

We must remind ourselves frequently that Christianity transcends identities and memberships in blood and land, and it offers no necessary cultural, political, or economic pattern. In the Old Testament God gave Israel detailed laws concerning their culture, politics, and economy. The New Testament has no such laws.[51]

Membership in the new covenant community is "in *Him*, with *Him*, by *Him*, and through *Him*." The implications of this tectonic shift in identity and membership cannot be overestimated. Chiefly, it delegitimizes xenophobia and political, economic, racial, ethnic, religious, or linguistic triumphalism.[52] No blood, land, culture, or political or economic system is more special to God. Peoples and cultures are *superior* only when they ensure justice, reward virtue, and punish vice.

Societies reflect the full range of grandeur (mature self-sacrificial love) and mendacity (neurotic narcissism) typical of fallen human beings.[53] For this reason, they are subject to criticism, as human constructions should be protected and nourished when they redound to human flourishing. However, when they promote injustice they must be criticized and resisted. Christians may insist that the Bible is precisely what postmoderns deny is possible: a knowable transcultural viewpoint from which to judge cultures. Historically, the problem is that Christians rarely turn that light on their own cultures. Culture does shape perception and worldview, but if the Bible is true, Christians have a good basis for criticizing any culture, especially their own. Historically injustices arise when Christians shine the light of justice on alien cultures too critically and not adequately on their own.

Christians must build vital counter- or sub-cultures to correct injustices, without cultivating contempt for culture, or for other cultures. In America, fundamentalist "separation from the world" did not keep such Christians from worldliness—it just created a subculture lacking thoughtfulness, integrity, beauty, and justice. Christians should have always recognized the ambivalence of cultures, thus avoiding tribalist *hubris*. The international character of the Church should have caused Christians to embrace a wide variety of cultural forms. Sadly, civilizational arrogance has been a colossal source of misery, scapegoating, oppression, and persecution, especially for the peoples whose land and labor was expropriated and exploited—or stolen!

Liberalism only liberates virtuous people. Citizens of modern democracies must be mindful that they, too, always teeter on the edge of reverting to identities of blood and land. Only sixty years ago the Nazis—in the world's most *liberal* society—reverted to a racist ideology that created a cauldron of carnage. Modern societies paced by cell-phones, petroleum production, and the internet can devolve into societies bent on the eradicating Jews, Hutus, Hindus, Armenians or anyone else in the name of blood and land. Tribalism, which is the root of fundamentalism, is responsible for most of the world's violence today.

Christians, living fearlessly in the midst of profound differences, can ap-

199

proach the task of ensuring social justice with deep humility and civility because they know their hope is in Jesus Christ. The only way ahead is civility—working with others to create more just social systems. In this spirit I proposed recognizing the rights of membership as one step on that road—as one possible way through the ideological gridlock plaguing theorists on the *Right* and the *Left*. Liberalism has no firm basis for arguing that some obligations are beyond individual consent, and that some rights are beyond all bargains. Christian theology does.

The greatest human good—the *summum bonum*—is virtue, especially love for God and ones neighbor. To be able to pursue virtue in a State where liberties of person, property, and the freedom of membership are protected is good. However, Jesus commanded His hearers to be virtuous (holy) during their occupation by the frequently unjust military forces of Rome—the very forces that illegally executed Him. The purpose of liberty is to serve God and our neighbor more openly. As an excuse for narcissism, liberty is desultory. Liberty and membership are not ends in themselves but means on the way to bring what we can of the common good to all. All ideologies that reside under Liberalism's mantle—Republican or Democrat, Left or Right—are subject to criticism where they fail to protect people from harm. The first calling of a Christian is to love God and our neighbor in justice.

A Collect for Peace

O GOD, from whom all holy desires, all good counsels, and all just works do proceed; Give unto thy servants that peace which the world cannot give; that our hearts may be set to obey thy commandments, and also that by thee, we, being defended from the fear of our enemies, may pass our time in rest and quietness; through the merits of Jesus Christ our Savior. Amen.

— Service for Evening Prayer

Book of Common Prayer, 1928

---

[1] General Confession, Service of Morning/Evening Prayer, *Book of Common Prayer.*

[2] John Donne, "Devotion XVII," in *John Donne: Selections from Divine Poems, Sermons, Devotions, and Prayers,* 272. Ed. John Booty, Paulist Press.

---

[3] The word *redemption* specifically means the price Christ paid to manumit His people out of slavery to sin, death, and judgment. Cf. Leon Morris, *The Apostolic Preaching of the Cross*, Eerdmans.

[4] On the forbidding of tattoos and ritual cuttings, Lev 19:28; cf. Dt 14:1; Jer 16:6.

[5] Tattooing has become a rite of passage among marginalized groups, like urban criminal gangs (from East Los Angeles to the Yakuza in Japan), as well as into popular culture. In our postmoderns societies it is currently a rite of passage into the ranks of those who are 'cool', which is the mark of adult hipness.

[6] It violates the first and the third commandments, Exodus 20: 1-3.

[7] Cf. Gen. 31:42; Gen. 31:53; Ex. 3:6 Ex. 3:15; Ex. 3:16; Ex. 4:5; 1Kings 18:36; 1Chr. 29:18; 2Chr. 30:6; Psa. 47:9; Matt. 22:32; Mark 12:26; Luke 20:37; Acts 7:32. Indeed, in ancient Semitic cultures covenants were 'cut', if not in human flesh then in animals.

[8] Gen 1:26-27.

[9] This is developed at length in Stephen Paul Kennedy, "From Religious Rights to Indigenous Rights: Protecting the Rights of Native Peoples to Religious Worship," in Ed. Michael T. Cooper, *Perspectives on Post-Christendom Spiritualities*, 180ff.

[10] Gen 2:18-25.

[11] Mt 16:18; Jn 17:6-18.

[12] I Co 12:4-27.

[13] "To have a viable community, or as you say a "genuine membership," its members [e.g., members of a "viable community"] must need one another's help and must be practically useful to one another." Wendell Berry, Morris Allen Grubbs, Ed. *Conversations with Wendell Berry*, University of Mississippi Press, 2007. 207

[14] This is in quite stark contrast to much of what is said about these gifts in the modern church. Entire seminars and retreats often focus formulas for defining and identifying who has what gift on the dubious assumption that they hold a key to what one is good at. In a culture dedicated to pigeon-holing and the quest for expertise this makes sense, but it utterly misses the point of the metaphor, which is that no one is useless in the Church. The point of the metaphor is not that a gift or two become ones identity. This is surely the consequence of life in a commercialized world where everything is thought to be a commodity. I am indebted to my colleague professor Myron Steeves for this insight.

[15] 1 Cor 3:23.

[16] 1 Pet 2:9-10.

[17] BADG, *A Greek-English Lexicon*. The difference between *genos* and *ethnos* is probably limited to the fact that *genos* is focused on ethnological physical characteristics, and *ethnos* is focused on cultural identity. This passage clearly reveals that genos is transcended by equal membership between the different peoples in the Church. In re: *ethnos*, the Church is the *nation* through which God pursues His providential action in the world. I am convinced that the Church is a *spiritual* nation.

[18] John 13:34-35. Cf. Francis Schaeffer calls this, "The Mark of the Christian," in *The Church at the End of the Twentieth Century*, 134-153; and David Watson calls it "the mark of the church" in *I Believe in the Church*, 58.

[19] Lev 19:18; Mt 19:19; 22:39; Mk 12:31; Rom 13:9; Gal 5:14; Jas 2:8.

[20] Schaeffer, *Ibid*. 135

[21] John 17:20-21.

[22] Philosophically this is known as *Nominalism*, which denies universals, and asserts that only individual things are real. Society is not a 'real' thing. All groups are reducible to the sum of their constituent (individual) parts. In other words, groups are only a collection of individuals—they have no character of their own.

[23] This belief is captured exquisitely in the great Eucharistic prayer for the Church in the *Book of Common Prayer*, "We beseech Thee also, so to direct and dispose the hearts of all Christian rulers, that they may truly and impartially administer justice, to the punishment of wickedness and vice, and to the maintenance of Thy true religion, and virtue." Holy Communion Service, 1928.

[24] The Christian version of this theory—Natural Law theory—claims more: that human beings made in God's image are designed and fitted for virtue. Virtue is mature character: the best *character* a human being is capable of achieving. Vice is its opposite. Virtue is *good* character; vice is bad or immature character. Virtues and vices are habits of the heart. For example, love is a virtue. Love is a skill learned by practice. The vices opposed to love, indifference and hatred, are also habits learned by practice. Love is learned by practicing longsuffering, kindness, generosity, gentleness, humility, seeking the good of the other, patience, etc. Vice is learned by practicing peevishness, orneriness, roughness, impatience, parading oneself, insisting on ones way, rudeness, envy, jealousy, etc. (Cf. I Co 13:4-8) Love and hate not merely affective states into which one falls. They are an ensemble of skills one may cultivate with great effort. Of course the differences in views on virtue and vice between Protestants and Catholics were

and are very minor indeed. The real issue was a power struggle between the Vatican and the rising nationalist movements vivified by the new Protestant rulers.

[25] Thomas Hobbes, *Leviathan*, 13.9. Hobbes is the first philosopher to assert that people have a right to what they desire.

[26] For the Christian aggression and violence are a *natural* consequence of human self-seeking—of sin and vice—creating a fundamentally *unnatural* human condition. For Liberalism, aggression and violence are *natural* to the human condition and while selfishness makes matters worse, it is to be expected due to overcrowding, scarcity, and competition.

[27] Contrary to the opinion of some, rights are most decidedly not a recent invention. The above definition is admirably consistent with that found in the Bible.

[28] Otherwise people will not part with enough rights to keep peace, and they will renege on the results of their negotiations. The extent to which this compulsion is heavy-handed differs among the founders of social contract theory: Hobbes, John Locke, Jean-Jacques Rousseau, David Hume, and Immanuel Kant.

[29] That rights are claims of belonging is further developed in, *In the Shelter of God's Hand: Human Rights in Christian Perspective* (forthcoming).

[30] In modernity all reality is perspectival, so one cannot know others as they are in themselves.

[31] Many Christians know that their religious duties are not dependent on their consent, but they have not carried this doctrine through consistently to their *public* lives. The public implications are more complicated, but certainly our duties to others in justice are not exclusively a private matter. Furthermore, the antinomianism rampant in the modern Church may have its roots in the complex webs of human obligation.

[32] Philip Edgcumbe Hughes, *The True Image: The Origin and Destiny of Man in Christ*, Grand Rapids: Eerdmans, 1989. 52. The ways all this influenced fundamentalist theology is not our purpose here. It need only be noted that it was profoundly so.

[33] *Ibid.*

[34] It is no small irony that the 'knowledge class' in liberal societies is so hesitant to insist on the goodness of this system in their educational efforts with the migrants who arrive from nations where such developments do not exist.

[35] David Hackett Fischer, *Liberty and Freedom: A Visual History of America's Founding Ideals*, Oxford University Press. 2005. 5

[36] *Ibid.* 6 Cf. also Ac 22:29, where the soldier explains the cost of his Roman citizenship to St. Paul.

[37] Fischer, *Ibid.*

[38] Fischer, *Ibid.* 7

[39] This corresponds to the development of the Greek word agape (especially the adjective *agapetos*, meaning *beloved*) as it collided with Hebrew in the Septuagint. "Love in this context means devotion towards one's neighbour for his sake, accepting him as a brother and letting him come into his own. This aspect is illustrated by the social legislation, which is particularly concerned with the rights of aliens (Lev. 19:34), the poor (Lev. 25:35) and orphans." Colin Brown, *DNTT*, Vol. II, 540. The social legislation spoken of here was designed to avoid exclusion from the rights of social participation.

[40] Fischer, *Ibid.* 8

[41] It is fashionable in some academic circles to call nationality an 'accident' of birth, and, so, as relevant to where one belongs. Whether it is accidental or not, it is certainly a meaningful category of belonging, as any Syrian refugee or Sudanese displaced person knows.

[42] I use the word *race* in the subsequent discussion only when referring to international treaties due to its imprecise and contestable scientific basis. Race is an idea invented in the seventeenth century for the purposes of exclusion. Instead, I refer herein to ethnicity.

[43] Human government is a 'natural' necessity, Rom 13:1ff.

[44] Cf. United States Constitution: "We the people of the United States, in order to form a more perfect Union, establish Justice, insure domestic Tranquility, provide for the common defense, promote the general welfare …" Under international law States have some duties to citizens of other nations and to stateless persons, but those duties are articulated in treaties.

[45] Family, marriage, and religion are separable from blood and land because people do marry outside their clans, etc.

[46] There is a local freeway sign advertising a church claiming to be "for people like you!"

[47] They must hate sin, not people. Luke 6:27-28, *But I say to you who hear: Love your enemies, do good to those who hate you, bless those who curse you, and pray for those who spitefully use you.*

[48] We cannot help but be builders of society. Even hermits and monastics in the ancient Church participated in the building of early medieval societies built around monasteries!

[49] The word 'culture' is not necessarily coterminous with the word 'world' as it is used in the New Testament. The Christian's relationship with cul-

ture is more complicated than that simple equation. The *world* is all the ideas and institutions in a given culture that violate God's design for His creation.

[50] Jesus' last command was that His followers be "witnesses in Jerusalem, and in all Judea and Samaria, and to the end of the earth." (Ac 1:8)

[51] Indeed, the bane of St. Paul's existence was the Judaizers who constantly dogged his steps trying to require that Christians adopt the social practices of the Jewish nation.

[52] And cultural, political, or economic superiority as well.

[53] As in the Sudan.

About the Press

THE TIMOTHY CENTER PRESS is the publishing arm of The Timothy Center for Sustainable Transformation. The Timothy Center is a network of Christian social innovators dedicated to catalyzing ventures that raise the quality of life and dignity of the world's marginalized. Our vision as a business and training center is to focus on the care of the impoverished, estranged, and imprisoned by the formation of new 360 degree ventures and the creation of opportunities to engage in sustainable Christ-centered social transformation. We believe that behind every societal problem is a person who has the need for Christ.

The Timothy Center Press publishes in the areas of human rights, social responsibility, entrepreneurship, and social venture creation, as well as cultural engagement. Our books are highly selective and our authors are first-rate scholars in their fields. The press utilizes ebook platforms compatible with Sony Reader, Kindle, Nook, iPad, and other ebook readers. This technology makes our books available on a global level as well. As an aspect of our commitment to the environmental good, we value technological advances that have made it possible to conserve energy and natural resources yet still deliver high quality products. We also publish paperback volumes on demand for the traditionalist.

You can learn more about the Timothy Center at www.thetimothycenter.org. Proceeds from the sale of this book go toward our efforts of lifting lives from both spiritual and economic poverty.

- rules on US Pharma corporations?
  → risk of outsourcing
- requirements on all drug companies
  to reveal specific details
  on their research.

- "This could be us"

- compassion gone bad

- incorporate into human rights activities

- "anemic theology" re: contraception
  — med schools
  — churches

Autonomy ←→ Relationship, Community
Beneficence ←→ Duty, Obligation
Justice ←→ Fairness

redound
desultory